Why Terr

Also by Alan M. Dershowitz

Psychoanalysis, Psychiatry, and Law
(with Jay Katz and Joseph Goldstein)

Criminal Law: Theory and Process
(with Joseph Goldstein and Richard D. Schwartz)

The Best Defense

Reversal of Fortune: Inside the Von Bülow Case

Taking Liberties: A Decade of Hard Cases, Bad Laws, and Bum Raps

Chutzpah

Contrary to Public Opinion

The Advocate's Devil: A Novel

*The Abuse Excuse: And Other Cop-Outs, Sob Stories,
and Evasions of Responsibility*

Reasonable Doubts: The Criminal Justice System and the O. J. Simpson Case

*The Vanishing American Jew: In Search of Jewish Identity
for the Next Century*

*Sexual McCarthyism: Clinton, Starr, and the
Emerging Constitutional Crisis*

Just Revenge: A Novel

*The Genesis of Justice: Ten Stories of Biblical Injustice That Led to the
Ten Commandments and Modern Morality and Law*

Supreme Injustice: How the High Court Hijacked Election 2000

Letters to a Young Lawyer

Shouting Fire: Civil Liberties in a Turbulent Age

Alan M. Dershowitz

Why

understanding the threat

Terrorism

responding to the challenge

Works

Yale University Press   New Haven and London

Designed by Sonia L. Shannon.
Printed in the United States of America by R. R. Donnelley & Sons Co., Inc.

Library of Congress Cataloging-in-Publication Data
Dershowitz, Alan M.
Why terrorism works / Alan M. Dershowitz.
p. cm.
Includes bibliographical references and index
ISBN 0-300-09766-2 (cloth : alk. paper)
0-300-10153-8 (pbk. : alk paper)
1. Terrorism. 2. Terrorism—Prevention. I. Title.
HV6431 .D473 2002   303.6'25—dc21   2002006387

A catalog record for this book is available from the British Library.
The paper in this book meets the guidelines for permanence and durability
of the Committee on Production Guidelines for Book Longevity of the
Council on Library Resources.

10 9 8 7 6 5 4 3

This book, my eighteenth, is warmly dedicated to the

nearly ten thousand students I have been privileged to teach

during my thirty-eight years at Harvard Law School.

You have inspired me, taught me, and made me proud.

You are our future.

Preserve it from our enemies.

Contents

Introduction

"The success of terrorists in one part of
the terror network emboldens terrorists
throughout the network."
—Benjamin Netanyahu,
former prime minister of Israel

"[The world must] never yield to suicide
bombing as a new diplomatic tool."
—Ehud Barak,
former prime minister of Israel

The greatest danger facing the world today comes from religiously inspired terrorist groups—often state sponsored—that are seeking to develop weapons of mass destruction for use against civilian targets. These loosely knit groups are especially difficult to combat because they often employ suicidal terrorists who are not subject to the usual deterrent threats—of death or other severe punishment. They also lack a "return address"—a known location where they can be attacked without civilian casualties. The grave dangers posed by this kind of "poor man's warfare" are different from any previously faced, and we are unprepared to confront them, because we refuse to recognize and eliminate the reason why terrorism persists.

Terrorism is often rationalized as a valid response to its "root causes"—mainly repression and desperation. But the vast majority of repressed and desperate people do not resort to the willful targeting of vulnerable civilians. The real root cause of terrorism is that it is successful—terrorists have consistently benefited from their terrorist acts. Terrorism will persist as long as it continues to work for those who use it, as long as the international community rewards it, as it has been doing for the past thirty-five years.

Global terrorism is thus a phenomenon largely of our own making. The international community—primarily the European governments and the United Nations, but also, at times, our own government—made it all but inevitable that we would experience a horrendous day like September 11, 2001. We are reaping what we sowed. It is of course the terrorists themselves who bear the full moral responsibility for their murderous deeds, but since we cannot directly control their actions, except by our own counteractions, it is our policy toward terrorism that will determine whether their terrorism succeeds or fails. It is we who must change our failed approach to terrorism if the world is not to become swept up in a whirlwind of violence and destruction. I believe we *can* reduce the frequency and severity of terrorist acts, provided we take significant steps now. What is more, we can do it while preserving our fundamental liberties.

The first part of this book explains why terrorism works. It demonstrates how the international community served as midwife to the birth of international terrorism, beginning in 1968, by encouraging it, providing incentives for its continuation, and refusing to take the steps necessary to curtail it. The second part shows how we could easily wipe out international terrorism if we were not constrained by legal, moral, and humanitarian considerations. The third part proposes a series of steps that can effectively reduce the frequency and severity of international terrorist attacks by striking an appropriate balance between security and liberty.

In a recent decision by the Supreme Court of Israel forbidding the use of "physical pressure" to secure information deemed necessary to prevent future terrorist acts, the president of the court, Aharon Barak, observed: "Although a democracy must often fight with one hand tied behind its back, it nevertheless has the upper hand."

Following up on this apt metaphor, the first part of this book shows how the international community has been confronting international terrorism for at least thirty years, by tying one hand behind its back while extending another hand of encouragement to the terrorists. The second part shows how we could defeat terrorism if we were willing to use both of our hands, our fingernails, our teeth, and our feet, without following the Marquess of Queensberry rules. The third part shows how democracies can do far more than they are actually doing, even if law and morality require us to fight terrorism with one hand tied behind our backs. Although I am not as sanguine as Justice Barak, I am convinced that we can do much more than we are doing to reduce the horrors—present and future—of international terrorism.

But there are many obstacles in the way. One of these is the refrain, "One man's terrorist is another man's freedom fighter." We have heard this theme and its variations so often that it has been impossible to fix on a single definition of terrorism that satisfies everyone. Part of the blame lies with the United Nations and its politicization of the term, as we shall see later. There are certain components that tend to appear in most serious attempts to define this elusive term, but none is without its difficulties. The first focuses on the nature of the targeted victims. The deliberate killing of innocent civilians is a central element in most definitions of terrorism, but if this were the only criterion, then the bombings of Hiroshima, Nagasaki, and Dresden by the armed forces of the United States and Great Britain would have to be considered terrorism. Whatever else these actions may constitute, most readers would not consider them terrorism. On the other hand, the recent attacks on the Pentagon and the Marine barracks in Lebanon and Saudi Arabia are widely regarded as acts of terrorism—certainly by the U.S. government—even though the targets were primarily military.

Another element that often figures into the definition of terrorism is the nature of those who commit the violence. According to many definitions of terrorism, only groups that are not part of the official apparatus of the state can commit terrorism. A distinguishing characteristic of what many people regard as terrorism—and the characteristic that makes it so difficult to punish—is its shadowy nature. Most acts of terrorism are difficult to pin on nation-states. Instead, they are committed by unofficial groups that have no standing army and no "return address" where preventive or retaliatory actions can be focused. The terrorist kills and then blends back into the civilian population or is himself killed. Increasingly, the terrorist may be a woman, a teenager, or even a child. All efforts to retaliate or prevent future terrorism are labeled "collective punishment" and are often condemned. The word "terrorism" itself has its historical origins not in the actions of shadowy groups but in acts of terror inflicted by the state on its own citizens: the "reign of terror" conducted by the revolutionary government of France was the paradigm. Terror was also an integral part of the Stalinist, Nazi, Peronist, and other totalitarian and authoritarian regimes.[1]

Yet a third aspect of many definitions of terrorism includes the mechanism by which those who engage in violence seek to influence the actions and attitudes of their intended audiences. Terrorists seek to attract attention to their cause by employing, or threatening, dramatic acts of violence that capture the attention of the media and terrorize large populations. One scholar characterized terrorism as "propaganda by the deed"—to which I would add, by violent and deadly deeds, often against the most vulnerable and innocent of victims, and often only as an initial step in a multifaceted program of violence. If "war is a mere continuation of policy by other means," as Clausewitz once observed, then terrorism is war by other means. Criminal organizations, such as the Mafia or Colombian drug cartels, also employ terror as a technique, but their object is more financial than military, religious, or nationalistic. They are different in kind from the global terrorists we fear most, because their use of violence is narrowly designed to terrorize competitors and police.[2]

Fortunately, for our purposes it is not necessary to come up with an all-encompassing definition of "terrorism" or "terrorist" that applies to every situation.[3] It is enough to describe the phenomenon. My focus may be on only a part of the overall phenomenon of terrorism, but it is the part that poses the greatest danger to the world. My focus is on groups, not individuals (which excludes those like the Unabomber, and twosomes like Timothy McVeigh and Terry Nichols). More specifically, it is on groups that receive some sponsorship and support—though it may be only indirect—from nation-states (so right-wing neo-Nazi groups are excluded).[4] More-

over, these state-sponsored terrorist groups are inspired by religious, nationalistic, or political zealotry and are prepared to use any
means—including suicide and mass murder—to achieve their goals.
Their targets include, but need not be limited to, civilians. The
object of this "organized terrorism" is to attract attention to the terrorists' cause, to terrorize their enemies into submission, or to
defeat an "evil" state that has more powerful conventional weapons.

Among the principal differences between the current war
against terrorism and more conventional wars is that this war may
never end. Previous wars against nation-states have eventually concluded at a specific time, with surrender, peace treaties, and decla-
rations of victory. Some end with a bang, others with a whimper.
Some are over quickly, others drag on. But eventually there comes
a time when we can say the war is over, or at least see a termina-
tion of hostilities even if there is no definitive resolution. There will
be no such clear demarcation date in the war against terrorism.
Individual terrorists will surrender or be killed. We will declare
that certain terrorist bases or cells have been destroyed, but international terrorism—as a dangerous and frightening technique of
seeking change—will continue. Indeed, "poor man's warfare" may
well proliferate, becoming the tactic of choice for many disaffected
groups incapable of waging effective conventional warfare.

Terrorism will persist because it often works, and success
breeds repetition. Terrorism is certainly not a new phenomenon: it
dates back to the earliest history of humankind. Samson may have
been the first recorded suicide terrorist, but terrorism in its broadest sense has been common throughout much of history.[5] Much of
it has been small scale—"retail" assassinations of individuals and
ambushes or explosions directed against specific groups. The
"retail" nature of terrorism in the past was largely a function of the
available weaponry. Before the advent of dynamite and automatic
weapons, killing had to be done essentially on a one-to-one basis. It
took one terrorist (or soldier) to kill one enemy or perhaps a hand-

ful of enemies (except in unusual cases, such as Samson bringing down an entire temple, or the failed Gunpowder Plot of Guy Fawkes).[6] The weapons of choice for earlier terrorists were the dagger, the noose, the sword, and the poison elixer. The introduction of the hand-thrown bomb and the pistol, and more recently the machine gun and plastic explosives, enabled terrorists to kill much more efficiently. Now, weapons of mass, or "wholesale," destruction allow terrorists to "leverage" their personnel, as proved by the events of September 11, 2001, in which a relatively small number of highly trained individuals armed with primitive box cutters and prepared to give up their own lives were able to use passenger jets as weapons of mass murder.

Over its long history, terrorism has had a checkered record of stunning successes and dismal failures—at least as judged by the achievement of the goals proclaimed by its practitioners. Recently, terrorism's successes have been more visible than its failures, and the international community—diplomatic, religious, academic—has been selective in its condemnation of terrorists. For these reasons aggrieved groups and individuals have increasingly found terrorism an acceptable, even attractive, option. Nearly every nation has made some use of terrorism. Nearly every cause has supported or benefited from some form of terrorism. Many individuals have terrorist groups they "approve of," "refuse to condemn," "understand," or apply a more permissive standard to than the one they use for other terrorist groups. The United States has supported, financed, and trained groups that are widely regarded as terrorist, such as the contras in Nicaragua, the mujahideen in Afghanistan, UNITA in Angola, and Samuel K. Doe in Liberia/Sierra Leone. Many Jews supported the Irgun and the Stern Gang during Israel's struggle for independence. The anti-apartheid movement in South Africa employed terrorism, with widespread support from many African-Americans (and others as well). To a far lesser extent, small numbers of blacks supported, or at least refused to condemn, such

American terrorist groups as the Black Panthers, the Revolutionary Action Movement, and the Black Liberation Army. Some Irish-Americans have assisted Catholic terrorists in Northern Ireland, while some have quietly admired their actions. A small number of Jews supported the Jewish Defense League during the late 1960s and the early 1970s. A substantial number of American Muslims have contributed money to Islamic terrorist groups.

The important point is that terrorism *as a mechanism of change* has never been universally condemned—at least before September 11. It is true, of course, that not all terrorism is the same. The use of terrorist tactics against the Nazis by the French, Polish, and Jewish undergrounds was different from the attacks on the World Trade Center in several ways. First, members of the anti-Nazi underground targeted primarily Nazi military and police personnel. Moreover, they were literally fighting for their lives, not for some abstract political goal; their killing was done in self-defense (if not in the legal sense, certainly in the moral sense).

If one seeks to construct a continuum of condemnation for terrorist acts, several factors would have to be considered. Among them would be the nature of the people being targeted, with the most innocent and vulnerable civilians (babies, children, old people, and so on) being at one end, and active military personnel at the other. In the middle would be political, diplomatic, civil service, and police personnel. In his moving play *The Just Assassins*, Albert Camus describes a Russian terrorist who has been assigned to throw a bomb at a villainous grand duke. But on the day of the carefully planned assassination, the duke is accompanied in his carriage by two young children. The just assassin refuses to throw the bomb. Today's terrorists deliberately target children.

Another factor would be whether terrorism is being used in self-defense against state-supported terrorism, genocide, or mass murder of innocent people. Had the Jews in Nazi Germany blown up German kindergartens and threatened to continue to do so unless the gas chambers were shut down, they would be less deserving of condemnation (though perhaps still deserving of some) than those who blow up kindergartens to retrieve captured land or even to end an oppressive occupation not accompanied by mass murder. But if Jews blew up German kindergartens *after* the war ended, in revenge against what the Germans did to their children, that would be far more deserving of condemnation than the use of terrorism in an effort to prevent further genocide.

There are other factors as well that might figure into any effort to construct a continuum of condemnation for terrorism, with reasonable people disagreeing about some and agreeing about others. The point is that nearly everybody supports some terrorism and opposes other terrorism. For some, it depends on self-serving considerations, while for others there are somewhat more objective criteria. Moreover, attitudes may change over time and with experience. Whether the world's selective tolerance toward terrorism continues will depend, at least in part, on our reaction to current terrorist threats. Since terrorists and their supporters generally regard *their* terrorism as justified, no objective continuum of terrorism will ever receive universal acceptance. All terrorism must be condemned, if condemnation of any terrorism is to have an impact.

The nature of terrorism will continuously change in the future, as it has in the past. Yesterday we worried about retail acts of terror—assassinations, bombings, and hijackings. Among the most difficult dilemmas was whether or not to give in to specific demands of the terrorists—usually the freeing of other terrorists. Today we fear wholesale acts of terror—such as the use of passenger planes as airborne missiles directed against densely populated targets. These acts are rarely accompanied by specific demands. They are not contingent or conditional threats, or if they are, the conditions are deliberately set so high as to be unrealistic. Instead, their object is massive destruction and mass murder of hundreds,

even thousands, of civilians. Tomorrow we may be faced with terrorist mass weapons—nuclear, chemical, and biological—capable of
destroying entire cities and more. In October 2001 there were
reports of a plan to detonate a ten-kiloton nuclear weapon, stolen
from a Russian arsenal, in New York City, and it is a sign of the
times that the United States government took the threat seriously.[7]

Professor Ehud Sprinzak of Israel's Interdisciplinary Center
in Herzliya has written that the attacks of September 11, 2001, represent "an intellectual failure to identify an entirely new category
of terrorism," which he calls "megalomaniac" hyperterrorism.
Sprinzak acknowledges that "the vast majority of terrorists and terror organizations still behave according to the logic portrayed in
hundreds of academic studies, scholarly models, and intelligence
profiles. They are political, conservative in their use of weapons,
and are low-casualty perpetrators ... [that] prefer to avoid catastro-
phes in order to secure sympathy in the post-terrorism stage." But
he insists that the Islamic terrorist group al-Qaeda does not fit this
conventional profile. Whether he is right or wrong, it is clear that
we will never again be able to lower our guard against the kind of
massive terrorism we experienced on September 11, 2001. This is
an endless war with ever changing enemies, always moving from
place to place.[8]

An important tenet of civil liberties is that the greatest dangers to liberty come from the powerful state. The greatest disasters
throughout history have been inflicted by states. The Crusades, the
Spanish Inquisition, the Stalinist murders, the Holocaust, the Cambodian genocide—all were inflicted by governments. Hence, the
focus of civil libertarian concerns has always been on the abuse of
power by state actors.

The relatively new phenomenon of terrorist groups—organizations that are not themselves states but that are nonetheless
waging war and seeking access to weapons of mass destruction—

challenges that paradigm for the first time. The new paradigm—terrorist groups capable of wreaking havoc of the kind that only states could previously inflict, but without the accountability of states—requires civil libertarians to rethink our exclusive focus on state action. To be sure, the most dangerous forms of global terrorism are still state sponsored, but identifying the sponsoring states is often difficult and subject to plausible deniability. Such denials are more often implausible, but they are conveniently "believed" by opportunistic governments. In Chapter 5, I will propose new ways of thinking about how to strike the appropriate balance between liberty and security in the context of entirely new threats posed not only by states but by comparably dangerous terrorist groups as well.

The "emergency" steps that we take today to combat terrorism—the "temporary" compromises we strike with our liberties—are likely to become part of the permanent fabric of our legal and political culture. Sunset provisions written into laws restricting our freedoms will be less effective in the context of terrorism than in other contexts, because the sun will never set on terrorism and the fears it provokes. Before September 11, 2001, many wise politicians and pundits advised us to learn to live with terrorism and not to let it unduly influence our policies and attitudes. They reminded us that far fewer people were killed or injured in retail terrorist attacks than in automobile accidents. Although that is still the case, it is no longer possible to ignore or downplay terrorism, because we have experienced its wholesale version and we now understand—emotionally as well as intellectually—its potential for even greater mass destruction. Terrorists are trying to kill our children and our grandchildren. They are trying to change our way of life and to diminish our liberties. It is possible they may succeed, at least in part. In the face of this all too realistic prospect, it is no longer feasible to go about business as usual. How we deal with international terrorism is quickly becoming the defining issue of our age. The terrorists have gotten our attention, and we have gotten theirs. We are in a mortal struggle, one that will be fought primarily not on conventional battlefields but rather in dark alleys, shadowy streets, crowded airports, high-rise buildings, and secret weapons laboratories. It will also be fought in courtrooms, legislative chambers, and executive mansions. Finally, it will be fought in the hearts and minds of people throughout the world.

If we are to win the war against terrorism—or, more realistically, not to lose it—we will have to be smart, cautious, and open to new ways of thinking. There will be no panaceas, quick fixes, or simple solutions. The only possible "final" resolution of this struggle would be cataclysmic defeat—the nuclear, chemical, or biological destruction of the planet or large segments of it. Victories will be incremental, temporary, uncertain, and largely invisible. But there are steps we can—in fact must—take. There are also steps we could take but should not—at least until our very survival is imminently at stake. We should strive to strike an appropriate balance between preserving our security and preserving our liberty, because surely these important values will sometimes clash. The steps we take today are likely to affect the lives of future generations. We cannot assume they will be merely temporary. We have tough choices to make, and we should make them wisely, based on the fullest information, the most experienced advice, and the most creative thinking.

In this book I am bringing to bear my forty years of experience in thinking about terrorism, crime, and justice. I have advised governments on these issues. I have defended terrorists. I have consulted with the victims of terrorism. And I have studied, taught, and written about terrorism and civil liberties over many years. I have even been a terrorist target myself. As a criminal defense lawyer I have been close to evil, and I think I understand what motivates terrorists to take innocent life. To understand is not, however, to justify; understanding is empirical, whereas justification is normative. This book is the product of a lifetime of experience in thinking about crime and violence—from the perspective of a defense lawyer and a professor of criminal law and a student of psychology. Most of all, the issue is so important that I am willing to think the unthinkable and move beyond the kind of conventional wisdom that has failed us up to now in our losing battle against terrorism.

But I do not claim the dubious mantle of "expert" on the broad issue of terrorism, because there are no all-purpose experts in this multifaceted and ever-changing subject. Nearly everything we thought we knew about terrorism changed on September 11, 2001. Many experts are now scrambling to update their treatises and to qualify their predictions.[9] Although we can learn much from scholars who have studied terrorist groups for many years, the problem of terrorism is too important to be left to experts alone. Let us begin to confront the future by remembering the past and learning from our mistakes. For as George Santayana observed, those who cannot remember the past are condemned to repeat it. Following the catastrophe of September 11, many have developed a collective amnesia regarding their toleration, indeed encouragement, of terrorism. This is especially so in Europe, but it is also true among some segments of American society. Unless we remember and rectify our past attitudes, we will be condemned to reexperience events similar to those of September 11. But next time it may be worse—much worse.

chapter one

Deterring Terrorism

"[Terrorists] need to know that these
crimes only hurt their cause."
—President George W. Bush,
after learning that Islamic terrorists
had murdered reporter Daniel Pearl

"The first several hijackings
[accomplished more for the Palestinian cause]
than twenty years of pleading
at the United Nations."
—Palestine Liberation Organization's
chief observer at the United Nations

Although state-sponsored global terrorism is a relatively new phenomenon, and is in some ways quite different from other evils previously confronted, it is still subject to the basic rules of human nature and experience that teach us how to reduce the frequency and severity of harmful conduct. This chapter sets out some fundamental rules of deterring crime in general and then shows how these rules relate to terrorism in particular. The next chapter shows how the international community, and especially the United Nations and our European allies, have refused to follow these obvious rules since at least 1968, and in fact have deliberately violated them, thereby encouraging increased resort to terrorism, both in frequency and in severity.

How to Stop Harmful Conduct

For thousands of years, human societies have sought to reduce the frequency and severity of such harms as murder, robbery, and rape. Various techniques for dealing with such crimes have evolved over time. Broadly defined, these techniques have had much in common across societies and over time. They may be outlined in the following familiar terms.

The first technique is to ensure that the potential criminal understands that he has far more to lose than to gain from committing the crime. This serves to *disincentivize* the act, or *deter* the actor, by sending a clear and unequivocal message: not only will you not benefit from the act, but if you are caught doing it you will be severely disadvantaged. (A disincentive seeks to eliminate the benefit seen as an incentive by the offenders. A deterrent seeks to impose a negative cost on them and their cause.) A useful example of this mechanism is the treble or punitive damage remedy, which disgorges all gains from the person who secured them improperly and imposes a punitive fine.

The second technique is to *incapacitate* those who would carry out the actions by imprisoning them, killing them, keeping them away from the places they wish to target, or otherwise making it impossible for them to be in a position to undertake the undesirable actions. A useful metaphor for incapacitation is the zoo, where wild animals are kept behind bars. We are not seeking to change the animal's propensities but are simply erecting an impermeable barrier between it and us.[1]

A third technique is to *persuade* the actor not to undertake the action, by rehabilitating, reeducating, or shaming him, convincing him that the action is wrong. A good example of this mechanism is requiring drunken drivers to attend classes or enter programs designed to influence behavior.

Another traditional technique is *proactive prevention*. The word "prevention" carries broad implications, including eliminating or reducing the causes of crime, such as poverty. I am using "prevention" in the more specific sense of gathering intelligence about plans or impending crimes. Secret service agencies throughout the world plant spies in terrorist organizations to gather such information. They also bribe or extort actual members of these organizations to serve as double agents. Sometimes they engage in scams or stings calculated to get the criminals to commit the crimes under controlled situations (such as selling drugs to an undercover agent, or hiring a hit man who turns out to be a government agent). Intelligence agencies also gather information by means of high technology, such as satellite photography, electronic intercepts, and the like. A useful metaphor for this mechanism is building a trap for a wolf that is eating a farmer's sheep and baiting it with a dead animal.

There are clearly overlaps among these methods. The death penalty, for example, incapacitates and punishes the specific offender (this is called "specific deterrence") while also, it is hoped, deterring other potential offenders (this is called "general deterrence"). The age-old rule disallowing a murderer to inherit money from his victim disincentivizes killing for those who would do it in order to inherit more quickly. Imprisonment incapacitates (at least during the period of confinement, and at least against those on the other side of the bars) while also deterring both the offender and others. Even the mandatory class or program deters as well as rehabilitates (and may even incapacitate at least during time the person is in the program). Sometimes these mechanisms conflict with one another. Although imprisonment incapacitates during the period of confinement, it may increase the likelihood of recidivism among some inmates by exposing them to a criminal culture, even as it decreases that likelihood among others by demonstrating the horrors of prison. Paying double agents may help prevent some crime, but it may also promote others at the same time.[2]

The goal of removing all positive incentives (disincentivizing) while also imposing negative consequences (deterring) is to send the following powerful message to any person or group contemplating the commission of a harmful act: you, your group, your family, and everything you hold dear will be considerably worse off if you commit the prohibited act than if you forbear from committing it. That was the intent of the following statement made by President Bush on April 4, 2002: "I call on the Palestinian people, the Palestinian Authority and our friends in the Arab world to join us in delivering a clear message to terrorists. Blowing yourself up does not help the Palestinian cause. To the contrary, suicide bombing missions could well blow up the best and only hope for a Palestinian state." Anything that mutes this message, or undercuts it, diminishes the impact of this age-old technique for reducing the frequency and severity of harmful conduct. For example, if a bank robber's family (or the cause he was robbing for) were allowed to keep the proceeds of the robbery, the deterrent message would be decidedly mixed, even if the robber himself is caught and imprisoned.[3]

The major difference between the disincentive-deterrent approach, on the one hand, and the incapacitation approach on the other is that deterrence relies on a rational calculus—a cost-benefit analysis—by those contemplating the harmful act. Incapacitation relies exclusively on the physical impossibility of certain acts being carried out by people who are confined, exiled, or killed.[4] Again, think of a zoo as incapacitating the wild animals, and think of an animal trainer who threatens the whip and promises the food as more akin to the disincentive-deterrent model. Or think of the hospital for the criminally insane as incapacitating a dangerous person who cannot be deterred by the threat of future punishment, while at the same time trying to reduce his propensity toward violence by treating his aggressive mental condition.

In addition to these techniques of harm reduction, all of which focus directly on the behavior in question, there are also some "softer" approaches that tend to be oriented more toward the longer term and have a more subtle impact on the harmful conduct. This kind of approach includes such efforts as education, positive reinforcement, negative reinforcement, religious indoctrination, and so on.

In the next chapter I will focus on how the international community not only failed to disincentivize terrorism but went so far as to incentivize it, by rewarding it rather than punishing it. In subsequent chapters, I will discuss the other techniques.

Can Terrorism Be Deterred?

The theory of deterrence—reducing the frequency of an undesirable action by threatening and inflicting pain on those contemplating the action—operates along a continuum. At one end of the continuum is the calculating state. The conventional theory of nuclear deterrence, for example, hypothesizes a state, whose actions are rationally determined by self-interest, acting so as to maximize this self-interest and to minimize negative consequences.[5] The theory depends largely upon actors making calculations and counter-calculations based on each other's contemplated actions and reactions. Near the other end of the continuum are largely futile attempts to deter impulsive actions by irrational actors. These actions may be caused by such factors as passion, impulse, and mental illness. For the most part even the most passionate, impulsive, and mentally ill actors are capable of being deterred from taking *some* actions, under some circumstances, at some points in time, but the impact of long-delayed punishment is likely to be minimal. At a point even farther along this continuum are suicidal actors, although whether they can ever be deterred is a question that is rarely considered in deterrence theory. We shall return to this complex matter later.

Between the extremes of this continuum lies a wide range of actors and actions that are more or less subject to deterrence, based on a wide variety of factors. In the context of the kind of terrorism I am focusing on in this book, there is also a long continuum whose terminal points parallel those on the more conventional continuum. Some terrorists are exquisite calculators and will engage in terrorism only if the benefits (as defined by them) outweigh the costs (also as defined by them). As George Habash, the leader of the Popular Front for the Liberation of Palestine, told a reporter:

> The main point is to select targets where success is 100% assured. To harass, to upset, to work on the nerves through unexpected small damages. . . . This is a thinking man's game. Especially when one is as poor as the Popular Front is. It would be silly for us to even think of waging a regular war; imperialism is too powerful and Israel is too strong. The only way to destroy

them is to give a little blow here, a little blow there; to advance step by step, inch by inch, for years, for decades, with determination, doggedness, patience. And we will continue our present strategy. It's a smart one, you see.[6]

To the extent that terrorism is "an entirely rational choice" and "a calculated move in a political game"—as some have concluded—it should be subject to the usual rules of deterrence theory. As I will show later, however, not all terrorism is the same, and some may be subject to somewhat different calculations. The benefits contemplated by some terrorists may vary, both in kind and in degree, from those contemplated by the more conventional criminal or by other terrorists. Moreover, the costs may also be defined and calibrated differently. The 1972 terrorist attacks against the Israeli Olympic team in Munich, for example, might be considered an absolute failure according to conventional standards of success. The demands of the terrorists were rejected, and nearly all of the terrorists were killed, either on the spot or thereafter. In the short term, world opinion quickly turned against the terrorists and those who sponsored them. But, as I will show, in the intermediate and long term, the world's reaction to the Munich massacre served the interests of the terrorists to such an extraordinary degree that it encouraged many future acts of terrorism, both by Palestinians and by other aggrieved groups incentivized by the success of this apparent "failure."

Terrorism Is Different—But Not That Different

The kind of terrorism we are talking about is different in many respects from other crimes such as murder, rape, and robbery. The difference is that terrorism is generally more calculated, more premeditated, and more goal-oriented than impulsive crimes or crimes of passion. Criminal justice expert Philip Heymann has observed:

> As a crime, terrorism is different. Most crimes are the product of greed, anger, jealousy, or the desire for domination, respect, or position in a group, and not of any desire to "improve" the state of the world or of a particular nation. Most crimes do not involve—as part of the plan for accomplishing their objectives—trying to change the occupants of government positions, their actions, or the basic structures and ideology of a nation. Some would argue that violence carried out for political purposes is more altruistic; others would vigorously deny that. But all would agree that political violence is different from ordinary crime, in that it is planned to force changes in government actions, people, structure, or even ideology as a means to whatever ends the perpetrators are seeking with whatever motivations drive them towards those ends. It is in that sense that the U.S. State Department definition says that the violence is usually "perpetrated for political reasons."[7]

Terrorism—at least of the kind described by Heymann—is thus more, not less, subject to disincentive and deterrence techniques than most ordinary crimes. To be sure, some acts of terrorism are revenge-driven and impulsive, but most are carefully calculated to achieve a goal. Sometimes the goal will be specific and immediate, while other times it may be more general, long term, and apocalyptic. But whatever the object, if it becomes clear that it will be *dis*-served by terrorism—that the cause will be worse off—then it will be only a matter of time until co-supporters of the cause turn against those who resort to terrorism. Without widespread support from within the cause they are seeking to promote, terrorists cannot long thrive. Certainly if there is widespread opposition to terrorism within the cause, it will soon dry up.[8]

When we look at terrorism simply as a technique whose frequency and ferocity we seek to diminish—without necessarily making any moral judgments about particular terrorists or causes—certain conclusions seem beyond dispute. The first is that those who employ terrorism should always be worse off—by their own criteria—for having employed it than if they had not employed it. President Bush's rhetoric, that terrorist crimes "only hurt their cause," must become reality.

Not only must terrorism never be rewarded, the cause of those who employ it must be made—and must be seen to be made—worse off as a result of the terrorism than it would have been without it. The way calculating terrorists define and calibrate the cost and benefits may be different from the way common criminals decide whether to rob, cheat, or bully, but society's response must be based on similar considerations. Those who employ terrorism have their own criteria for evaluating success and failure, and in implementing the immutable principle that those who employ terrorism must be worse off for having resorted to this tactic, we must make them worse off by their own criteria. It will not always be possible to do this. If the terrorists' criteria for success is massive publicity, for example, it will be difficult for a democracy to control the amount of publicity a terrorist act generates. (Totalitarian regimes, such as China and the former Soviet Union, have enforced a blanket policy of disallowing media reports of terrorist acts, precisely to deny the terrorists what they want.) But publicity is generally not an end in itself. It is a means toward furthering the terrorists' cause. (Garnering publicity is generally part of the initial phase in a multiphased process for achieving substantive goals.) The end of achieving these ultimate goals can be controlled, at least to some degree, by those determined to disincentivize or deter terrorism.

The Root Causes of Terrorism

The current mantra of those opposed to a military response to terrorism is a plea to try to understand and eliminate the root causes of terrorism. There are several reasons why this is exactly the wrong approach.

The reason terrorism works—and will persist unless there are significant changes in the responses to it—is precisely because its perpetrators believe that by murdering innocent civilians they will succeed in attracting the attention of the world to their perceived grievances and their demand that the world "understand them" and "eliminate their root causes." To submit to this demand is to send the following counterproductive message to those with perceived grievances: if you resort to terrorism, we will try harder to understand your grievances and respond to them than we would have if you employed less violent methods. This is precisely the criterion for success established by the terrorist themselves. Listen to the words of Zehdi Labib Terzi, the Palestine Liberation Organization's chief observer at the United Nations: "The first several hijackings aroused the consciousness of the world and awakened the media and the world opinion much more—and more effectively—than twenty years of pleading at the United Nations." If this is true—and the Palestinians surely believe it is—then it should come as no surprise that hijackings and other forms of terrorism increased dramatically after the Palestinians were rewarded for their initial terrorism by increased world attention to its "root causes"—attention that quickly resulted in their leader being welcomed by the U.N. General Assembly, their organization being granted observer status at the United Nations, and their "government" being recognized by dozens of nations.[9]

We must take precisely the opposite approach to terrorism. We must commit ourselves *never to try to understand or eliminate its alleged root causes,* but rather to place it beyond the pale of dialogue and negotiation. Our message must be this: even if you have legitimate grievances, if you resort to terrorism as a means toward eliminating them we will simply not listen to you, we will not try to understand you, and we will certainly never change any of our policies toward you. Instead, we will hunt you down and destroy your capacity to engage in terror. Any other approach will encourage the use of terrorism as a means toward achieving ends—whether those ends are legitimate, illegitimate, or anything in between.

Nor is there any single substantive root cause of all, or even most, terrorism. If there were—if poverty, for example, were the root cause of all terrorism—then by fixing that problem we could address the root cause of specific terrorist groups without encouraging others. But the reality is that the "root causes" of terrorism are as varied as human nature. Every single "root cause" associated with terrorism has existed for centuries, and the vast majority of groups with equivalent or more compelling causes—and with far greater poverty and disadvantage—have never resorted to terrorism. There has never even been a direct correlation—to say nothing of causation—between the degrees of injustice experienced by a given group and the willingness of that group to resort to terrorism. The search for "root causes" smacks more of after-the-fact political justification than inductive scientific inquiry. The variables that distinguish aggrieved groups willing to target innocent civilians from equally situated groups unwilling to murder children have far less to do with the legitimacy of their causes or the suffering of their people than with religious, cultural, political, and ethical differences.[10] They also relate to universalism versus parochialism and especially to the value placed on human life. To focus on such factors as poverty, illiteracy, disenfranchisement, and others all too common around our imperfect world is to fail to explain why so many groups with far greater grievances and disabilities have never resorted to terrorism.[11]

Instead, the focus must be on the reality that using an act of terrorism as the occasion for addressing the root causes of that act only encourages other groups to resort to terrorism in order to have *their* root causes advanced on the international agenda. Put another way, the "root cause" of terrorism that must be eliminated is its *success*.

It may well be true that desperation contributes to the willingness of individuals to become suicide bombers, but it is the success of this tactic that incentivizes those who recruit and send the suicide bombers on their lethal missions. It is crucial to distinguish between the motivations of the bombers themselves and those of the leaders who decide to employ the technique of terrorism to achieve political and diplomatic goals. It would seem to follow from this reality that an act of terrorism should never be the occasion for addressing the substantive root causes of terrorism. The unequivocal message to all terrorists should be that the *only* response to acts of terrorism will be to make certain that it never succeeds, to inflict severe punishment on the terrorists, and to interdict their future terrorist acts by incapacitating them and undertaking effective proactive preventive measures. Just as we don't address the root causes of a bad marriage that may have led a man to murder his wife—we hunt down the murderer and punish him—so too we shouldn't consider the root causes that may have motivated the violence of the terrorists. We must hunt them down and punish and incapacitate them, without regard for the possible substantive justice of their cause. That is the only way to send the message that no cause—no end—justifies resort to the unacceptable means of terrorism. If we deviate from this principle, we become complicit in encouraging further terrorism.

This tough approach toward terrorism does not mean that root causes should never be addressed. If the cause is just, it should be considered—in the order of its justness compared with that of other causes, discounted by the penalty that must be imposed for resorting to terrorism. Again an analogy to ordinary crimes: we recognize that poverty and unemployment may contribute to the causes of street violence—that they are among its root causes. But we don't use the occasion of a drug-related murder to address these root causes. Instead, we punish the murderer and redouble our efforts to deter and interdict future murders. At the same time, we continue to try to address poverty and unemployment, because that is the right thing to do, even in the absence of drug-related murders. There are many just causes throughout the world. Those who advocate or resort to terrorism should be moved backward—not forward—on the list of just causes warranting consideration by the international community.

This is especially so if the terrorists are representative of the cause, rather than peripheral to it. An act of terrorism should be the occasion only for punishment and incapacitation, not for negotiation and consideration of root causes. The message must be that nothing will be gained by terrorism, and much will be lost. The cause will be set back, not furthered, by resort to terrorism. Here an analogy to child rearing is useful. Suppose you have two children, each of whom has an equally legitimate grievance. One of them discusses it rationally with you, while the other one hits you over the head with a stick. The latter will surely get your attention, but only a terrible parent would give preference to the grievance of the violent child over that of the peaceful one. To do that would be encouraging further violence by both children. (A concerned parent might pay more attention to the violent child, because his violence may reflect pathology, but the concern would not take the form of giving in to his demands.)

This would seem an obvious and simple first principle in dealing with terrorism (as it is in dealing with other crimes). But, as we shall see in the next chapter, the international community has responded in precisely the opposite manner. Terrorism has generally moved its cause forward rather than backward. And it con-

tinues to do so—even after September 11. The more horrible the
nature of the terrorism, the greater has been the forward movement. Terrorists—especially terrorist leaders—have been honored
rather than punished. Indeed, at least three terrorist leaders have
been awarded the Nobel Peace Prize. Some have received hon-
orary degrees from leading universities. Several have been made
heads of state or government. Some have been embraced by religious leaders. The message has been clear: if you believe your
cause is sufficiently just to resort to terrorism, you must be right.
The very decision to resort to terrorism is seen as a confirmation
of the justness of the cause. The more horrible the nature of your
terrorism, the more just your cause must be. Terrorism leapfrogs its
cause over other equally or more just causes whose advocates have
not resorted to terrorism.[12] It's no wonder, therefore, that some
aggrieved groups employ it as a first, rather than a last, resort.

There is also another reason why terrorism advances its
cause. Terrorism frightens us into seeking quick solutions. If we
give in to the demands of the terrorists, maybe they will stop using
terrorism.

The combination of these reasons—some moral, others prag-
matic—understandably inclines decent and thoughtful people to
opt for an approach that advances the cause of terrorists, by giving
in to their demands and advancing consideration of their root
causes over the root causes of other groups. The long-term effects
of this approach have been to legitimate terrorism as a means of
achieving certain ends and to encourage other groups to resort to
it. The recent history of terrorism demonstrates that this is how we
have responded to it, and how terrorists have responded to this
approach. This history of advancing the causes of terrorists, honoring their leaders and giving in to their demands—rather than punishing and repressing them, while at the same time moving their
cause backward on the international agenda—has been an important contributing factor in the recent proliferation of international

terrorism. This paradox—that by addressing the root causes of one group of terrorists we encourage others to resort to terrorism—should become an important foundation for any policy designed to reduce the frequency and severity of terrorism.

Suicide Terrorism

One major difference between ordinary crime and terrorism—and therefore in a society's approach to preventing or reducing the incidences of either—is that religiously motivated terrorists are often willing, sometimes even eager, to give up their lives in the interests of their holy cause. In this situation, the usual deterrent strategy of threatening death to the perpetrator will not work. Indeed, for those who desire a martyr's death, the threat may provide something of an incentive, especially if it is coupled with the promise of reward for the martyr's family or cause.[13]

But a desire for martyrdom need not eliminate all possibilities of deterring the act by threatening severe punishment. It merely requires that the severe punishment be directed against someone, or something, other than the potential martyr himself—such as his cause, or those who harbor him. In theory, the punishment could also be directed against his family, but such a strategy would raise daunting questions of morality and fairness.

There would be various steps, at least in theory, that could be taken to deter many suicide terrorists, *if* one were prepared to act amorally. Punishment of kin or friends is one obvious tactic that has been successfully used by tyrannical regimes throughout history. Putting aside these extreme tactics, there are entirely moral ways of deterring suicide actors as well. These tactics require that we think beyond the individual suicide terrorist, who probably cannot be effectively deterred by means acceptable to a moral society, and that we understand that the vast majority of individual suicide terrorists do not act on their own. They are part of complex organizational structures. They are sent to engage in their suicide terrorism by the organizations that have recruited them, persuaded them to become martyrs, promised them and their families rewards (in this world or the next), and selected the target, time, and place for the terrorist act. Often, their terrorism has widespread support within the cause, manifested through financial contributions, logistical assistance, and harboring. Few, if any, suicide bombers act on their own as a result of uncontrollable rage. They may volunteer to act because of rage, but the decision to send them is almost always calculated by others. The question therefore is not whether the individual suicide terrorist can be deterred from suicide terrorism. The questions that must be asked are whether the *organization* can be deterred from *sending* him on a suicide mission, and whether the *supporters* can be deterred from rendering needed assistance. The answer to the first question is generally going to be yes—*if* we can figure out effective threats and carry them out with sufficient public demonstration that terrorism does not benefit, and indeed harms, the organizations that opt for it, and the causes they represent. The answer to the second question can also be yes, *if* we are prepared to punish those who assist terrorism through material and other support.

When the terrorist organization is believed to be state sponsored or supported—as it often is—the deterrent threat can be directed against the state. This will not always be easy, for several reasons: state sponsorship or support is often a matter of degree, the evidence supporting the belief is often difficult to secure, and other factors—diplomatic, legal, economic—will sometimes militate against strong action.[14]

The Impact of September 11

Any attempt to understand the dynamics of terrorism, and to seek to minimize its future threats, requires us to distinguish between terrorism before September 11, 2001, and terrorism after the cataclysmic events of that date and the international reaction to them. Before September 11, terrorism worked—not in every case and not for every group, but often enough to be seen as a successful tactic for bringing about considerable change. It worked for the Jews in British-controlled Palestine. It has been working, to some degree, for the Irish in British-controlled Northern Ireland. It has been working for the Palestinians in the West Bank and Gaza. It has not worked for the Armenians, the Kurds, and some other groups. (In Chapter 2 we will explore the reasons why terrorism works for some groups and not for others.) It is the nature of terrorism that its successes are far more important than its failures, because they are more visible and thus more influential in encouraging further terrorism. And some of the successes of terrorism before September 11 were dramatic and observed throughout the world.

Before September 11, terrorism worked because those who sponsored it too often benefited from the terrorist acts. The sponsors were rewarded because the dramatic nature of the acts got our attention and brought their perceived grievances to the forefront of public consciousness.

This attention caused many decent people—religious leaders, academics, politicians, ordinary citizens—to seek to gain a better understanding of terrorists' grievances and to address the root causes of the terrorism. The very brutality and desperation of the acts led many in the international community to believe that the terrorists represented "a cause that could no longer justifiably be denied." Because their grievances and causes were addressed in response to terrorism, other groups with perceived grievances saw the benefits of terrorism and were more likely to resort to it, rather than to opt for other less visible and hence less successful mechanisms of change. Success begets repetition and imitation. (We will also see, in Chapter 2, that terrorism works because the short-term self-interest of some countries inclines them to make self-serving deals with terrorists that set back what should be a universal and coordinated attack on terrorism. This variation on the "prisoner's dilemma" encourages terrorists to believe they can always extort benefits from some countries, especially, it seems from experience, France, Germany, and Italy.)[15]

This, then, is the first paradox of dealing with terrorism: Terrorism does, of course, have substantive root causes. Every act of violence, criminality, and evil has root causes. By addressing and fixing the root causes of a *particular* terrorist group, we may sometimes—though not always, as we shall see—reduce or eliminate the specific terrorist threat of that group (and those who share its goals). But in doing so, we encourage other potential terrorists to resort to this unacceptable means of having their root causes addressed and fixed.

There is, however, another paradox of dealing with terrorism, which may point in the opposite direction. The more brutal and repressive we are toward the terrorists, the more we make them martyrs to be emulated by other potential terrorists. Punishing rather than honoring terrorists and moving their claims backward rather than forward may contribute to the breeding of new terrorists willing to sacrifice their lives to the cause. If both of these paradoxes are equally true, then it would seem to follow that neither of the obvious approaches to dealing with terrorism will work, at least not without at the same time encouraging new terrorism and breeding new terrorists.[16]

Actually, this conclusion is false, as we shall see, because paradox I is far more powerful than paradox II. Paradox I is far more powerful because it influences the conduct of *leaders* of the cause and it affects the ultimate goals of the cause. Paradox II, on the other hand, influences only the *followers* and may make them more susceptible to the calls of the leaders for martyrdom volunteers. In this kind of "organized terrorism," leaders are far more important than followers, because such terrorism is more authoritarian than democratic. It is a top-down, not a bottom-up, phenomenon. Individual martyrs in search of a leader can be dangerous, but far less so than charismatic leaders capable of persuading followers to risk or forfeit their lives.

chapter two

The Internationalization of Terrorism

How Our European Allies Made September 11 Inevitable

"In light of the result, we have made one
of the best achievements of Palestinian commando
action. . . . The choice of the Olympics, from the
purely propagandistic viewpoint, was
100 percent successful."
—Statement by Black September following
the murder of eleven Israeli Olympians

On July 22, 1968, three armed Palestinian terrorists hijacked an Israeli passenger airliner flying from Rome to Tel Aviv. The terrorists belonged to the Popular Front for the Liberation of Palestine (PFLP), one of the groups that made up the Palestine Liberation Organization. The hijacking marked the advent, according to the director of the Rand Corporation's terrorism research unit in Washington, D.C., of the modern era of international terrorism.[1]

Although this was not the first airplane hijacking—many airplanes had been temporarily diverted from their intended destinations in order to get the hijackers somewhere else, generally Cuba—it was the first one designed to terrorize a nation into changing its policy and to force world attention on a cause. The hijacking on July 22, 1968, was the first in a series of dramatic and well-coordinated attacks planned and approved at the highest levels of the Palestine Liberation Organization. The purpose of these hijackings was subsequently acknowledged, indeed proclaimed, by the PLO's chief observer to the United Nations: to bring public attention to the Palestinian cause, as an initial step in a multifaceted program of terror, the goal of which was the establishment of a Palestinian state.[2]

The systematic campaign of terrorism, begun in 1968 and continuing to the present, was so successful in achieving sympathy and support for the Palestinian cause that it "has since served as a model for similarly aggrieved ethnic and nationalistic minority groups everywhere," in the words of Bruce Hoffman, the Rand Corporation's director of terrorism research. Accordingly, the thrust of this chapter will be on Palestinian terrorism, especially in its global aspects, and the international community's responses to it. It is impossible to understand the terrible events of September 11, 2001, without understanding the dynamics—and the success—of Palestinian terrorism.[3]

Palestinian terrorism had begun well before the Six Day War in 1967 and Israel's subsequent occupation of land previously controlled by Jordan and Egypt. Immediately following the establishment of Israel in 1948 and the cease-fire that ended the first Arab-Israeli war, Egypt began training commandos known as fedayeen to cross the border from Gaza into Israel to attack civilian targets.[4] These attacks were localized and received little attention outside Israel. But after Israel occupied the West Bank and the Gaza Strip in 1967, the Palestinians internationalized their terrorism, beginning with attacks on the Israeli airline El Al, and then moving to other international airlines.

As George Habash, the founder of the PFLP, put it: "When we hijack a plane it has more effect than if we killed a hundred Israelis in battle." It was also far easier to kill unarmed and vulnerable civilian airline passengers than well-armed and protected Israeli soldiers.[5]

The Initial Hijackings and Airline Attacks: 1968–72

The initial hijacking of July 22, 1968, was regarded as a great success by the PLO, focusing world attention on the Palestinian cause for the five weeks during which twenty-one Israeli passengers and eleven crew members were held hostage in Algiers. Finally, the hostages were released in exchange for sixteen Arab prisoners being held in Israeli jails. The hijackers too were released.

Success begets repetition. So it should not have been surprising when, before the end of the year, Palestinian gunmen attacked another El Al airplane at the Athens airport, killing one Israeli and wounding another. The perpetrators were arrested, but they were freed after other hijackers seized another plane.

Two months later, yet another El Al plane was attacked, at the

Zurich airport, leaving the pilot and three passengers dead. One of the perpetrators was killed, one was freed almost immediately, and the other three were released following another hijacking.

Six months after this attack, Palestinian terrorists hijacked a TWA plane from Rome, ordering it to land in Damascus, where the passengers were released but a bomb was detonated in the cockpit. The lead hijacker, a woman named Leila Khaled, was released and shortly thereafter participated in another hijacking.

A week later, two thirteen-year-old Arab boys threw hand grenades at the El Al office in Brussels. The two, who had been recruited by al-Fatah, the largest of the groups composing the PLO, took refuge in the Iraqi embassy and later escaped.

Less than three months later, another hand grenade attack was directed against the El Al office in Athens. A Greek child was killed and thirteen other people were injured. Two Jordanians were convicted of the murder but were released after another hijacking.

In December 1969 an attack was planned on an airplane in Jordan, but this one was prevented. Four terrorists were arrested, and it is not known what happened to them. Another hijacking was thwarted at Athens in the same month, and the hijackers were arrested but freed following yet another hijacking.

In addition to the attacks on international aviation, Palestinian terrorists carried out numerous bombings in Israeli shopping markets and malls, and against other civilian targets, during 1968 and 1969. At the end of 1969, as Palestinian terrorism was increasing, the U.N. General Assembly adopted a resolution, long sought by Arab members, recognizing the "inalienable rights" of the Palestinian people. The initial phase of Palestinian terrorism had been successful.

Nineteen seventy was another banner year for terrorism. It began with the hijacking of a TWA plane from Beirut to Paris. The hijacker was quickly released.

Six weeks later, an airplane bus taking passengers to an El Al plane at the Munich airport was attacked. One Israeli was killed and eight people were wounded. Three Arabs were arrested but quickly freed following another hijacking.

Eleven days after that, Palestinian terrorists blew up a Swissair jet bound from Zurich to Tel Aviv, killing all forty-seven people on board. The same day, a bomb exploded in the luggage compartment of an Austrian Airlines plane flying from Frankfurt to Vienna. Palestinian terrorism was entering a new and more deadly phase: instead of hijacking planes and demanding concessions, the terrorists were now simply murdering innocent civilians. The success of the initial phase produced an escalated second phase.

A week later, three Arabs were arrested for conspiring to hijack an El Al plane in Munich. They were sentenced to three months' imprisonment but were released after two months.

On June 10, the Popular Front for the Liberation of Palestine murdered the U.S. assistant military attaché in Jordan.

On July 22, 1970, an Olympic Airlines plane was hijacked to Athens. The six PFLP terrorists were freed, as were seven other defendants who were involved in previous hijackings.

On September 6, 1970, the PFLP tried to hijack an El Al flight from Amsterdam to New York. Israeli security agents thwarted the hijacking, killing one of the hijackers and wounding Leila Khaled, who had been freed by Syria after her first hijacking a year earlier. Following her capture she was held in a British prison where she was, by her own account, treated "as if I were an official state guest," and she knew that she would be quickly released—which she was, after less than a month.[6]

September 6 was a major day in the history of terrorism, with the PFLP also hijacking three other planes (Pan Am, TWA, and Swissair) and forcing two of them to land in Jordan, and the third in Egypt. Three days later a BOAC plane was hijacked and also flown to Jordan. All the planes were blown up. Several imprisoned terrorists were released and the terrorists responsible for the multiple hijackings were allowed to go free.

In December 1970, five Arab terrorists were arrested for conspiring to sabotage an El Al plane. They served a three-month sentence in Germany.

Between the end of 1970 and the Munich Olympics in the late summer of 1972, there were a number of additional attacks against international airlines, including the hijacking of a Sabena plane that was forced to land in Israel. A rescue by Israeli security guards resulted in the killing of two of the hijackers and the long-term imprisonment of the other two. Six Israelis died during the rescue. Three weeks later, three Japanese terrorists, working in coordination with the PFLP, machine-gunned passengers at the terminal in Israel, killing twenty-seven and wounding eighty. Two of the terrorists were killed and the third is serving a life term in an Israeli prison. Then in August 1972, a booby-trapped phonograph exploded in the baggage compartment of an El Al flight from Rome to Israel, injuring four. The Italian government freed the two Arab terrorists who were responsible.

The pattern was becoming quite discernible. Terrorists who hijacked, blew up, or otherwise attacked commercial airliners would, if captured, quickly be released by most countries. Only Israel (and presumably the United States, though it had not to that point caught any hijackers) would keep captured terrorists in prison for substantial terms. The message was clear. Terrorist attacks committed outside Israel would go unpunished and would generally achieve the desired result. Terrorist attacks committed in Israel were less certain to succeed—the Sabena hijacking had failed, though the shootings by the Japanese terrorists had succeeded—and far more certain to result in long-term imprisonment. Individual terrorists were neither being deterred by any realistic threat of punishment nor incapacitated by being kept confined. Indeed, they could expect to be released after a brief detention and returned home where they were treated as heroes. Moreover, their cause was benefiting from the attention the terrorist acts brought to it. On June 12, 1970, for example, *Life* magazine devoted its cover to the Palestinian cause and featured a positive interview with George Habash, who had orchestrated many of the most lethal terrorist attacks. The interviewer concluded her story with the following observation: "Dr. Habash's lips began to tremble and his eyes filled with tears, and one of them descended along his nose. What can I add? Human nature is the ultimate mystery, and the boundary between good and evil is such an elusive line." Terrorism—whether it took the form of conditional hijackings or unconditional mass murders—was turning out to be a winning tactic for those willing to kill civilians.[7]

September 5, 1972: Black September

It was against this background that Palestinian terrorist organizations planned the most dramatic act of international terrorism up until that time: the attack on the Israeli Olympic team in Munich. The attack was masterminded by Mohammed Oudeh, a onetime associate of Yasser Arafat. According to Oudeh, "Arafat was briefed on the scheme." It was part of the PLO's overall strategy to bring world attention to the Palestinian cause. Its specific purpose was articulated by one of its planners, Faud al-Shameli: "Bombing attacks on El Al offices do not serve our cause.... We have to kill their most important and most famous people. Since we cannot come close to their statesmen, we have to kill artists and sportsmen."[8]

Based on the reaction to international terrorism over the previous four years, the terrorists planning the Munich operation could expect to succeed in attracting the world's attention and be relatively certain that if any of the terrorists were captured they would not be held for long. It did not matter whether the terrorists threatened to kill unless specified demands were met, or simply killed to make a point. They could expect to be treated as heroes by supporters of their cause, and as "official state guests" by the European governments that held them for a brief period before sending them home. One authoritative study of international terrorism summarized the "extreme indulgence" shown to Palestinian terrorists by European countries: "Terrorists captured enroute to missions were frequently released after interrogation. Those captured during or after the execution of missions were often jailed for brief periods of time, their release obtained by subsequent terrorist acts or motivated by European fears that continued detention would inevitably encourage such acts. In cases where prison sentences were actually imposed, they were usually light." According to one survey, "of the 204 terrorists arrested outside the Middle East between 1968 and 1975, only three remained in prison at the end of 1975." That trend was already apparent by the summer of 1972. If terrorists were seeking targets "where success is 100 percent assured," as Habash described his approach, then the Munich Olympics seemed to satisfy the criterion. But even those who planned the Munich massacre could not have imagined how successful their bloody actions would prove for their cause, or how promptly the captured terrorists would be released and returned home as conquering heroes.[9]

Although global terrorism had made its debut several years earlier and had increased in frequency and ferocity between 1968 and 1972, the West German government was woefully unprepared to protect the security of the Olympics held in Munich. German security officials had been specifically warned of a possible terrorist attack on the Olympics by Palestinian groups. Yet they refused Israel's request to provide its own security to its team. At least eight armed Palestinian terrorists—almost certainly assisted by East German officials—easily scaled the security fence erected to protect the Olympic village. (They were also inadvertently helped by some American athletes who had broken curfew and were returning from a late-night drinking spree.) The terrorists, armed with automatic weapons, immediately murdered one of the Israeli coaches and threw his naked, machine-gunned body out the window. Shortly thereafter they shot an Israeli athlete, leaving him to bleed to death in front of his seven colleagues. They threatened to kill the remaining athletes unless approximately two hundred imprisoned terrorists—Germans, Palestinians, and others—were immediately released.[10]

Following hours of futile negotiation, the terrorists demanded that they and their hostages be flown to an Arab country. German authorities, after turning down Israel's requests to conduct its own rescue operation with a highly trained antiterrorist group, pretended to agree to the terrorist demand, instead planning a rescue operation of their own at the airport. The Germans had failed to train any antiterrorist police and left the operation in the hands of totally unprepared border guards. Several armed guards, who were necessary to the success of the operation, voted to abandon their posts moments before the rescue was to begin, refusing to risk their lives to save Israelis. Others were wrongly positioned, and there was an insufficient number of snipers assigned to the operation. Moreover, armed vehicles that were supposed to rush the terrorists got stuck in traffic and did not arrive until it was too late. There was a brief shootout in which several German snipers shot each other and two or three of the terrorists, and following this the remaining terrorists murdered all of the Israeli athletes in cold blood. Three of the terrorists were captured. But not one of them was ever brought to trial.

Less than two months after the murders, Chancellor Willy Brandt made a secret deal with the Palestinian terrorists. Together they arranged for other Palestinian terrorists to hijack a Lufthansa plane from Beirut carrying eleven German men and a skeleton crew and to hold these Germans hostage, threatening to kill them unless the three Munich murderers were flown to freedom in an Arab country. (The Lufthansa flight had originated in Damascus with no passengers and seven crew members and had picked up eleven male passengers and the two hijackers in Beirut.) Feigning terror at the prospect of Germans being murdered on a Lufthansa plane, Brandt gave in to the "demands" of these terrorists. Many observers suspected that the Lufthansa hijacking had been staged by the Brandt government to concoct an excuse for releasing the three terrorists, as a way of avoiding a real hijacking. Until recently there was no proof of this cynical secret deal between the government that had botched the rescue of the Israeli Olympic team and the terrorists who had murdered the Israelis, but it has now been confirmed by both Palestinian and German sources that the Lufthansa hijacking was a sham and that the Germans were all too eager to free the murderers.[11]

The captured terrorists were released, receiving a hero's welcome when they returned home. The bodies of the terrorists who had been killed in the shootout were sent to Libya, where they were given martyrs' burials. Israel, which became aware of the deception of the Lufthansa hijacking, was in no position to protest the immoral actions of the German government, since Germany, especially under Brandt, was a strong ally and an important supplier of reparation funds. The Israeli government, however, was determined to try to deter future terrorist actions. (Recall that at this time terrorism was conducted not by suicidal religious zealots but primarily by Palestinians with radical political views.) The Israeli secret service subsequently assassinated two of the three surviving Munich terrorists.[12] The third remains alive, residing somewhere in Africa with his wife and two children.

The prime minister of Israel, Golda Meir, reacted strongly to the news of the German decision to release the Munich murderers.

Simon Reeve, in a recent book about the Munich massacre, wrote: "Meir said she 'was literally physically sickened.' Perhaps some indication of the isolation felt by Meir and her government can be seen in her later thoughts on the release of the three terrorists. 'I think that there is not one single terrorist held in prison anywhere in the world. Everyone else gives in. We're the only ones who do not,' she said in disgust."[13]

The Munich massacre proved to be an unqualified success for the Palestinian cause in general and for Palestinian terrorism in particular. In the immediate aftermath of the murder of the Israeli athletes, "thousands of Palestinians rushed to join the terrorist organizations," according to Bruce Hoffman. There was some short-term criticism of the terrorists, but the Palestinians understood how effective their strategy had turned out to be. Hoffman has argued:

> The real lesson of Munich ... was a somewhat counter-intuitive one. The Olympic tragedy provided the first clear evidence that even terrorist attacks which fail to achieve their ostensible objectives can nonetheless still be counted successful provided that the operation is sufficiently dramatic to capture the media's attention. In terms of the publicity and exposure accorded to the Palestinian cause, Munich was an unequivocal success—a point conceded by even the most senior PLO officials. According to Abu Iyad, the organization's intelligence chief, long-time confidant of Arafat and co-founder with him of al-Fatah, the Black September terrorists admittedly "didn't bring about the liberation of any of their comrades imprisoned in Israel as they had hoped, but they did attain the operation's other two objectives: World opinion was forced to take note of the

Palestinian drama, and the Palestinian people imposed
their presence on an international gathering that had
sought to exclude them."

Indeed, despite the worldwide condemnation of the
terrorists' actions at the time, it soon became apparent
that, for the Palestinians, Munich was in fact a spectacu-
lar publicity coup. The undivided attention of some four
thousand print and radio journalists and two thousand
television reporters and crew already in place to cover
the Olympiad was suddenly refocused on to Palestine
and the Palestinian cause. An estimated 900 million persons in at least a hundred different countries saw the
crisis unfold on their television screens.[14]

Black September, the group that carried out the Olympic massacre,
issued the following communiqué a week after the killings:

In our assessment, and in light of the result, we have
made one of the best achievements of Palestinian commando action. A bomb in the White House, a mine in
the Vatican, the death of Mao tse-Tung, an earthquake
in Paris could not have echoed through the consciousness of every man in the world like the operation at
Munich. The Olympiad arouses the people's interest and
attention more than anything else in the world. The
choice of the Olympics, from the purely propagandistic
viewpoint, was 100 percent successful. It was like paint-
ing the name of Palestine on a mountain that can be
seen from the four corners of the earth.

A Palestinian refugee put it more directly: "From Munich onwards
nobody could ignore the Palestinians or their cause."[15]

But international reaction went beyond merely "taking note"

of the Palestinian cause. Even decent people cannot ignore inde-
cent events. It is only natural to talk about evil. What many in the
international community did was to ascribe a positive moral content to the evils of Palestinian terrorism. The assumption seemed to
be that any group of people willing to resort to such extreme measures must have a just and compelling cause.

The Aftermath of Munich

Not long after the Munich murders and the contrived hijacking that
brought about the release of the surviving murderers, Palestinian
terrorists invaded a diplomatic reception at the Saudi Arabian
embassy in Khartoum, Sudan, kidnapping two American diplomats
and a Belgian diplomat in March 1973. The same group that had
massacred the Israeli athletes at Munich, Black September, conducted the attack in Khartoum. The United States, which intercepted a direct communication between Yasser Arafat and his
operatives in the Khartoum office of al-Fatah, has long known that
Arafat personally planned the kidnapping of the diplomats. One of
the men involved in the interception was James Welsh, then an
official of the National Security Agency. According to a recent
newspaper account:

> Welsh was involved in a signals intercept between
> Arafat in Beirut and Khalil al-Wazir in the Khartoum
> office of al-Fatah. According to Welsh, the two were dis-
> cussing an operation about to occur in Khartoum. In
> addition to the logistics, the intercepts revealed the code
> name for the operation. It was Nahr al-Bard, or Cold
> River. Based on the intercept, a warning was issued on
> Feb. 28, 1973, but owing to some mix-up between the
> NSA and the State Department, it was downgraded

from "Flash" precedence to a communication of lesser
urgency. As a result, by the time it reached Khartoum
on March 2, the three diplomats were dead.[16]

The terrorists sought the release of Sirhan Sirhan, the murderer of
Robert Kennedy. When President Nixon refused this demand,
Arafat personally ordered the murder of the diplomats. The diplomats—one of whom was the highest-ranking African-American in
the foreign service—were taken to the embassy basement and tortured and killed in cold blood. The torture they suffered was so
barbarous that, later, "authorities couldn't tell which was black and
which was white." Although Arafat publicly denied any complicity
in these murders, he talked about them during a private dinner
with Romanian dictator Nicolae Ceauşescu in May 1973. The dinner was also attended by General Ion Mihai Pacepa, a high-ranking Romanian intelligence officer who later defected to the United
States. Pacepa subsequently wrote an article, published in the *Wall
Street Journal* in 2002, in which he stated that the Munich massacre had been led by "Arafat's liaison officer for Romania, Ali
Hassan Salameh," and that at the dinner "Arafat excitedly bragged
about his Khartoum operation." After reviewing Arafat's history,
including his involvement in a shipment of Iranian-made arms captured by the Israelis in 2002, Pacepa concluded that "Yasser Arafat
remains the same bloody terrorist I knew so well during my years
at the top of Romania's foreign intelligence service." Based on the
evidence now available, Arafat could be tried and convicted for the
first-degree murder of an American diplomat—a crime with no
statute of limitations.[17]

Between the Arafat-ordered murder of the diplomats and the
end of 1974, Palestinian terrorists attacked another airline office, a
passenger terminal, a train carrying Soviet Jews to Vienna, a jumbo jet
from New Delhi, a Pan Am office in Rome, and a DC-10 from Dubai.

They also took Israeli children hostage at schools in Ma'alot and Qiryat Shemona in Israel, killing dozens of children in the process.

Only six months after Palestinian terrorists killed these schoolchildren, and a year and a half after he ordered the murder of three Western diplomats, Arafat received the legitimization he had long been seeking: an invitation to speak at the U.N. General Assembly, where he was greeted like a hero and a statesman, not as a cold-blooded murderer with the blood of American diplomats, Israeli Olympians, and Jewish children on his hands.

Soon afterward, the United Nations granted observer status to the PLO—the first terrorist organization to be so honored. Recall that all this was taking place while the PLO was still boasting of its reliance on terrorism as its primary mechanism of "diplomacy." Hoffman saw a likely causal relation between the willingness of the Palestinians to resort to terrorism and their acceptance by the United Nations: "It is perhaps not entirely coincidental, then, that eighteen months after Munich the PLO's leader, Yassir Arafat, was invited to address the UN General Assembly and shortly afterwards the PLO was granted special observer status in that international body. Indeed by the end of the 1970s the PLO, a non-state actor, had formal diplomatic relations with more countries (eighty-six) than [did] Israel (seventy-two). It is doubtful whether the PLO could have achieved this success had it not resorted to international terrorism."[18] More important than what any expert thinks, the Palestinians believe that their acceptance and legitimation by the international community would not have come about so quickly had they not resorted to terrorism and instead played by the rules. An organization committed to peace and a world that claimed to eschew terrorism were rewarding their terrorist acts.[19] At about the same time, Arafat met with the French foreign minister, who said he had a "favorable and encouraging impression" of him and hoped he would end his terrorism.

If anyone actually believed that honoring Arafat and legitimizing his terrorist organization would persuade them—or anyone
else—to abandon terror, they were quickly proved wrong. Within
ten days of Arafat's speeches—on the very day the General
Assembly voted to grant official observer status to the PLO—
Palestinian terrorists continued their pattern of terror by hijacking
a British airliner in Dubai. The plane was eventually flown to
Tunisia, where a passenger was killed. Over the half decade following the legitimation of Arafat and his cause, Palestinian terrorists
attacked Orly Airport, hijacked a plane to Entebbe, Uganda
(where Israeli commandos rescued all but three passengers),
attacked a passenger terminal at Istanbul, hijacked a Lufthansa
plane, hijacked an Israeli bus, killing twenty-six civilians, attacked
an El Al plane in Paris, and shot passengers in Brussels. During
this same half decade, the United Nations declared its first International Day of Solidarity with the Palestinian people, and Arafat met
with Austrian chancellor Bruno Kreisky, former West German
chancellor Willy Brandt, the prime minister of Spain, and the president of Portugal. Palestinian terrorism was working. It was prov-
ing itself more effective than any form of diplomacy.

The 1980s: Escalating Violence

The European policy of appeasing terrorists and encouraging their
acts continued unabated through the 1980s, as did Palestinian terrorism. On June 13, 1985, Arab terrorists hijacked a TWA jet full
of passengers and flew it to Beirut, where they murdered an American and threw his body on the tarmac. American efforts to send in
a Delta Force rescue squad were frustrated by the unwillingness of
the Italian government to allow it to land at a NATO base in Italy.
The terrorists were freed, their demands satisfied, and efforts to
extradite them denied.[20]

Perhaps the most publicized instance of this European "policy" of appeasing terrorists came on the heels of the the hijacking of an Italian cruise ship, the *Achille Lauro*. In October 1985 armed PFLP terrorists boarded the ship as it left Alexandria, Egypt. In one of the most cowardly acts in the history of terrorism, they murdered a Jewish-American man in a wheelchair. (The murder of journalist Daniel Pearl, after making him acknowledge that his parents were Jewish, has to rank a close second.) Once again American plans for a rescue were thwarted by the Italian government, whose "foreign policy required it to maintain very close relations with the Arab states and the PLO," according to Philip Heymann. The terrorists were freed, with the approval of Italian prime minister Bettino Craxi, who "later said somewhat implausibly [that he did not know] that they had murdered a wheelchair bound American, Leon Klinghoffer," Heymann wrote. But even that absurd excuse was not available to Craxi when he once again frustrated efforts by the U.S. government to bring the terrorists to justice. After the hijackers were freed in Egypt, a small Egyptian plane was flying them to a hero's welcome in another friendly Arab country. The U.S. military intercepted the plane in midair and forced it to land at a NATO base in Italy, where American C-141 troop transports were waiting to fly the terrorists to the United States to stand trial for the hijacking of the ship and the murder of Klinghoffer. But Italian soldiers blocked the Americans from approaching the Egyptian plane. Finally, after the Italians promised to bring the hijackers to justice, the United States backed down, and the four hijackers were taken into Italian custody. Among them were two important terrorist leaders with rivers of blood on their hands. The Italians released them immediately. The others were tried, convicted, and allowed to "'escape' while on leave from Italian prisons," in Heymann's words.[21]

The selective killing of Jews was not merely incidental to Palestinian terrorism. It was an integral part of a philosophy taught to Palestinian children from their earliest education.[22] As George Habash said: "We believe that to kill a Jew far away from the battleground has more effect than killing 100 of them in battle; it attracts more attention."[23] In the early 1980s Palestinian terrorists began a series of attacks throughout Europe on Jews at prayer. The bombing of a Paris synagogue in October 1980 killed four Jews and injured twelve. The machine-gunning of a Vienna synagogue in August 1981 killed two and wounded seventeen. During the next year, synagogues in Brussels and Rome were attacked. And in September 1986, an attack on the main synagogue in Istanbul wiped out much of the tiny Jewish religious leadership in that city, killing twenty-two and wounding four. Threats were leveled against synagogues throughout Europe.

Even Yasser Arafat did not try to justify these actions as part of a national liberation struggle. Its targets were not occupying anyone's land, nor were they potential soldiers. This was simply terrorism directed at Jews and Jewish targets in much the same way that the Ku Klux Klan directed its deadly attacks against black children in churches.

In 1982, I called on Arafat to conduct an investigation of the terrorist attack on a Rome synagogue, in which a two-year-old baby was murdered and dozens of people were seriously injured. Although the PLO denied complicity, I thought the Palestinians should pursue an independent inquiry of the kind that Israel had conducted following the massacres at the Sabra and Shatila refugee camps, because reports at the time showed that certain neo-fascist terrorists—the very kind of anti-Jewish extremists who target synagogues—were trained in the same locations as PLO terrorists and received funding from the same sources as the PLO. The international network of terrorists is made up of extremists from both the far right and the far left, and high among their common goals is the destabilization of Western governments. Because the PLO was responsible for training terrorists in much of the Arab world, I argued that it had a responsibility to investigate synagogue attacks that killed innocent civilians but had no evident purpose in furthering the PLO's avowed goal of statehood.[24]

No such inquiry was ever conducted by the PLO, but as a result of my call for an investigation I became the target of a terrorist plot by several North African Arab students who were attending school in the Cambridge area. The plot was thwarted when another student notified authorities about what he had heard.

Rewarding Terrorism

As the Palestinian reliance on terrorism increased, most of the international community became more—not less—supportive of the Palestinian cause. Indeed, there seemed to be almost a direct, one-to-one correlation between the targeting of innocent civilians by Palestinian terrorists and the legitimation, even lionization, of the Palestinians and their leaders who were employing terrorism as their primary tactic for securing recognition for themselves and their cause.

In midst of the systematic attacks on Jewish houses of worship, Pope John Paul II decided to welcome Arafat to the Vatican. The invitation came in 1982, just a year after the Vienna synagogue attack. Six years later, the pope welcomed him again, despite the mass murder of Jews at prayer in the Istanbul synagogue in 1986. In 1994, Israel began turning over governing in the West Bank and Gaza Strip to Arafat and his newly created Palestinian Authority, and in 2000 the pope visited a "beaming Yassir Arafat" in the Palestinian-controlled territory.[25] The pope has met with Arafat on at least six occasions, far more than he typically meets with heads of state. (To show that moral naïveté, if not obtuseness, is not limited to any one faith, in 1999 a major Jewish organization actually considered honoring Arafat but finally decided not to do so, following protests from families of his victims.)

In 1988, Arafat was again invited to address the U.N. General Assembly, despite continuing Palestinian terrorism, including numerous attacks against international aviation through the 1980s. The 1990s saw renewed attacks on Jewish religious institutions, including a community center in Argentina in which eighty-six people were killed and nearly three hundred were injured. Argentine authorities believe this attack was perpetrated by Palestinian terrorists working with local neo-Nazi anti-Semites. No one has yet been convicted of this crime. There were also more Palestinian attacks on international aviation.

Again the message being sent by the international community to the terrorists was unmistakable: we will not punish you or your cause for your use of terrorism; to the contrary, we will reward you, honor your leaders, and further your cause. If this was the message—and how can any reasonable observer deny that it was?—then what did the international community expect the terrorists to do? What would any calculating criminal or terrorist do if given that message? If a tactic is working, why change it, especially if the international community seems to approve of it?

The U.N. General Assembly even went so far as to encourage Palestinian terrorism directed against Israeli and Jewish civilians. In 1979, it approved an exception to the international convention against the taking of hostages. The amendment, which was expressly intended to *permit* hostage taking by Palestinians, went as follows: "The present Convention shall not apply to an act of hostage-taking committed in the course of armed conflicts, . . . in which people are fighting against colonial occupation and alien occupation and against racist regimes in the exercise of their right of self-determination." This formulation then became part of several antiterrorist resolutions, all of which implicitly exempted acts of terrorism committed by Palestinians against Israelis and Jews. Some Arab countries even tried to pressure the General Assembly into declaring that foreign occupation "was the ugliest form of terrorism" and that killing civilians in order to end such occupation was not terrorism at all—an Alice in Wonderland inversion of the plain meaning of words. Although the General Assembly has not included the exception permitting hostage taking in any resolutions adopted since the Oslo Accords of 1993, and the Security Council condemned "all acts of terrorism, irrespective of motive" in 1999, as things now stand many Palestinians believe that killing Israeli and Jewish civilians for the purpose of securing a better deal than Israel is offering has been approved by the General Assembly and does not constitute terrorism. In late March 2002, a Palestinian suicide bombing of a Passover seder killed at least twenty-six Israelis and wounded more than a hundred. Following the bombing, the Arab League proposed a definition of terrorism designed to exclude attacks like this one, which it said was "not terrorism but 'resistance.'" The "living model" of terrorism, according to the proposed definition, is Israel. The *Washington Post* reported that "no one disagreed."[26]

Not surprisingly, in the years following the legitimation of Palestinian terrorism—first by the United Nations, then by European governments, the Vatican, numerous Protestant churches, academics, and others—not only did Palestinian terrorism increase but terrorism became the tactic of choice for numerous other groups with grievances. Relying on a huge archival database on terrorism maintained at the University of St. Andrews in Scotland, Hoffman has summarized the situation since the Munich massacre this way:

> During the weeks that followed the incident, thousands of Palestinians rushed to join the terrorist organizations.

. . . Within four years, a handful of Palestinian terrorists had overcome a quarter-century of neglect and obscurity. They had achieved what diplomats and statesmen, lobbyists and humanitarian workers had persistently tried and failed to do: focus world attention on the Palestinian people and their plight. They had also provided a powerful example to similarly frustrated ethnic and nationalist groups elsewhere: within the decade, the number of terrorist groups either operating internationally or committing attacks against foreign targets in their own country in order to attract international attention had more than quadrupled. According to the RAND–St Andrews Chronology of International Terrorism, the number of organizations engaged in *international* terrorism grew from only eleven in 1968 (of which just three were ethno-nationalist/separatist organizations, the remainder radical Marxist-Leninist or left-wing groups) to an astonishing fifty-five in 1978. Of this total, more than half (thirty, or 54 per cent) were ethno-nationalist/separatist movements, all seeking to copy or capitalize on the PLO's success. They ranged from large, international communities of displaced persons with profound historical grievances, such as the Armenian diaspora, to minuscule, self-contained entities like the obscure expatriate South Moluccan community in the Netherlands. What they all had in common, however, was a burning sense of injustice and dispossession alongside a belief that through *international* terrorism they too could finally attract worldwide attention to themselves and their causes.[27]

To illustrate why so many Palestinians (and others) believe that terrorism has accomplished far more for their cause than nonviolent methods ever could, the following table shows graphically how positive developments for the Palestinians have flowed almost inevitably from their terrorist attacks. The column on the left lists the major terrorist actions on behalf of the Palestinian cause since July 22, 1968, and the column on the right lists the major benefits the Palestinians received following these acts. Whether the benefits were a direct result of the terrorist acts is, of course, impossible to prove, but the important point is that many Palestinians—and others considering the use of terrorism rather than nonviolent or less violent methods—believe that it was the terrorism that brought about the benefits.

Palestinian Benefits Following Terrorist Acts

Palestinian terrorist acts	Benefits to Palestinian cause
July 22, 1968 Three PFLP terrorists hijack an El Al flight from Rome.	
September 4, 1968 Three bombs explode in central Tel Aviv, killing one civilian and wounding seventy-one.	
November 22, 1968 Al-Fatah terrorists bomb Mahaneh Yehuda market in Israel, killing twelve civilians and injuring fifty-two.	

Palestinian terrorist acts   Benefits to Palestinian cause

December 26, 1968
   A PFLP machine-gun attack
   on El Al aircraft at Athens
   airport kills one Israeli.

February 18, 1969
   Palestinian terrorists attack
   El Al Boeing 707 on runway
   at Zurich airport, raking the
   fuselage with gunfire and
   killing the pilot and three
   passengers.

February 21, 1969
   Palestinian terrorists explode a
   bomb in a crowded supermarket
   in Jerusalem, killing two people
   and injuring twenty.

May 22, 1969
   Attempt to assassinate David
   Ben-Gurion in Copenhagen.

August 29, 1969
   PFLP terrorists hijack a TWA
   flight after it takes off from
   Rome.

September 8, 1969
   Two thirteen-year-old Arab
   boys, recruited by al-Fatah,
   throw hand grenades at the
   El Al office in Brussels.

<u>Palestinian terrorist acts</u>   <u>Benefits to Palestinian cause</u>

October 22, 1969
    Palestinian bombs kill four civilians
    in two apartments in Haifa.

November 27, 1969
    A hand grenade attack on
    an El Al office in Athens kills
    one Greek child and wounds
    thirteen.

                  December 10, 1969
                    U.N. General Assembly
                    resolution recognizes the
                    "inalienable rights of the
                    Palestinian people."

February 10, 1970
    Three Arab terrorists attempt
    to hijack an El Al Boeing 707
    at Munich airport, killing one
    Israeli and wounding eight others.

February 21, 1970
    PFLP terrorists blow up a
    Swiss airliner just after it takes
    off from Zurich, killing all
    forty-seven people on board.

May 4, 1970
    An attack on the Israeli
    embassy in Asunción, Paraguay,
    kills the wife of an Israeli
    diplomat and a secretary.

Palestinian terrorist acts

Benefits to Palestinian cause

July 22, 1970

Six members of the Palestine
Popular Struggle Front hijack
an Olympic Airlines plane
from Beirut to Athens.

September 6, 1970

"Skyjack Sunday": The PFLP
hijacks TWA, Swissair, and
Pan Am airliners, with more
than four hundred hostages, and
orders them to Jordan and Egypt
to punish the United States for
supporting Israel. The terrorists
blow the planes up on the ground.

September 9, 1970

Members of the PFLP hijack a
BOAC plane from Bombay to Rome.

November 28, 1971

Black September terrorists shoot and
kill Jordanian prime minister Wasfi
Tal at the Sheraton Hotel in Cairo.

May 8, 1972

Israeli commandos storm a
hijacked Belgian Sabena
airliner at Ben-Gurion Airport,
near Tel Aviv, killing two of the
four terrorists and freeing the
hostages. One passenger and
five Israeli soldiers are killed.

<u>Palestinian terrorist acts</u>   <u>Benefits to Palestinian cause</u>

May 30, 1972
    PFLP and Japanese Red Army
    terrorists open fire in a passenger
    terminal of Lod Airport, Israel,
    killing twenty-seven civilians and
    wounding eighty.

September 5, 1972
    Eight Black September ter-
    rorists seize eleven Israeli
    athletes at the Munich Olympics,
    killing two of them. A bungled
    rescue attempt by West German
    authorities results in the deaths
    of nine of the hostages and four
    of the terrorists.

September 9, 1972
    A Palestinian letter bomb kills a
    member of the Israeli embassy
    staff in London.

October 29, 1972
    Members of al-Fatah,
    acting under the cover
    name National Youth
    Group for the Liberation
    of Palestine, hijack a Luft-
    hansa plane on a flight
    from Beirut to Ankara,
    diverting it to Zagreb.

Palestinian terrorist acts	Benefits to Palestinian cause

March 2, 1973
Members of Black September
murder the U.S. ambassador to
Sudan, Cleo A. Noel, at the
Saudi Arabian embassy in
Khartoum.

March 12, 1973
Black September terrorists
murder an Israeli business-
man on Cyprus.

April 27, 1973
A Palestinian attacks the
El Al office in Rome,
killing an Italian clerk.

May 20, 1973
Two Arabs send letter bombs
to the addresses of Jews
and Israelis in Britain and
Holland.

August 5, 1973
Black September suicide
squad attacks passenger
terminals at Athens airport,
killing three civilians and
injuring fifty-five.

September 5, 1973
Five Arabs attack the Saudi
Arabian embassy in Paris.

Palestinian terrorist acts	Benefits to Palestinian cause

September 28, 1973

Aboard a train bound for
Vienna, two Palestinians seize
three Jewish immigrants from
Russia as hostages.

November 25, 1973

Three Arabs hijack a KLM
jumbo jet from New Delhi
and force it to fly to Abu Dhabi.

December 17, 1973

Palestinian terrorists bomb
Pan Am office at the Rome
airport, killing thirty-two and
injuring fifty.

April 11, 1974

PFLP General Command
terrorists seize part of the
Qiryat Shemona settlement
in northern Israel. During a
rescue attempt, the terrorists
detonate explosives that kill
eighteen Israelis.

May 15, 1974

PFLP terrorists hold ninety children
as hostages at a school in Ma'alot,
Israel. Negotiations break down;
Israeli troops storm the dormitory,
and the terrorists machine-gun the
children, killing twenty-seven people
and wounding seventy.

Palestinian terrorist acts   Benefits to Palestinian cause

June 13, 1974

The PFLP raids Shamir kibbutz
in Israel; the four terrorists and
several Israelis are killed in the
ensuing gun battle.

June 26, 1974

Al-Fatah terrorists land by boat
near Nahariya, Israel, and attempt
to take civilians hostage. Three
Israelis and all the terrorists are
killed in a firefight.

October 21, 1974

French foreign minister
Jean Sauvagnargues, in
Beirut, tells Arafat to stop
"'terrorist activities' against
Israel"; but the *New York
Times* describes the meeting
as a "gesture of official recognition," and Sauvagnargues
says he has a "favorable and
encouraging impression" of
Arafat.

October 28, 1974

Arab summit in Rabat
declares PLO the "official
representative of the
Palestinian people."

Palestinian terrorist acts	Benefits to Palestinian cause
	November 13, 1974 Arafat speaks before the U.N. General Assembly, becoming the first nonstate leader to do so.
	November 22, 1974 United Nations grants observer status to the PLO; only the United States and Israel oppose it.
November 23, 1974 Palestinian Rejectionist front terrorists hijack a British DC-10 airliner at Dubai, diverting it to Tunisia, where a German passenger is killed.	
January 19, 1975 Arab terrorists attack Orly Airport in Paris, seizing ten hostages in a terminal bathroom.	
	November 10, 1975 General Assembly passes its resolution equating Zionism with racism. It also establishes the Committee on the Exercise of the Inalienable Rights of the Palestinian People.

Palestinian terrorist acts	Benefits to Palestinian cause
	November 22, 1975 U.N. Secretary General Kurt Waldheim travels to Damascus to meet with Arafat.
June 27, 1976 The PFLP and the German Baader-Meinhof gang hijack an Air France airliner, forcing the crew to fly to Entebbe airport in Uganda. On July 4 Israeli commandos fly to Uganda and rescue most of the hostages.	
August 11, 1976 PFLP and Japanese Red Army terrorists attack a passenger terminal at Istanbul airport, killing four civilians and injuring twenty.	
October 13, 1977 Four Palestinian terrorists hijack a Lufthansa Boeing 737 and order it to fly around a number of Middle East destinations for four days. The plane's pilot is killed.	

Palestinian terrorist acts	Benefits to Palestinian cause
	January 4, 1978 President Jimmy Carter recognizes "legitimate rights" of the Palestinian people and their need to "participate in the determination of their own future."
March 11, 1978 An al-Fatah seaborne raiding party of nine lands in Israel and hijacks a bus, killing twenty-six civilians and wounding seventy.	
May 20, 1978 Three terrorists from the PFLP open fire on El Al passengers at a Paris airport, killing a French policeman and a French civilian and wounding two other civilians.	
August 20, 1978 PFLP terrorists ambush an El Al crew bus outside the Europa Hotel in London, killing a stewardess.	
	November 29, 1978 United Nations marks its first-ever International Day of Solidarity with the Palestinian People.

Palestinian terrorist acts	Benefits to Palestinian cause

April 16, 1979
El Al passengers are attacked at Brussels airport, with twelve wounded.

July 6–8, 1979
Arafat meets in Vienna with Austrian chancellor Bruno Kreisky and former West German chancellor Willy Brandt; Kreisky is the first serving Western head of state to meet with Arafat.

September 13–15, 1979
Arafat visits Spain and meets with its prime minister and foreign minister; the Spanish say that Arafat's visit was not "official," but also issue supportive statements.

November 2, 1979
Arafat visits Lisbon and meets with Portuguese president Ramalho Eanes, in Arafat's first visit to a NATO-member country.

January 2, 1980
Director of the El Al office in Istanbul is killed.

Palestinian terrorist acts	Benefits to Palestinian cause
	June 13, 1980 European Economic Community's Venice Declaration states that the Palestinian people "must be placed in a position . . . to exercise fully its right to self-determination."
October 3, 1980 A Palestinian bomb attack on a synagogue in Paris kills four Jews and injures twelve.	
August 29, 1981 A machine-gun attack on a Vienna synagogue kills two and wounds seventeen.	
	December 14–16, 1981 Arafat arrives in Greece on an official visit; Greece "decided to grant diplomatic status to Palestine Liberation Organization office in Athens."
June 3, 1982 Terrorists from the Abu Nidal organization critically injure the Israeli ambassador to the United Kingdom in an attack in London.	

Palestinian terrorist acts

Benefits to Palestinian cause

September 15, 1982
Pope John Paul II receives
Arafat in Rome, and Arafat
meets with the Italian
president.

September 19, 1982
Attack on a synagogue in
Brussels. The Abu Nidal
terrorist group is believed
responsible.

October 9, 1982
A grenade and machine-
gun attack on a Rome
synagogue injures ten
people and kills one child.
Abu Nidal is believed
responsible.

May 18, 1983
Suicide terrorists explode
a 400-pound truck bomb
at the U.S. embassy in
Beirut, killing 63 people,
including the CIA's
Middle East director, and
injuring 120.

Palestinian terrorist acts	Benefits to Palestinian cause

October 23, 1983

Suicide terrorists simultaneously attack the American and French compounds in Beirut with truck bombs. A 12,000-pound bomb kills 242 Americans and destroys the U.S. compound; a 400-pound bomb kills 58 French troops at the other base.

March 16, 1984

Islamic Jihad kidnaps and murders American official William Buckley in Beirut.

July 1, 1985

Abu Nidal terrorists bomb a British Airways ticket office in Madrid, killing one person and injuring twenty-seven.

September 13, 1985

A bomb is exploded in an El Al office in Amsterdam.

September 16, 1985

A grenade attack on a Rome café wounds thirty-eight people.

September 25, 1985

PLO Force 17 commando squad kills three Israeli tourists aboard a yacht at Larnaca marina, Cyprus.

Palestinian terrorist acts   Benefits to Palestinian cause

October 7, 1985
Four PFLP terrorists seize
the Italian cruise liner *Achille
Lauro* in the Mediterranean Sea,
taking more than seven hundred
hostages. One American passenger
is murdered.

November 23, 1985
Members of Abu Nidal hijack
an Egyptian airplane flying from
Athens to Malta.

December 27, 1985
Abu Nidal terrorists attack
passenger terminals at Rome
and Vienna airports with grenades
and gunfire, killing sixteen and
injuring more than one
hundred civilians.

March 30, 1986
A Palestinian splinter group
detonates a bomb as TWA
flight 840 approaches Athens
airport, killing four U.S. citizens.

September 6, 1986
Attempted hijacking of a Pan
Am flight at Karachi leaves twenty-
two dead. Abu Nidal operatives attack
a synagogue in Istanbul, killing
more than twenty-two worshipers.

Palestinian terrorist acts   Benefits to Palestinian cause

December 22, 1987
U.N. Security Council
resolution condemns
Israeli practices in putting
down the first intifada,
which had begun two
weeks earlier.

September 13, 1988
Arafat speaks before the
Socialist Group of the
European Parliament.

December 13, 1988
Arafat addresses the
General Assembly, which
had moved to Geneva after
the United States denied
Arafat a visa to speak in
New York; after Arafat says
Israel has a right to exist,
the Reagan administration
begins quiet dialogue with
him.

December 23, 1988
Arafat visits Pope John Paul
for the second time.

May 2, 1989
Arafat visits Paris and
meets with French president
François Mitterrand.

Palestinian terrorist acts	Benefits to Palestinian cause

May 2, 1992
An Islamic Jihad terrorist
kills a tourist at the Israeli
resort of Eilat on the Red
Sea.

May 17, 1992
Hezbollah claims responsibility
for a blast that levels the Israeli
embassy in Buenos Aires,
killing 29 and wounding 242.

September 13, 1993*
Arafat signs the Oslo
Accords on the White
House lawn.

September 17, 1993
With Yitzhak Rabin and
Shimon Peres, Arafat
wins UNESCO's Félix
Houphouët-Boigny Peace
Prize, which honors those
who contribute to building
and keeping the peace.

* The number of terrorist attacks following the signing of the Oslo Accords
in 1993 and the Camp David talks in 2000 is too great to be listed in full. A
complete listing of these attacks can be found at http://www.jcrc.org/main/
terror.htm.

Palestinian terrorist acts

Benefits to Palestinian cause

July 18, 1994

Eighty-six civilians are killed
in a bomb attack on a Jewish
social center in Buenos Aires.
Iranian diplomats in the city
are expelled after being
connected with the incident.

December 10, 1994

Again with Rabin and Peres,
Arafat accepts the Nobel Peace
Prize in Oslo.

December 24, 1994

Members of the Armed Islamic
Group seize an Air France
flight to Algeria.

October 24, 1995

Arafat speaks at Harvard
University, his address organized by an institute funded
partly by a grant from an
American Jewish charity.

February 25, 1996

Two Palestinian suicide bombers
blow up a bus in Jerusalem and a
soldiers' post in the coastal city of
Ashkelon, killing twenty-three
Israelis, two Americans, and a
Palestinian, and wounding more
than eighty. Hamas claims
responsibility.

Palestinian terrorist acts	Benefits to Palestinian cause

March 3, 1996
> A suicide bomber kills
> at least eighteen people
> on a Jerusalem bus and
> wounds ten others. Hamas
> claims responsibility.

May 1, 1996
> Arafat meets with President
> Bill Clinton at the White
> House on his first official
> United States visit.

June 3, 1996
> Arafat speaks at Oxford
> University, sponsored by
> its famed Oxford Union.

February 23, 1997
> A Palestinian gunman
> opens fire on tourists at
> an observation deck
> atop the Empire State
> Building in New York,
> killing a Danish national
> and wounding visitors
> from Argentina, Switzer-
> land, France, and the
> United States.

March 5, 1997
> Arafat speaks at Rice Univer-
> sity in Houston.

Palestinian terrorist acts

Benefits to Palestinian cause

July 30, 1997

Two bombers kill themselves and fifteen others at an outdoor market in Jerusalem.

September 4, 1997

Three explosions, one after another, kill at least four Israelis and three suicide bombers in Jerusalem's main outdoor shopping mall.

March 23–25, 1998

U.N. Secretary General Kofi Annan visits Palestinian areas and meets with Palestinian leaders.

March 30, 1998

Arafat speaks at Erasmus University of Rotterdam with Dutch prime minister Wim Kok; receives a small statue as "prize for his efforts to promote peace," a Palestinian diplomat says.

July 7, 1998

General Assembly upgrades Palestinian status; Palestine remains an observer but gains many of the rights of the member states.

Palestinian terrorist acts	Benefits to Palestinian cause
	December 14–16, 1998
	President Bill Clinton visits Gaza and Bethlehem and addresses the Palestinian parliament and other leaders.
	August 31, 1999
	Maastricht University in the Netherlands awards Arafat an honorary Ph.D. in business administration.
	March 22, 2000
	Pope John Paul visits Arafat in Bethlehem.

In light of the success of terrorism as a tactic, it should have come as no surprise that Arafat would once again play the terrorism card after walking away from the Camp David negotiations in 2000, when Israeli prime minister Ehud Barak's government, with the support of the Clinton administration, had offered the Palestinians nearly everything they were seeking. Rather than trying to negotiate some additional concessions—or compromising their maximalist claims—the Palestinians reverted to the terrorist tactics that had brought them so far already. These included the renewal of the intifada of the late 1980s—only this time featuring much more deadly violence against Israeli civilians than before. The hijacker Leila Khaled, interviewed for a newspaper article published in the *Guardian*, recalled: "Until [we began hijacking airplanes], the world only dealt with us as refugees. We demonstrated and screamed and shouted to make the world listen, but the only answer we got was more tents and humanitarian aid. The hijackings were only a short-lived tactic, but I think they were successful in getting international opinion to ask: 'Who are these people?' Now the intifada is giving the answer." The decision to resort to terrorism again "was planned in advance."[28] The communications minister of the Palestinian Authority acknowledged as much at a symposium in Gaza:

> The PA had begun to prepare for the outbreak of the current Intifada since the return from the Camp David negotiations, by request of President Yasser Arafat, who predicted the outbreak of the Intifada as a complementary stage to the Palestinian steadfastness in the negotiations, and not as a specific protest against [Ariel] Sharon's visit to Al-Haram Al-Qudsi [Temple Mount]. . . . The Intifada was no surprise for the Palestinian leadership. The leadership had invested all of its efforts in political and diplomatic channels in order to fix the flaws in the negotiations and the peace process, but to no avail. It encountered Israeli stubbornness and continuous renunciation of [Palestinian] rights. . . . The PA instructed the political forces and factions to run all matters of the Intifada.[29]

In other words, terrorism was the tactic selected "to fix the flaws in the negotiations." It was being used as an adjunct to diplomacy. And why not? It had worked in the past. Why should it not continue to work? The resulting epidemic of suicide bombings—killing many Israeli civilians and wounding even more—was not a result of any "desperation." It was a carefully worked out policy designed to increase the bargaining power of the Palestinians. *New York Times* columnist Thomas Friedman characterized it this way: "The world must understand that the Palestinians have not chosen suicide bombing out of 'desperation' stemming from the Israeli occupation. That is a huge lie. Why? To begin with, a lot of other people in the world are desperate, yet they have not gone around strapping dynamite to themselves. More important, President Clinton offered the Palestinians a peace plan that could have ended their 'desperate' occupation, and Yasir Arafat walked away."[30]

It is important to distinguish among several elements that contribute to the deployment of suicide bombers. The one emphasized by Palestinian supporters is the desperation of the bombers themselves. There are reasons to be skeptical of this claim, since there are people all over the world who are far more desperate than the Palestinians and yet would never consider blowing themselves up and taking innocent civilians along with them. The alleged desperation of the Palestinians is exploited by their religious and political leaders who drive them to become suicide bombers by turning mass murder into a religious obligation and by glorifying those who carry it out.

In April 2002, Sheikh Muhammed Sayyed Tantawi, the leading Islamic scholar at al-Azhar University in Cairo, declared that "martyrdom operations"—which means suicide bombings—were the "highest form of jihad operations," and that suicide attacks were "an Islamic commandment until the people of Palestine regain their land and cause the cruel Israeli aggression to retreat." Dr. Ahmad al-Tayyeb, Egypt's leading religious jurist, declared that the solution to Israel's aggression lies in a proliferation of suicide attacks "that strike horror into the hearts of the enemies of Allah." He ruled that "Islamic countries, peoples and rulers alike, must support these martyrdom attacks."[31]

An example of the political glorification of suicide bombing is the statement made by Yasser Arafat's wife, who is living in luxury with her daughter in Paris. Though far from desperate, she said that if she had a son there would be "no greater honor" than for him to become a suicide bomber. She did not say whether she wanted her daughter to become a martyr.[32]

Islamic religious and political leaders also make it easier for these suicidal killers to engage in the mass murder of civilians by dehumanizing Israelis and Jews in their schools, mosques, and media. As Charles Krauthammer wrote in the *Washington Post,* "Arafat has raised an entire generation schooled in hatred of the 'Judeo-Nazis.'" This indoctrination includes "the rawest incitement to murder, as in this sermon by Arafat-appointed and Arafat-funded Ahmad Abu Halabiya broadcast live on official Palestinian Authority television early in the Intifada. The subject is 'the Jews.' (Note: not the Israelis, but the Jews.) 'They must be butchered and killed, as Allah the Almighty said: "Fight them: Allah will torture them at your hands." . . . Have no mercy on the Jews, no matter where they are, in any country. Fight them, wherever you are. Wherever you meet them, kill them.'" Palestinian educators, too, incite their students to murder. An end-of-the-year ceremony for 1,650 kindergarten students run by the militant Palestinian Islamic group Hamas "included a skit by children that encouraged the murder of Jews as a religious commandment." This combination of religious, political, and media messages helps explain why, among the many desperate peoples of the world, only the Palestinians are lining up to commit suicide and homicide.[33]

But it does not explain why the Palestinian leaders have turned to suicide bombing as the tactic of choice for achieving their goals. Here the answer is clear: because it has worked. And it has worked because the international community has fallen hook, line, and sinker for the Palestinian exploitation of the cruel fact that death produces sympathy for its cause whenever Israelis *or* Palestinians are killed. The goal of suicide terrorism is to create a "cycle" of violence—or at least the illusion that the violence and counterviolence are part of the cycle of morally equivalent actions and counteractions. But the actions of the Palestinians, who glorify homicide and dehumanize its Jewish victims, are not morally equivalent to the actions of the Israelis, who put their own soldiers at risk in order to minimize the inevitable killing of civilians that accompanies any military response to terrorism, especially when terrorists hide among civilians and use them as human shields.

As expected, the calculated use of terrorism worked. The international community was initially critical of Arafat's refusal to accept the deal offered at Camp David in 2000, but after the terrorist attacks and the predictable Israeli military response, much of European opinion once again turned against Israel. It worked exactly as planned. According to the *New York Times,* Hamas was "almost welcoming of the Israeli attacks."[34] It was part of their strategy to regain support both at home and abroad. In March 2002, following the massive increase in suicide bombings that killed scores of Israeli citizens, the U.N. Security Council rewarded the Palestinians by, for the first time, unanimously voting in favor of establishing a Palestinian state. Secretary General Kofi Annan, also for the first time, insisted that Israel "must end the illegal occupation" of the West Bank and the Gaza Strip. Although he warned the Palestinians that terrorism was "doing immense harm to your cause by weakening international support," the reality is that terrorism was helping their cause and strengthening international support. Once again terrorism accomplished what negotiation had not—at least from the Palestinian perspective.[35]

As understandable as it may be for the United Nations to try to do something about the cycle of violence, the bottom-line message to the Palestinians is still the same: terrorism works. One diplomat told the *New York Times:* "The Palestinians have mastered a harsh arithmetic of pain. . . . Palestinian casualties play in their favor, and Israeli casualties play in their favor. Nonviolence doesn't pay." And he may be right—at least in the short term: "After using the stick for months to get Mr. Arafat to crack down on terrorism, there are signs that the [Bush] administration is trying the carrot." In light of this and other rewards for their previous acts, Palestinian attitudes unsurprisingly tilt toward the use of terrorism above all other options. A poll taken at Najah University in Nablus recently found that "87 percent of Palestinians surveyed were in favor of continuing terror attacks," and "87.5 percent were in favor of 'liberating all of Palestine.'"[36]

All this has come after the terrible events of September 11, 2001. Many observers had expected America's powerful response to those murders to serve as a deterrent to future terrorism. The Bush administration's policy of treating as terrorists those who harbor or support terrorists would seem to include the Palestinian Authority, especially after it was caught smuggling a shipload of Iranian weapons for use in terrorist acts. The Palestinian Authority is to the suicide bombers what the Taliban was to al-Qaeda. The United States went after the Taliban, with a vengeance, but imposed constraints on Israel's military response to terrorism, particularly after the European community, the United Nations, and the Vatican strongly opposed the response. Terrorism against Israel has killed more of its citizens, as a proportion of its population, than the number of Americans killed in the World Trade Center attacks.

One reason for the double standard concerning Palestinian terrorism is that many world leaders refuse to acknowledge the cynical Palestinian manipulation of the arithmetic of pain. Instead, they claim to see a moral equivalence between those who deliberately target innocent civilians and those who respond to such provocations and inadvertently kill innocent—along with not so innocent—civilians. By emphasizing the "body count" of those killed in the clashes between civilians and terrorists, the Palestinians made it appear that Israel bore the primary moral responsibility for the terrorism. More Palestinians than Israelis were in fact killed, but that is not the morally relevant calculus. Virtually all the dead Israelis were completely innocent noncombatants, such as the teenagers blown up at a disco or the women murdered at a pizza restaurant or the guests at bat mitzvah and Passover celebrations.

Many of the dead Palestinians were armed terrorists and bomb throwers. (The Palestinians' official count of those killed on their side includes approximately two hundred suicide bombers who blew themselves up along with their Israeli civilian victims; it also includes Palestinians killed by other Palestinians because of suspicion that they may have collaborated with the Israelis.) Most of the others were caught in crossfire—like one young child whose tragic death was seen around the world on videotape shown by news broadcasts. His death was mourned throughout the world, including in Israel. By contrast, the deaths of innocent Israelis were applauded throughout the Palestinian territories (as was the al-Qaeda attack on the United States).

Moreover, it should be expected that when criminals unlawfully attack a state, and the state responds, the criminals will suffer more casualties than the state. The ratio of criminals to police killed or wounded in any democratic society should be high. A low ratio would represent a failure of law enforcement. The same is true of a military response to terrorism.

Those who suggest a moral equivalence between the terrorist targeting of civilians and the traditional responses to terrorism—which always carry the risk of accidentally killing noncombatants—actually encourage the use of terrorism.[37] The United States is feeling the sting of this false moral equivalency in criticisms of its military response to the attacks of September 11, 2001—a response that has necessarily entailed some collateral damage and inadvertent civilian casualties. Those who focus on body counts, without distinguishing between the deliberate targeting of civilians and the inadvertent killing of some civilians along with terrorists, play directly into the hands of those who employ terrorism as a tactic for securing the moral high ground.

The same thing happens in the news media, when reporters try to demonstrate their objectivity by using "terminological neutrality" in reporting on terrorism. The phenomenon is described by Bruce Hoffman in *Inside Terrorism:*

> The reporting of terrorism by the news media, which have been drawn into the semantic debates that divided the U.N. in the 1970s and continue to influence all discourse on terrorism, has further contributed to the obfuscation of the terrorist/"freedom fighter" debate, enshrining imprecision and implication as the lingua franca of political violence in the name of objectivity and neutrality. In striving to avoid appearing either partisan or judgemental, the American media, for example, resorted to describing terrorists—often in the same report—as variously guerrillas, gunmen, raiders, commandos and even soldiers.[38]

In all, the international community responded to terrorism between 1968 and 2001 by consistently rewarding and legitimizing it, rather than punishing and condemning it. Seen in this light, it is no wonder we had to suffer the horrors of September 11, 2001. Those who bestowed these benefits on the Palestinians following their terrorism, especially our European allies and the United Nations, made September 11 unavoidable. By continuing to reward Palestinian terrorism even after September 11, they have continued to make future terrorist attacks more likely. As one diplomat put it: "If they think it's going to buy off the militancy of the Palestinians, it's mistaken. It's going to increase it, because it gives it legitimacy." Thomas Friedman warned, "Either leaders of good will get together and acknowledge that Israel can't stay in the territories but can't just pick up and leave, without a U.S.-NATO force helping Palestinians oversee their state, or Osama wins—and the war of civilizations will be coming to a theater near you."[39]

What If ... ?

What if the international community had responded to the initial acts of global terrorism with universal condemnation and an absolute refusal to recognize the PLO and its cause? What if it had *punished* the Palestinian cause instead of rewarding it? What if the promise of President George W. Bush following the murder of Daniel Pearl—"These crimes will only hurt their cause"—had been implemented by the Europeans, the United Nations, the Vatican, and others, who instead rewarded terrorists between 1968 and 2001? We will, of course, never know for certain. But it is highly likely that an immediate and firm negative, rather than positive, response to terrorism would have reduced its frequency and severity. If the cause of the terrorists had been set back, rather than furthered, by their murderous acts, it is possible that in the short term such punishment would have caused resentment (as it does with most common criminals). But in the long run, punishing the cause of the terrorists—and promising to continue do so—would have led the leaders of the cause to eschew terrorism as a self-defeating technique for achieving their goals. If terrorism is an entirely rational choice calculated to achieve a political objective, then it becomes especially important to disabuse terrorist leaders of their "unswerving belief in the [positive] efficacy of violence." This requires unambiguous action that sends only one clear message— namely, that terrorism *never* pays, that it *always* sets back the cause, and that, if the cause is to succeed, then its leaders must resort to other techniques for bringing about change.[40]

What if, in addition to setting back the causes for which the terrorists had risked their lives, the terrorists themselves had been imprisoned for life instead of quickly released? As it happened, many of the most "successful" and experienced terrorists who committed the attacks described here were caught and then released.[41] Had they not been released, it is true that others might have taken their place. But it is not so easy to train terrorists, especially for complicated missions.

Not every act of terrorism perpetrated on behalf of the Palestinian cause was specifically authorized by its formal leadership. It may even be true that some of these acts may have been committed in violation of the leadership's orders. But there can be absolutely no doubt that the general tactic of global terrorism, targeting airline passengers and other innocent civilians, was expressly approved, indeed devised, by the Palestinian leadership.

In April 2002 the Israeli government captured a large cache of documents in raids on Palestinian Authority buildings in the West Bank. These documents, which were provided to the Bush administration and placed on the Internet, appear to show that Yasser Arafat, the Palestinian Office of Preventive Security, and other elements of the Palestinian Authority are closely linked to the suicide bombings. "According to Israeli officials, the document showed that Mr. Arafat and his deputy approved cash payments to Al Aksa Martyrs Brigades. One appeal for financial assistance on stationery bearing the name of that group was dated September 16, 2001, just 5 days after the terrorist attacks in the United States. It requested money for electrical components and chemicals for making bombs. Suicide bombings by the Aksa Brigades began in November. Another memo on Aksa Brigade stationery . . . asked for money to set up a bomb factory." On April 12, 2002, the *New York Times* published a chart illustrating what the Israelis claim the captured documents prove: namely, that Yasser Arafat is at the top of the Palestinian terrorist network.[42] Another newspaper report quoted Maslama Thabet, one of the leaders of the Aksa Brigade, saying: "Our group is an integral part of Fatah," the organization that Arafat heads. "We are the armed wing of the organization. We receive our instructions from Fatah. Our commander is Yasser Arafat himself."[43]

Even those specific terrorist acts that were not approved by the leadership brought tactical victories to the Palestinians. In having the international community advance their cause while at the same time detaching themselves from particularly gruesome acts of terrorism, their leaders were able to have it both ways. They achieved increased leverage on account of the terrorism, while also achieving increased legitimacy by "condemning" the acts. In this way they were able to speak out of both sides of their mouths. The international community was able to view these leaders as publicly trying to stop the terrorist attacks, even as their own constituents understood that they were tacitly approving them.

Every movement that employs both nonviolent and terrorist means toward achieving its goals understands how to use the terrorism—even if not directly supported by the formal leadership—as part of a carrot-and-stick approach to help them in negotiations. So long as the international community continues to reward this approach, it will persist. The only way it can be thwarted is by eliminating the incentives for terrorism and enforcing disincentives, severely punishing and incapacitating the terrorists themselves, and delegitimizing their leaders. If the international community had taken these measures—instead of rewarding terrorist acts, releasing the terrorists, and honoring their leaders—it would almost certainly have made a considerable difference in how terrorism was viewed by those contemplating its continued use as a tactic for change.

Why Terrorism Fails

Palestinian terrorism is the paradigmatic example of terrorism that has worked. In order to understand better the factors that contribute to the success of terrorism, it is useful to compare Palestinian terrorism, and the international reaction to it, with the unsuccessful use of terrorism by other groups.

Perhaps the most relevant comparisons are with Armenian and Kurdish groups. The Turkish Armenians and the Kurds have long sought states of their own. Although each of the two has a population considerably larger than that of the Palestinians, both have suffered far more at the hands of those who they claim occupy their homeland. The Armenians suffered genocide by the Turks, who killed as many as 1.5 million of their people. The Kurds were gassed and slaughtered by the Iraqi military, with as many as 110,000 deaths. The Palestinians have also been victims of mass slaughter, for as many as 20,000 of them were killed in September 1970—by the *Jordanian* military. The total number of Palestinians that Israel has killed since 1948 does not constitute even a tiny fraction of this, even by the most exaggerated "body count," and it is far less than the number killed in any other comparable group engaged in a similar armed struggle anywhere in the world—yet Palestinian leaders speak as if no group in history has suffered as much as they have. Thomas Friedman, who has been quite sympathetic to the Palestinian cause, has nevertheless observed that Muslims seem to be far more outraged when Israelis kill a handful of Muslims than when Hindus kill hundreds of Muslims, or when fellow Muslims kill thousands of their own. He asked:

> Why is it that when Hindus kill hundreds of Muslims it elicits an emotionally muted headline in the Arab media, but when Israel kills a dozen Muslims, in a war in which Muslims are also killing Jews, it inflames the entire Muslim world?
> ... This is a serious issue. In recent weeks, whenever Arab Muslims told me of their pain at seeing Palestinians brutalized by Israelis on their TV screens every night, I asked back: Why are you so pained about Israelis brutalizing Palestinians, but don't say a word

about the brutality with which Saddam Hussein has snuffed out two generations of Iraqis using murder, fear and poison gas? I got no good answers.[44]

The Armenians have sought an independent state since at least 1920, when the short-lived Armenian Republic, which had been established in 1918, was absorbed by the Soviet Union. The Soviet Armenians achieved independence, along with other Soviet ethnic enclaves, following the breakup of the Soviet Union, but the Turkish Armenians and their ancestral lands remain under the control of Turkey. The Kurds have been struggling for statehood since at least the end of World War I, when Woodrow Wilson promised them a state and the Treaty of Sèvres said they would have it if a majority of Kurds supported statehood.[45]

The Palestinians, on the other hand, were offered their own state by the United Nations in 1948, when Israel declared statehood. The Palestinians chose instead to join other Arab nations in seeking to destroy Israel. After Israel defeated the combined Arab armies—at great cost to itself in casualties—a truce was declared and the vast majority of Palestinians lived under Jordanian and Egyptian occupation. The Palestinians made no realistic effort between 1948 and 1967 to achieve statehood from their Jordanian occupiers on the West Bank or the Egyptians in the Gaza Strip. It was only after Israel occupied these territories in June 1967—following its victory in a defensive war—that the Palestinians began to seek statehood in earnest.[46]

Far from being a last resort, the very first strategy the Palestinians employed was terrorism. They never tried civil disobedience or other nonviolent means of the kind used by Mohandas Gandhi or Martin Luther King, Jr. Friedman argues that such an approach would have worked: "If Palestinians had said, 'We are going to oppose the Israeli occupation, with nonviolent resistance, as if we had no other options, and we are going to build a Palestin-

ian society, schools and economy, as if we had no occupation'—
they would have had a quality state a long time ago. Instead they
have let the occupation define their whole movement and become
Yasir Arafat's excuse for not building jobs and democracy." The
fact that Friedman believes that nonviolence would have worked
better than terrorism is not nearly as important as the tragic reality
that most Palestinians have been led to believe that terrorism has
worked and will continue to work. Their leaders exaggerate their
grievances as a way of justifying the most extreme responses.
Habash said in 1970, "after what has happened to us we have the
right to do anything, including what you call acts of terrorism."
And they did do "anything," including the deliberate targeting of
children at school and people at prayer—a tactic they share with
the Ku Klux Klan! Habash even went so far as to say he was not
bothered by the prospect "of triggering a *third* World War." If the
grievances of the Palestinians justify killing children and triggering
a world war, it is hard to imagine what the Armenians, the Kurds,
and the victims of Cambodian or Nazi genocide would be justified
in doing.[47]

Although their substantive claims are weaker and of more
recent standing than those of the Armenians and the Kurds, the
Palestinians had several important advantages over them. Their
enemy was a Jewish state, not an Arab or Muslim one. This difference was crucial in garnering international support for the Palestinians. The Jewish state had some support in Europe in the years
following the Holocaust, but this support was based on considerations of morality and guilt—considerations that do not long endure
in the world of realpolitik. Arab and Muslim states have vast quan-
tities of oil and enormous populations—factors that weigh heavily
and do not diminish in force over time. To support the Palestinian
cause meant opposing a small nation with no oil and with a population consisting primarily of Jews, who were still the object of prej-
udice in many parts of the world. To support the Armenian or Kur-

dish causes, on the other hand, meant opposing Arab and Muslim nations with oil and with large populations that shared a common religion with a significant percentage of the world's inhabitants.

Consequently, the international community responded very differently to Palestinian terrorism than it did to Armenian or Kurdish terrorism. An Armenian terrorist group, the Secret Army for the Liberation of Armenia, conducted a number of high-profile attacks, including bombing a Turkish Airlines ticket counter at Orly Airport in 1983. But in spite of this there were no invitations to the United Nations, no legitimation by European governments, and no releasing of prisoners. It quickly became clear that the international community would not respond to Armenian terrorism as it had to Palestinian terrorism, and by the end of the 1980s "none of the Armenian terrorist groups were still actually engaged in international terrorism."[48]

Kurdish attempts to use terrorism were similarly rebuffed. The primary Kurdish terrorist group is the Kurdish Workers' Party, or the PKK, which was founded in the late 1970s. In the early 1990s, the PKK initiated a series of attacks against Turkey, not only inside the country but in other parts of Europe as well. The response to these attacks, however, was largely negative: Germany and France outlawed the group, and the French arrested twenty of its members. Today there is little global terrorism attributed to Kurdish groups.[49]

Armenian and Kurdish terrorist groups have not enjoyed the kind of state sponsorship and support that Palestinian terrorism has, which is another important factor in their lack of success. But the primary reason is that the international community has simply not rewarded Armenian or Kurdish terrorism, as it has Palestinian terrorism.[50]

Other groups and causes have employed terrorism with more success than the Armenians or the Kurds, but less than the Palestinians. These have included the Jews in the British mandate of Palestine following World War II, the anti-apartheid movement in South Africa, and Catholic Republicans in Northern Ireland. None of these groups used global terrorism, each limiting itself to more localized attacks. All three had some support from governments and widespread backing from their own constituents, but none of them achieved conclusive, concrete results.

In Palestine, the Irgun and the Stern Gang attacked British military and administrative targets primarily, seeking to make it so difficult for the British to rule that they would simply give up and leave. Terrorism certainly contributed to the achievement of this goal, but other factors were much more important, and many historians believe that the British would not have remained in Palestine very long in any case.

The African National Congress employed terrorism against the apartheid regime in South Africa, with similar results. Many factors coalesced to make the end of apartheid and minority control of South Africa inevitable; terrorism alone did not bring Nelson Mandela to power, and in fact it may even have delayed it.

The situation in Northern Ireland is more complex and not yet completely resolved. Terrorism on both sides has certainly contributed to the urgency ending the conflict, but unlike with the Palestinian cause it has not been the determining factor. The use of terror by the Irish Republicans has focused much attention from Great Britain and the rest of the world on their plight, but it has not so far succeeded in gaining them the release from British rule that they seek.

Of all these groups that have had some recourse to terrorism, the Palestinian cause is the only one that has gotten where it is primarily as the result of its willingness to resort to global terrorism. It is also the most visible manifestation of the success of terrorism as a mechanism for achieving the goals of a group.

Terrorism's Goals Are Flexible

The objectives behind terrorist acts can change over time. In the late 1960s and early 1970s, for example, the self-proclaimed goal of Palestinian terrorism was to bring attention to the Palestinian cause. Black September, in its communiqué following the Munich massacre in 1972, explicitly said that publicity was the goal of the attack. After the international community placed the Palestinian cause on the front burner of its concerns as a direct result of the terrorism, it was no longer necessary simply to bring attention to it. The object of the continuing terrorism shifted to coercing concrete results, such as the creation of a Palestinian state, the end of the Israeli occupation of territory captured in the 1967 war, and the return of refugees who had left Israel during the 1948 war. Following the breakdown of the Camp David talks in 2000, the object of Palestinian terrorism shifted once again. The Palestinian Authority now controls much of the territories, including the bulk of the Palestinian population. The goal of terrorism since 2000 has been to extort even greater concessions from the Israeli government, by making life in Israel and in the settlements unlivable. Terrorism was now being used as leverage in the ongoing negotiations.

Al-Qaeda's terrorism has always had very different goals from those of Palestinian terrorism. Its claimed objectives have included the removal of American troops from Islamic lands, the overthrow of certain Arab governments, and the creation of Islamic states uncorrupted by the West. More recently, al-Qaeda has included the resolution of the Israeli-Palestinian dispute, as an afterthought calculated to broaden its base of support. But al-Qaeda's real goals seem far less specific and far more apocalyptic. In some respects, al-Qaeda terrorism reflects a somewhat different genre of violence: terrorism as a substitute for conventional warfare. Al-Qaeda is waging war against the United States and its allies by means of the only weapons available to it. It is truly a "poor man's warfare." The war does not appear to be conditional— no realistic demands are made as a prerequisite for ending the hostilities. The object seems to be maximum destruction of American symbols of power and of people associated with these symbols. Like the religiously inspired terrorists of old, the means and the ends seem to be the same: mass murder for its own sake, based on religious zealotry.

The Japanese doomsday cult Aum Shinrikyo is using terrorism for yet another end: to bring about an apocalypse that will hasten the end of days and the appearance of some messianic personage or era. There are similar groups in other parts of the world, including the United States, that base their apocalyptic visions on scriptural sources. These kinds of irrational terrorism may be the most difficult to deter, because they are typically not subject to the usual rules of human cost-benefit calculation.

Philip Heymann's view that "terrorism is generally a calculated move in a political game" has been more true of Palestinian (and Irish, Jewish, and South African) terrorism than in the cases of al-Qaeda and Aum Shinrikyo. It may be true that terrorism is an entirely rational choice, as Heymann says, for those who employ it, but it does not necessarily follow that the rational response in each case should be the same. Even if the object of the response is identical—to persuade those who would employ terrorism that they and their cause will be worse off than if they had opted for more peaceful means—it will still be necessary to tailor different responses to terrorism that has specific political goals and to terrorism that has generalized apocalyptic religious goals.[51]

In tailoring these responses to the goals of the terrorists, it is important to recognize that different groups may be seeking different results from their actions in the short, intermediate, and long terms. These may include bringing attention to an otherwise neglected cause. Short of censoring news accounts of dramatic

terrorist acts—which some tyrannical regimes have tried to do—
it will be impossible to counter this short-term objective. What
can be done is to try to make it counterproductive, by reporting
on the terrorist act in a negative, rather than positive, manner.
The media reported the Ku Klux Klan's attacks on black children
far more negatively than they generally did with comparable
Palestinian terrorist acts. No responsible journalists characterized
hooded Klansmen as freedom fighters, guerrillas, or commandos.
Democratic governments, of course, cannot dictate to journalists
how they report an event, but responsible journalists should
understand that glorifying terrorism may well serve the interests
of the terrorists and those who are contemplating future use of
this tactic.

Another short-term goal of terrorist acts has been to bring
about the release of prisoners, generally other terrorists who have
been captured previously. This goal has been almost completely
successful, thus creating a revolving-door system in which terrorists are arrested only to be released following another conditional
terrorist act, such as a hijacking, after which they are free to commit further attacks.

An intermediate objective of terrorism may include attracting new recruits. Osama bin Laden, in one of his famous videotape recordings, boasted about how many new warriors the September 11 attacks had brought to his cause. Palestinian suicide
bombings also generate young people eager to join the fight.
Hamas leaders have boasted that the Passover massacre and the
Israeli military response to it "will generate more recruits for
Hamas." They describe that massacre and another in which fifteen Jews and Israeli Arabs were killed in Haifa as the "most successful they have ever made." They now have "more than enough
recruits for suicide attacks," demonstrating once again that "success," far more than desperation, inspires suicide bombers. This
phenomenon may also be largely a function of how the media

report on terrorist acts and how the international community responds to them. Responsible religious leaders also must not encourage members of their faith to view terrorism as a positive duty or option in their religion.[52]

Another intermediate objective of terrorism may be raising money for future terrorist acts or for the cause in general. Several European countries have paid large sums of blood money to terrorist groups over the years. Serious efforts are now being made to stop the flow of money to terrorist groups and to seize their assets wherever they are found. Victim groups have also begun to file lawsuits against the terrorist groups and states that sponsor them, hoping to divert money away from terrorism and into the deserving pockets of victims.

Certain kinds of terrorism, such as those directed at an occupying power, may be calculated to make life so frightening and miserable for the citizens of the occupying country that they are encouraged to put pressure on their governments to end the occupation. The tactic works only with democratic countries in which the government is responsive to the demands of its citizens. This phenomenon, which contributed to the British decision to leave Palestine in the mid-1940s, is currently being used against Israel by the Palestinians. Professor Shibley Telhami has written: "Those who have tried to explain suicide terror by religious doctrines have been proved wrong. Increasingly, secular Palestinians are adopting this method because they think it is effective in making occupation unbearable to Israel. From nonreligious young women to members of the semi-Marxist Popular Front for the Liberation of Palestine to the secular Al Aksa Martyrs Brigades, groups and individuals have begun emulating the suicides of Hamas, the radical Islamist group."[53]

Less rational goals of terrorism may include taking revenge, a racist belief in killing specified others, a religious duty to kill infidels, and random acts of violence designed to bring about an apocalypse. These are the most difficult to combat by deterrents and disincentives because they do not fit into the kind of cost-benefit calculations that are conducive to rational responses. Prevention and incapacitation may be the responses of choice against such terrorism.

Finally, the kind of terrorism represented by al-Qaeda's attacks may be designed to destroy an enemy by weakening its economy, its infrastructure, and its symbols. For this type of warfare by unconventional means, there may be no effective response other than warfare employing more conventional means, as well as prevention and interdiction.

It is impossible to catalog every conceivable goal that any terrorist group may have in mind, but it is important to try to understand the goals of the particular group—in the short, intermediate, and long term—if there is to be any success in implementing the overall policy of making terrorism counterproductive.

Terrorism and the Prisoner's Dilemma

One explanation, though certainly not a justification, for why some nations deal with terrorism by capitulating to it involves a variation on the prisoner's dilemma. This heuristic model involves two hypothetical prisoners who are confined in separate cells awaiting trial. If neither prisoner cooperates with the police, they would both be better off, since there would be no direct evidence to convict them. But if either cooperates, then the cooperator would be better off, because he would get a deal, while the noncooperator would be convicted and get a harsh sentence. Since neither knows whether the other will cooperate, each must make a decision based on speculation as to what the other will do.[54]

I have had considerable experience with *real* prisoners' dilemmas, especially in white-collar conspiracy cases involving several suspects. Although each alleged conspirator knows that without the cooperation of one there will be no case, none of them trust the others to stand tall against the authorities who are offering a deal to the first cooperator. Generally, one of them breaks down and the prosecutor gets to make his case against the others. The reason one of them breaks down is that his lawyer tells him that experience shows that at least one will eventually cooperate and that he is better off "winning the race to the prosecutor's door," since the first cooperator gets the best deal and later cooperators may get no deal at all.[55] Benjamin Franklin may have been right when he told the signers of the Declaration of Independence, "We must all hang together, or assuredly, we shall all hang separately," but in the modern world of plea bargaining, the one who cooperates first can usually avoid hanging at all.

How does this prisoner's dilemma relate to terrorism? Every rational nation knows that the international community would be better off as a whole if no nation were ever to give in to terrorists. But every nation also knows that some nations, seeking short-term advantage, *will* give in to terrorists. The nations that do give in may be able to strike a deal with at least some terrorist organizations, sparing their citizens from being targeted. In the case of Germany, the Brandt government was even willing to participate in a staged hijacking, in which it knew no one would actually be hurt, rather than risk a real hijacking that would place its citizens at risk. Other nations have freed imprisoned terrorists, paid cash bounties, or otherwise helped the cause of terrorists. Some have generally refused to submit to terrorists' demands. The reality is that terrorists can count on some countries being more willing to capitulate than others.

These capitulating countries—such as France, Germany, and Italy—may in fact be subject to more instances of *conditional* terrorism, such as hijackings during which no one is hurt, if the government submits to the terrorists' demand to release prisoners. Everyone knows that these capitulating countries will quickly give in to the demands of the terrorists, so that it is not to the terrorists' advantage actually to hurt their citizens. Other countries, which have reputations as noncapitulators, will be subject to fewer instances of pure conditional terrorism but more instances of nonconditional violent terrorist acts, such as blowing up airplanes, shooting passengers, and destroying buildings. Some of these violent acts will be directed against the targets of noncapitulators that are located within the jurisdiction of the capitulators. Examples of this are quite common and include the hijacking of the *Achille Lauro* containing Americans and Jews, the blowing up of Americans in Germany, and the hijacking of American and Israeli planes from French, Italian, or Greek airports. The terrorists know that if they are caught in a country that capitulates, they will be quickly released, even if a noncapitulating country is seeking their extradition.

This cynical phenomenon, widely known both to terrorists and to the countries involved, determines—at least in part—the rules of the terrorist game. It would be far more difficult for the terrorists to play their dangerous game if they knew that no country would capitulate. But they know precisely the opposite: they can always count on France, Germany, Italy, and several other countries to place their own short-term parochial interests over those of the international community, especially since the international community has never sought to impose sanctions on those who capitulate to, or even cooperate with, terrorists.

These prisoner's dilemma rules apply more directly to the sort of terrorism engaged in by the Palestinians—that is, terrorism calculated to produce fairly specific and phased political results. They are less applicable to the kind of apocalyptic terrorism engaged in by groups like al-Qaeda and the Japanese Aum Shinrikyo cult.

Macro and Micro Approaches to Combating Terrorism

The more general, or macro, approach to combating terrorism requires a single-minded effort to eliminate all incentives for terrorism and to impose significant disincentives. This macro approach must be directed at the leaders who seek to further their cause by using terrorism. It will generally require the collaboration of many governments, although if one powerful government, such as the United States, has disproportionate influence on the success or failure of the cause, that government can also have disproportionate influence on disincentivizing and deterring the leaders from employing or tolerating terrorism. If the United States had, for example, refused to recognize the Palestine Liberation Organization so long as it encouraged or tolerated terrorism (or after recognizing it had withdrawn its recognition when it openly resumed terrorism), this policy—even if not supported by other countries—might well have influenced Palestinian decisions regarding the use of terrorism.

The macro approach will not end all terrorism, for several interrelated reasons. First, few nations will accept a rational, long-term approach toward disincentivizing and deterring terrorism. Short-term self-interest will too often induce governments to reward terrorism and create incentives for its continuation, as the Brandt government in West Germany did both before and after Munich. Moreover, there will always be some terrorists who are not subject to the usual disincentives and deterrent strategies. Accordingly, other approaches must be employed as well.

There are also micro approaches to combating terrorism, which assume that it will continue and which are directed at the terrorists themselves rather than at their leaders alone. These approaches include intelligence gathering, ranging from infiltrating terrorist cells to electronic surveillance, and improving security at airports and other vulnerable targets. None of these micro measures will be entirely successful either. No preventive action is ever foolproof. There will always be "leakage," but this does not mean that a considerable number of terrorist acts cannot be prevented.

Israel has had the most extensive experience with micro-managing terrorism. (Because of its small size and lack of influence in the international community, it can never have significant influence on the macro issues, beyond its general policy of not giving in to terrorist demands.) Despite enormous expenditures of resources (moral as well as economic and military), there has been a great deal of terrorism directed at its citizens, its supporters, and Jews around the world. This does not mean that its micro efforts have been a failure. They have succeeded in preventing many additional acts of terrorism, including some involving large numbers of people. The United States, too, has prevented many acts of terrorism. That it did not succeed in preventing the horrors of September 11 shows how deficient it is in several important aspects of its micro capacities to prevent terrorism, including its paucity of "on the ground" intelligence within radical Islamic groups, as well as its wholly inadequate airport security system. These are in the process of being upgraded, and it can be expected that our capacity to prevent disasters like September 11 will be much improved in the years to come.

Somewhere between the micro techniques and the macro techniques for deterring and disincentivizing terrorism lies a wide range of intermediate preventive strategies. These include planting spies in the terrorist groups, bribing or extorting members of the group to become double agents, "scamming" the terrorists into committing controlled crimes designed to catch them in the act, and intercepting their communications.

An effective combination of all these techniques holds the best promise for reducing the frequency and severity of global terrorism. Terrorist leaders must be made to understand that they and their cause will not be allowed to benefit from terrorism and that, on the contrary, they will both suffer severe setbacks in everything they hold dear. The terrorists themselves must be incapacitated or deterred, or otherwise prevented, from carrying out their deadly acts, even if they are willing—or eager—to die in the process. Our past policies—which have rewarded the causes of terrorists, honored their leaders, freed the actual terrorists, neglected on-the-ground intelligence, failed to secure our airports and borders, allowed terrorist groups and states that support them to obtain weapons of mass destruction, and refused to hold states that sponsor terrorism accountable for the actions of their surrogates—were prescriptions for creating more and worse terrorism.

No one who observed how the world responded to the globalization of terrorism between 1968 and 2000 should have been surprised by the attacks of September 11, 2001. The only surprise, and one I suspect the terrorists did not anticipate in light of the world's previous reactions to terrorism, was the swiftness and massiveness of our military response following those attacks. We are now, finally, engaged in an effort to send a message to terrorists—at least terrorists who target Americans—that they will pay a heavy price for their terrorism, that terrorism will only hurt their cause. This is a new message, and it remains to be seen whether we will continue to send it, and how it will be received by terrorist groups and those who harbor and sponsor them. Already Pakistan seems to have gotten the message. It has changed its policies in some important ways since witnessing the American determination to punish those who attacked its citizens—and those who helped them.

Much remains to be done on the macro, the preventive, and the micro levels if global terrorism is not to increase in frequency and ferocity. It is to the preventive and micro issues that we now turn.

chapter three

How an Amoral Society Could Fight Terrorism

"No one could possibly justify sacrificing millions
of lives to spare a murderous psychopath a brief spell
of intense pain, which he can end by his own choice.
When the threat is so gigantic and the solution
so simple, we are all in the camp of the
Shakespeare character who said,
'There is no virtue like necessity.'"
—Steve Chapman, *Washington Times*

T errorism is a tactic directed most effectively against open democracies. It is far less effective against closed tyrannies. One reason for this difference is that terrorism, to the extent that it is "propaganda by the deed," relies on widespread publicity, and such publicity is readily available in countries that permit freedom of the press. Closed societies—such as China, Iraq, North Korea, and the former Soviet Union—impose controls on what can be printed in state-run newspapers and shown on state-run television.[1] To be sure, there is often leakage, even in the most closed of societies. Fax machines, the Internet, satellite communication, samizdat publications, and word of mouth make it virtually impossible to impose total control on the flow of information today. But even with the expectation of some limited retail publicity in a closed society, terrorism is far less effective than in societies where widespread, wholesale publicity can be counted on.

Moreover, the effectiveness of terrorism relies, at least to some degree, on a bottom-up, grassroots phenomenon, whereby the public is terrorized into demanding change from the leadership. Tyrannical regimes, which operate in a top-down manner, are somewhat less susceptible to this tactic.

Finally, tyrannical regimes have few if any constraints on the responses they can make to terrorism. Unlike democracies, which are subject to civil libertarian, humanitarian, and constitutional limitations, tyrannical regimes can employ the most brutal countermeasures against terrorists, their supporters, their families, their co-religionists, and anyone else.

It should therefore come as no surprise that terrorism is directed more often against democracies than against tyrannies. At the very least we are more aware of terrorism directed against societies with a free press than against societies that censor the news, especially the bad news.

To see how an amoral society could reduce—perhaps even effectively eliminate—terrorism, let us imagine the following hypothetical situation: The dictator of a strong, amoral nation victimized by terrorism empowers an antiterrorism czar to do whatever it takes to eliminate terrorism. The czar's mandate is to do everything militarily and technologically feasible, without considering the moral or legal implications. It will be up to others to strike the appropriate balances among the feasible, the moral, and the legal. The czar's only job is to think outside the moral and legal box and propose *effective* means for achieving the agreed-upon goal—elimination of terrorism.

Controlling the Media

The czar might recommend total governmental control over the reporting of terrorist acts and the regime's response to them. Totalitarian regimes generally seek to control the flow of information both within the society and between it and the outside. Terrorists, therefore, cannot count on their message being received by its intended audience (unless that audience is the leadership or some small segment of the society directly affected by the terrorism). The regime can choose to publicize terrorist acts if publicity serves its purposes. It can exaggerate the damage done, or even contrive a terrorist act as an excuse for a massive "reprisal," the way the Nazis did with the Reichstag fire of 1933.[2] It can also report (and, if it chooses, exaggerate) the reprisal to achieve maximum deterrent impact.

Control of the media is a powerful weapon against terrorism—a weapon that has been used effectively by Hitler, Stalin, Mao, and other dictators, such as Kim Il Sung and Kim Jong Il in North Korea, Mengistu Haile Mariam in Ethiopia, Idi Amin in Uganda, Mohammad Siad Barre in Somalia, and Saddam Hussein in Iraq. Although it is somewhat more difficult today than it used to be to control the flow of information about terrorism, it is still far

easier for a closed society than for an open one to reduce the effectiveness of the publicity goal of terrorism. Acts of terrorism—especially conditional acts, such as hostage taking—are natural news
stories, because they create real-time drama involving individuals
whose identities are known, whose faces are shown, and whose relatives can be interviewed. These are not anonymous, faceless victims. Even when the terrorists engage in nonconditional acts of terrorism, such as blowing up buildings, the target is "everyman" and
"everywoman," so that the identification with the general public is
powerful. Each of us can imagine ourselves or a loved one in the
World Trade Center or one of the airplanes on September 11, 2001.
Moreover, the sheer number of those killed in a terrorist attack
like that one ensures that it will remain an enduring story. Even the
most tyrannical of regimes could not have prevented disclosure of
such a catastrophe. But terrorist acts on a smaller scale can be and
have been covered up in closed societies.

A regime that exercises total control over the media can also
disseminate false and damaging information against the terrorists,
calculated to turn the population—including those who support
their cause—against them. It can leak reports suggesting that the
terrorists are really agents provocateurs who are actually working
for enemies of the cause. Arab regimes, for example, often accuse
local indigenous terrorists of working for Mossad, the Israeli intelligence service, as a way of discrediting them. Even in the United
States, the FBI has occasionally tried to disparage local terrorist
groups by spreading disinformation about their being government
"informers" or agents provocateurs.[3] The adverse public reaction
to these tactics has largely discredited them in the United States,
and when the government floated the idea of a disinformation
office—even one directed against the September 11 terrorists—the
reaction was swift, and the secretary of defense had to retract it.

The important point is that open societies with freedom of
the press make it far easier for terrorists to get their message out

and far more difficult for the government to take secret actions against terrorists. This is a price we pay for our freedom. It is a price well worth paying, but we should not understate its high cost. If we were willing to cede total control over the media to our government, we probably could reduce the incentive terrorists now have to try to influence public opinion by resorting to terrorism. To do this most effectively, we would require the cooperation of other nations as well, which is, of course, unrealistic. The reality is that the kind of censorship regime it would take to control this important aspect of terrorism is not feasible, and certainly not desirable, in a democracy. We must fight terrorism in the open and with the full realization that terrorists will be able to provoke the publicity they seek from their acts. We must figure out ways of turning this publicity against them—of using the openness of our society as both a shield and a sword in the war against terrorism. In Chapter 5, I will propose some modest steps that an open democratic society can take in this direction, but they will never be as effective as the steps that could be taken by a closed, tyrannical regime. For now it is enough to understand that a society willing to dispense with freedom of the press could take certain steps that we cannot and should not take to combat terrorism.

Monitor All Communication

Another type of information control an antiterrorist czar might recommend would be for the state to monitor all private communications both within the country and between its residents and outsiders. A system of governmental censorship over the media imposes controls over public dissemination of information. Monitoring of phones, computers, and other means of communicating controls private dissemination. Together they constitute the kind of complete control over all information sought by totalitarian regimes.

To achieve this type of control requires both electronic and human monitoring—a high-tech system of wiretapping, bugging, satellite monitoring, face recognition software, and other gadgets, supplemented by spies, informers, and double agents. Hitler, Stalin, Mao, Saddam Hussein, and other tyrants have employed these tactics as effectively as the technology of their day permitted. Today's technology, especially in the United States, knows few bounds. We are capable of monitoring all telephone, e-mail, and other communications that employ wire or satellite transmission. We have, or are in the process of developing, software capable of identifying "dangerous" words, phrases, and even concepts. We could, if we chose to, implant in every person (or gun, or dollar bill, or car) a chip capable of tracking his or her (or its) every movement. Big Brother is now technologically feasible—if we were to opt to unleash him in the war against terrorism.

But in a democracy constrained by constitutional limitations we cannot opt to do everything we are technically capable of doing. The Fourth Amendment prohibits searches and seizures that are unreasonable and generally requires (subject to several exceptions) a judicially issued warrant based on probable cause and limited by some degree of specificity. What is "unreasonable" depends, of course, on the circumstances, and the courts have historically given law enforcement considerable latitude when national security is invoked. But there are limits. When Zacarias Moussaoui was detained after raising suspicions when he sought flying lessons, the FBI did not even seek a warrant to search his laptop computer, because agents believed that no judge would issue one based on the kind of vague information they had at the time.[4] A tyrannical regime would not have hesitated to search his computer, his home, or anything else. Nor would it have hesitated in torturing him, threatening his family, and employing other tactics that might have loosened his lips and perhaps even prevented the attacks of September 11, 2001.

Reasonable people can disagree about whether searching Moussaoui's computer on the basis of the suspicious information then available would have been justified, but no democracy can simply allow law enforcement agents free rein to search anyone and anything on nothing more than suspicion. Our Constitution makes it harder for us to prevent terrorism than it would be if we were entirely free to employ every technological and human means currently available. But there are reasonable steps we can take to expand our arsenal of technological and human monitoring weapons in the battle against terrorism, which we will come to in Chapter 5.

Criminalizing Advocacy

The First Amendment protects "advocacy" of violence but not "incitement" to violence. The distinction, though determinative, is often elusive. Advocacy is supposed to be directed to the rational mind, while incitement is aimed at the irrational gut. Shouting "fire" in a crowded theater, for example, is not an idea designed to stimulate debate; it is a clang sound that is supposed to stimulate immediate action. A popular professor urging his impressionable students to take over a computer center that is being used for war research may be advocating to some, while inciting others.[5]

To the tyrant these distinctions are meaningless. Anyone whose speech—even whose thought—poses any danger to the tyrant or his regime will be silenced. George Bernard Shaw's observation that "assassination is the ultimate form of censorship" has long been known to tyrants. Hitler, Stalin, and the tyrannical monarchs who came before them had their critics killed on the basis of the slightest suspicion. In common law, it was high treason even to "compass"—that is, imagine—the death of the king. Fearful that he who is capable of dreaming that the king is dead may also be capable of turning fantasy into reality, the tyrants of old took no chances. Our Constitution, on the other hand, sought to strike an appropriate balance between the security of the realm and the right to dissent. The Supreme Court has altered that balance many times over the course of our history, expanding the parameters of free speech considerably between the 1920s and the 1960s—and maintaining approximately the same balance over the past forty years or so. Pursuant to the current balance, an advocate of terrorism could make a speech arguing for the virtue of killing civilians and urging his audience to consider this course of action. He could not, however, incite a crowd of gun-toting zealots to shoot now into a crowded marketplace. The line between permissible advocacy and impermissible incitement is not always clear. As Oliver Wendell Holmes once observed: "Every idea is an incitement."[6]

To apply these abstract principles to the post–September 11 world, consider the issue of whether an imam who issues a fatwa calling for the death of a specific infidel (such as Salman Rushdie) or calling for terrorist attacks against general targets (such as American "institutions") is engaging in protected advocacy or unprotected incitement.[7] To the extent that a fatwa, or a religious order from any authorized leader, is felt to be obligatory by followers of that religion, it feels quite different from ordinary advocacy, which the listener is free to accept or reject on its merits or demerits. But it also feels somewhat different from classic incitement, which is generally face-to-face. A fatwa can be in writing, delivered in abstract theological terms and calling for nothing immediate to be done. If an actual fatwa case were to come before our courts, it would probably be decided on the basis of the particular facts of the case, including how close in time the terrorism followed the fatwa, how specific the religious command was, and how free the potential terrorists felt to reject it.

Or consider the following variations on the fatwa. A religious leader (imam, rabbi, priest, minister) is asked the following question by one of the faithful: Is it permissible for me to ... (you can fill in the blank—blow up an abortion clinic, murder a prime minister, fly a plane into a building)? If the religious leader honestly answers the question in the affirmative, has he become part of a conspiracy to do the criminal act?[8] Or is he merely exercising his free speech and religious rights? What if he adds, "but you are not obliged to do it, and you should not"? Or what if he adds, "not only is it permissible, it is obligatory for you to do it"? To extend the hypothetical, what if the potential terrorist asks the religious leader to bless his terrorist act? What if the potential terrorist says that without the blessing he will not do it?

An actual case in Israel following the assassination of Prime Minister Yitzhak Rabin adds an interesting wrinkle to these hypothetical situations. It turns out that, a month before the assassination, a Jewish religious leader put a "curse" on Rabin, imploring the angel of death to strike him down. Even though there was no evidence that the actual assassin was even aware of the curse, the man who uttered it was convicted of declaring that the ancient curse of *pulsa dinura* (Aramaic for "lashes of fire") applied to Rabin and was sentenced to four months in prison. He was also given a year's suspended sentence for inciting violence in violation of Israel's Prevention of Terrorism Act.[9] No such prosecution could be successful under American law.

The Israeli government, in addition to the foolish prosecution of the man who issued the curse on Rabin, has also prosecuted an Arab member of the Knesset, Azmi Bishara, for arguing that Hezbollah-type "resistance" should be taken up by Palestinians in the West Bank and Gaza.

An antiterrorist czar, unconcerned about law or liberty, would probably be inclined to criminalize any suggestion of terrorism, whether advocacy, incitement, or even a balanced and academic consideration of the virtues and vices of this tactic. He would certainly ban sermons praising terrorists or the depiction of suicide terrorists as martyrs to be emulated. The Egyptian government, which was plagued with terrorism ranging from the assassination of Anwar Sadat to the mass murder of tourists at Luxor, has cracked down on all advocacy of terrorism. As a result, Islamist terrorism in Egypt has decreased sharply since the mid-1990s. As Peter Beinart notes, "Most of Egypt's remaining Osama bin Ladens are in jail."[10]

The United States will not follow the Egyptian model, or even the far less restrictive Israeli model. But it is likely that we will see prosecutions that challenge the current broad interpretation of the First Amendment. This has certainly been the historic response to national emergencies. In Chapter 5 I will propose a small number of steps regarding expression that I believe may increase our security somewhat without diminishing our most important safeguard of liberty during times of emergency: the right of vigorous dissent.

Restricting Movement

An antiterrorist czar would probably recommend imposing airtight control and severe restrictions on the movement of people both within the country and at its borders. All tyrannical regimes impose geographical limitations on their citizens and visitors. The technical capacity exists for enforcing such limitations electronically, by implanting chips or requiring people to wear external devices that can be tracked. Already we are using electronic bracelets and anklets on some criminal defendants awaiting trial or appeal to assure that they cannot leave the jurisdiction without alerting the authorities.

More primitive methods of controlling movement involve frequent checkpoints, internal passports, periodic reporting requirements, and the like. The demand "your papers please" has become a symbol of this kind of tight control exercised by the authorities over the people. We now expect to be asked to show a photo ID—generally one secured from the government—when we go to the airport, to government buildings, and now even to private office buildings. These checks are designed not to restrict our movement but rather to check our identity. They are easily circumvented, because phony driver's licenses and other photo ID's are so readily available.

It is also relatively easy to slip into and out of this country, because our borders are so large and mostly unpatrolled, and the Immigration and Naturalization Service is so notoriously inefficient.[11] Movement inside the country is unrestricted, and anyone can crisscross it entirely by car without ever showing an ID or passing through a toll booth or a checkpoint. This makes it easy for potential terrorists to hide in plain view, waiting for an opportune moment to strike. Frequent checkpoints, coupled with foolproof ID's, would make this much more difficult—but at a price. The use of checkpoints by Israel has clearly saved lives, but it has also generated much resentment and has made the checkpoints themselves targets of suicide terrorists. One reason for the resentment is that the checkpoints and identification requirements are directed primarily at Arabs—and for obvious reasons, since the suicide bombers are Arabs. Palestinian terrorists have figured out ways of ratcheting up the resentment by expanding the profile of potential suicide bombers to include women, teenagers, and ambulance drivers. This requires the Israelis to conduct intrusive searches on women, teenagers, and ambulances, thus increasing the resentment and the international criticism. Now some imams have gone even further, urging Palestinians—according to the *New York Times*—

"to arm themselves *or their children* with explosive belts to pursue holy war against the Jews." And children have complied with this directive, as a fourteen-year-old and two fifteen-year-olds did on April 23, 2002, when they tried to blow up a Jewish settlement in Gaza with homemade bombs. They were shot by Israeli soldiers and a Palestinian outcry followed. Advocates of terrorism cannot, out of one side of their mouth, urge women and children to become suicide bombers and then, out of the other side of their mouth, pretend to complain when these terrorists are killed in self-defense. But that is precisely what some Palestinian leaders are doing—and they are benefiting from this calculated hypocrisy.[12]

Law enforcement officials in the United States have also used racial and ethnic profiling and selective checking, and it has generated understandable resentment here too. Even if the check-points and ID requirements were to be pervasive and neutral in their application, they would lack the feel of freedom to which Americans have become accustomed. We have a right to travel unrestricted from city to city and state to state. Even foreign travel, with some restriction, has been recognized as a right. This right would, of course, be subject to modification in the event of a genuine emergency, such as a biological attack necessitating some form of quarantine. In the immediate aftermath of September 11, 2001, New York City's bridges and tunnels were closed, and when they were reopened people using them were subject to ID checks.[13]

Absent an emergency, however, Americans would simply not accept the kind of movement restrictions and ID checks I experienced when visiting the Soviet Union, Czechoslovakia, and China in the 1970s and 1980s. But there are steps that could be taken to make it harder for potential terrorists to get into and move around this country, without violating constitutional rights or significantly reducing the feel of freedom we rightly cherish.

Collective Punishment

Perhaps the most effective—and at the same time the most immoral—technique for combating terrorism is collective punishment. This tactic would be particularly useful in deterring suicide terrorists, who are willing to die but may not be willing to have their loved ones punished for their actions. Hitler and Stalin employed collective punishment ruthlessly and quite effectively as an antidote to personal bravery by those willing to risk their own imprisonment or death. Hitler destroyed the entire Czech village of Lidice in response to the assassination of Reinhard Heydrich, shooting all men over the age of fifteen and sending everyone else to concentration camps.[14] By this action he sent a clear message to potential terrorists, assassins, or saboteurs: if you undertake any of the above acts, you will be responsible for the mass murder of your own people. The Gestapo also took hostages and executed them in response to terrorism or other threatening actions. It employed what it called Sippenhaft, the punishment of kin. These immoral tactics worked—not perfectly, but quite effectively. Stalin too would not hesitate to kill the family members of people that he believed posed a threat to him.

Tyrants understand that by killing innocent relatives, friends, countrymen, co-religionists, and supporters of terrorists' causes they can turn the people—the potential victims of the reprisal—against the terrorists. This is a particularly effective dynamic, especially when the terrorists themselves are beyond the reach of the tyrant, either because they cannot be caught or are willing to die.

Terrorism is itself one of the most immoral forms of collective punishment against innocent people based on their religion, nationality, or location. George Habash has explicitly argued that all Jews and Israelis are appropriate targets, as are all airline passengers: "And as for the non-Israeli passengers, they are on their way to Israel. Since we have no control over the land that was stolen from us and called Israel, it is right that whoever goes to Israel should ask for our permission. Countries like Germany, Italy, France and Switzerland, with many Jews among their population, allow their territory to be used as a base for the Jews to fight the Arabs. If Italy, for instance, is a base against the Arabs, the Arabs have a right to use Italy as a base against the Jews."[15]

Yet those who support terrorism are often among the most vocal critics of any response to terrorism that smacks of collective punishment. The terrorists use collective punishment both as a sword and as a shield. Because they understand that collective punishment against their supporters would be the only effective deterrent against their terrorism, they take advantage of the civilized world's abhorrence of any punishment that is not limited to the culpable perpetrators themselves—calling it "collective punishment," whether or not it actually fits that emotionally laden category. Punishment of kin is explicitly authorized by Islamic law, or Sharia, which according to one informed observer provides that "a murder committed by a Muslim must either be avenged or compensated by the murderer's family or clan."[16]

The concept of collective punishment has been condemned in Judeo-Christian law since Abraham tried in vain to dissuade God from punishing all the residents of Sodom. Abraham's powerful words—"Far be it from you . . . to bring death upon the innocent as well as the guilty"—ring true even today. Yet collective punishment, in its broadest sense, is commonplace. The innocent people of a nation suffer for the evil deeds of their unelected leaders, as the Iraqis do for the actions of Saddam Hussein and the Libyans do for Muammar el-Qaddafi's. Innocent wives and children suffer when their criminal husbands and fathers are executed, imprisoned, or fined. Innocent civilians become "collateral damage" when military targets are attacked.

There is a real difference, of course, between punishing criminals directly, with the realization that some innocents will also be hurt, and specifically targeting the innocent to deter or punish the guilty. Directly punishing the innocent raises the most pointed moral objections, but it is also most effective. Notwithstanding the effectiveness of this extreme form of collective punishment, we are morally constrained—and legally prohibited—from imposing it. But once again there are steps we can take, consistent with morality and law, to deter suicide terrorists by making their terrorism the trigger for reprisals against those who harbor, finance, or otherwise support them, or hope to benefit from their actions. Chapter 5 shows how a democratic society can employ a mild form of collective accountability without violating the principle that people should be punished proportionately to their personal culpability.

Targeted Assassinations

In one sense, the polar opposite of collective punishment is targeted assassination. This tactic seeks to prevent future terrorism by incapacitating those who are planning to carry it out but are beyond the reach of other methods of incapacitation, such as arrest. Tyrannical regimes have employed targeted assassination widely against perceived enemies at home and abroad. Hitler had his rivals, even some friends, murdered with impunity. Stalin took his campaign of targeted assassination around the world, even as far away as Mexico, where his thugs murdered Leon Trotsky.

The United States has certainly tried to assassinate foreign leaders over the years. Our hit list has included Fidel Castro, as well as Patrice Lumumba, Muammar el-Qaddafi, and Saddam Hussein. Although we did not directly murder Salvador Allende or Ngo Dinh Diem, we certainly played an active role in helping others to dispatch them.[17] Today we are considering again targeting Saddam Hussein, and we have put bounties on the heads of Osama bin Laden and Mullah Mohammad Omar.

Targeted assassination, like collective punishment, operates along a continuum. At the hard end is the widespread targeting of all perceived political opponents, as Hitler and Stalin practiced it. At the soft end is what Israel currently does—targeting specific terrorist leaders who are actively involved in planning or coordinating terrorist attacks and who cannot be arrested, such as Yehiya Ayash, known as "the Engineer," the chief bomb maker for Hamas whom Israeli agents killed in January 1996 by placing explosives in his mobile phone. In the middle is what the United States and Israel (and some other countries) have done in the past: target enemies who are thought generally to pose a danger or who may have participated in past atrocities and evaded justice.[18]

The vice of targeted assassination is that it is essentially lawless. Those who authorize the hit are prosecutor, judge, and jury—and there is no appeal. The virtue of targeted assassination, if the targets are picked carefully and conservatively, is precisely that it is targeted and tends to avoid collateral damage and collective punishment. Camus's "just assassin" was employing targeted assassination against an evil wrongdoer, and he refused to proceed in the face of collectively (or collaterally) punishing the evildoer's young niece and nephew. Even when there are collateral victims, there are fewer of them than in typical military reprisals.

Preemptive Attacks

Targeted assassination is closely related to—in fact is a subcategory of—the preemptive attack. The object of the preemptive attack is to disable or incapacitate potential terrorists from carrying out planned attacks by destroying their weapons, training bases, communication systems, and other facilities that are thought necessary to their success. Perhaps the most famous example of a preemptive attack was Israel's bombing of an Iraqi nuclear facility in Osirak in 1981. Israeli intelligence had discovered that Saddam Hussein was in the process of developing the capacity to produce nuclear weapons that could be directed at Israeli targets. Iraq already had the capacity to deliver such weapons, as evidenced ten years later when it rained Scud missiles on Tel Aviv during the Persian Gulf War. The Israeli air force attacked the Osirak facility and destroyed it. One French technician was accidentally killed. The United Nations condemned Israel for the attack.[19] The United States and Europe joined in the public condemnation, although over the years Israel has been praised privately for making the area safe from a Saddam Hussein with nuclear weapons. The United States has also tried to destroy Iraq's capacity to produce weapons of mass destruction, especially chemical and biological weapons. In 1991 it bombed the Kamisiyah facility, where U.N. inspectors have determined that the Iraqis stored chemical weapons.

The tactic of preemptive attack also functions along a continuum. Tyrannical regimes use it as an excuse for aggressive warfare, as Germany did in the late 1930s. Japan's attack on Pearl Harbor was rationalized as preventive. On the other end of the continuum are preemptive attacks made as part of a defensive war. Much of the world approved Israel's destruction of the Egyptian air force after Gamal Abdel Nasser had engaged in an act of war by closing the Strait of Tiran to Israeli shipping and threatening to "drive the Jews into the sea."

All democratic nations take preemptive military actions under some circumstances, and there is a role for some such actions in the war against terrorism, especially if they succeed in disabling weapons of mass destruction.

Massive Retaliation

Tyrannical regimes employ massive, disproportionate retaliation against those who take actions against them. The total destruction of Lidice by the Nazis in 1943 is, perhaps, the paradigm of much disproportionate retaliation. Even when retaliation is not intended as collective punishment, as it clearly was by the Nazis, its effect is to kill large numbers of innocent people. For tyrannical regimes, this is a plus. For moral governments it is an unfortunate cost that should be minimized as much as possible, consistent with the military objective of the retaliation.

The American retaliation in Afghanistan is an example of an effort to minimize collateral damage while at the same time sending a powerful message that no one can attack us without expecting to be punished, and that we will do everything reasonable to disable those who continue to threaten us, even if we know there will be some collateral damage. It is a difficult balancing act, as Israel has learned over the years. Terrorists—for whom no damage inflicted is "collateral"—understand that by provoking a democracy into retaliation they will inevitably suffer some collateral damage, which will result in the international community condemning the retaliation. Accordingly the terrorists take advantage of this collateral damage as both a sword and a shield. They understand that the arithmetic of death adds up to a benefit for them every time they kill a civilian as well as every time one of their civilians is killed as a collateral consequence of any military reprisal.

As with other potential responses to terrorism, massive retaliation is very much a matter of degree and intentionality. How an immoral, aggressive regime carries out massive retaliation, with no regard for civilian casualties or even with the intention of maximizing them, is very different from how a moral regime responds to attacks on its civilian population, with considerable effort to reduce to a minimum the inevitable collateral damage, even at the risk of death or injury to its own soldiers.

Secret Military Trials

Tyrannical regimes employ secret military trials, if they even bother with trials at all. Enemies, both domestic and foreign, are brought before special tribunals, which conduct their proceedings in secret, with few rules or rights. Efficiency is the object of these kangaroo courts. Aleksandr Solzhenitsyn once explained the Soviet legal approach to dissidents by likening it to a sewage system—it was to be evaluated according to its ability to rid the society of unwanted garbage.[20]

Some military tribunals are, of course, fairer than others. The system for court-martialing soldiers in the United States is widely regarded as a model of justice in most situations.[21] It provides for effective legal representation and protects, albeit imperfectly, against command influence. It also provides for appeal to a civilian court, outside the chain of command.

Our experience with military tribunals for our enemies has been decidedly more mixed. When German spies and saboteurs were captured in New York in 1942, President Franklin Delano Roosevelt ordered them tried by a military tribunal precisely because he wanted to be absolutely certain they would be convicted and executed. Roosevelt's biographer Joseph Persico described his instructions: "A military tribunal offered the advantages and the assured outcome that the President wanted. A civilian court was out of the question. FDR told [attorney general Francis] Biddle, 'I want one thing clearly understood, Francis: I won't give them up . . . I won't hand them over to any United States Marshall armed with a writ of habeas corpus. Understand!'"[22] George Washington and Abraham Lincoln did not act very differently during wartime, and the civilian courts generally defer to the commander in chief as long as the nation is involved in hostilities.[23]

There is little doubt that military tribunals are constitutionally permitted for enemy soldiers captured abroad, and even for enemy spies, saboteurs, or terrorists caught in this country (if they are not citizens or, perhaps, permanent residents). The real question concerns the nature of the tribunals and the desirability of employing them in particular categories of cases.

Torturing Suspects

Torture is a staple in tyrannical regimes. Enemies are tortured mercilessly for information and then killed. Political opponents are tortured to death to send a powerful deterrent message. For understandable reasons, torture has become a symbol of tyranny.

Most civilized people do not even want to think about torture as a matter of degree. Torture is torture, and it is an unspeakable evil, regardless of its specific nature or precise degree. Yet the word "torture" has no precise meaning. It can range from the most unmitigated cruelty as a prelude to death to the most antiseptic, nonlethal, and even nonphysical mind games that police play with suspects. "Psychological torture" is widespread in democracies and has even been approved by some courts in the United States. The all too commonplace "third degree" is a form of torture, as was the insertion of a broom handle into the rectum of Abner Louima by a New York City policeman.

The United States Court of Appeals for the Eleventh Circuit seems to have approved of torture as a way of securing information necessary to find a victim of kidnapping. In the case that led to this decision, *Leon v. Wainwright* (1984), the Miami police choked a suspect "until he revealed where [the victim] was being held." A dissenting state court judge characterized the policemen's actions as "'rack and pinion' techniques," but the federal appellate court unanimously held that it was merely "a group of concerned officers acting in a reasonable manner to obtain information they needed in order to protect another individual from bodily harm or death."[24] The truth is that both of the opposing views were correct—choking is a form of torture, and it *was* used to try to protect another person from harm.

Tyrannical regimes do not worry about distinctions or matters of degree. They are willing to employ any manner of torture for even the most minor infractions. The difficult issue, to be addressed at length in the next chapter, is how to consider whether a democracy can ever employ any form of torture to prevent any degree of harm.

How an Unlimited War on Terrorism Would Feel

A tyrannical regime is more than the sum of its parts. The feel of tyranny transcends individual violations of particular rights. Tyranny may be difficult to define, but its victims know it when they see it—and feel its impact.[25] The forms of law may apply, as they sometimes did in Nazi Germany or Stalinist Russia, but the reality of lawlessness is the norm. Sometimes, as in contemporary Iraq, there is not even the pretense of law. The rule of law is subordinate to the whim of the tyrant. The word of the dictator is the law.

An all-powerful nation willing to act on the recommendations of an amoral antiterrorist czar could go a long way toward rooting out most terrorist threats against it. By combining ruthless and disproportionate macro policies with proactive preventive and micro policies that reflect no concern for civil liberties or morality, such a nation could take maximum advantage of its superior military and technical capacities. It would attack militarily and conquer any area that harbored or supported terrorists, without regard to civilian or collateral casualties. It would round up and execute, or at least permanently imprison, all who support or sympathize with the terrorists or their cause. It would make reprisals against the relatives and others close to the terrorists and their supporters. It would make no deals with terrorists and it would severely punish any nation that did, or any that released a convicted or suspected terrorist. It would target opponents, at home or abroad, for assassination. It would close the borders of the country and severely restrict all movement within it, requiring every person to produce identification upon request. It would plant human spies and high-tech monitoring equipment everywhere. It would censor all dissenting speech. It would subject all suspects to secret military tribunals under the direct control of the antiterrorist czar. It would always resolve doubts in favor of the war against terrorism, without regard for civil liberties or the protection of the possibly innocent.

A nation conducting such an all-out war against terrorism would quickly lose both the feel of freedom and the reality of freedom. It would also reduce the risk of terrorism. Though some individuals might well persist in attacking the government, they would lack the infrastructure and support systems necessary to present any sustained terrorist threat, particularly one involving weapons of mass destruction.

The United States would be incapable of mounting an unlimited war against terrorism because we are constrained by our Constitution, our commitment to the rule of law, and our heritage of fairness, humaneness, and proportionality. Were we to face an imminent and near certain threat of nuclear, biological, or chemical destruction, we might well move in the direction of such an all-out war, but it would probably be too late. For a total, immoral approach to work most effectively, considerable lead time would be required. We are not about to goose-step down this road—and surrender our liberties and our heritage—on the basis of uncertain risks.

If we were absolutely sure that taking the kind of repressive steps an antiterrorist czar might recommend could have prevented the events of September 11, and would prevent comparable or worse events in the future, there would be considerable popular support for such measures. There is, of course, no such certainty, but neither is there any certainty that such measures would not work—at least enough to lower the risk somewhat. Civil libertarians who adamantly deny the possibility that repression can sometimes reduce terrorism are as agenda-driven as are those who favor repression and promise that it will end all terrorism. The reality is that repression—like terrorism itself—sometimes works, and the reason we should oppose it is that it carries too high a price tag.

I have outlined the above amoral "doomsday" scenario to help us understand and appreciate the heavy price we rightfully pay for our freedom and decency. In countries that are truly committed to the rule of law, there may be compromises with particular rights, and there may be restrictions placed on specific categories of people. But the feel of freedom will persist, even for those whose rights are restricted. They know that they can hold and express views in opposition to the government and that if they are prosecuted or otherwise targeted they will generally have access to an independent judiciary or a critical media.

Israel, for example, has the feel of freedom, not only for its Jewish citizens but for its Arab citizens and residents as well. Despite significant restrictions on the rights of Palestinians—including administrative detention, restriction of movement, identification checks, and other forms of discrimination—all Israelis, including Palestinian noncitizens in East Jerusalem and Arab citizens in other parts of the country, are free to express their support for the Palestinian cause, even for its terrorist tactics.[26] They know that the Supreme Court of Israel stands as an independent bastion of liberty, even when the military or the government seek restrictions. Indeed, the only court in the entire Middle East in which an Arab can expect justice against governmental repression is the Israeli Supreme Court.[27] Anyone who spends any time in Israel, and who reports fairly on the situation on the ground, will attest that the feel of freedom is far greater there—for both Jews and Arabs—than in any Arab or Muslim country, or even than in many other places with fewer formal restrictions but many more actual constraints on liberty.[28] One wag has said that Israelis and Iraqis have exactly the same right of free speech: they can both condemn Israel and praise Saddam Hussein.

Human rights organizations that try to quantify abuses or "rank" or "grade" countries by reference to specific "objective" criteria often miss the important qualitative difference. Yet it is apparent to those who spend time in various countries around the world.

Even during times when the United States has imposed significant restrictions on liberty, it has never lost the feel of freedom. To be sure, more than a hundred thousand Japanese-Americans lost this feel when they were interned during World War II, and parts of Hawaii lost it to a considerable degree when martial law was declared there following the attack on Pearl Harbor. Many immigrants, especially socialists and anarchists, very likely lost it during World War I and the Palmer raids that followed. And American communists and former communists certainly did not feel free during the McCarthy era. But these are the exceptions to a far more general rule of liberty in this country.

If our government were ever to impose tyrannical restrictions on our liberties, we would feel and recognize the change. It would not result from any specific restriction on our liberty. It would be the consequence of a change in attitude, a reduction in the checks and balances each branch of government imposes on the others, an abrogation of the rule of law. It is this reality that perhaps explains why so many Americans were rightly appalled to learn of the "shadow government" secretly put in place following September 11, 2001.[29] This "government" did not include a legislative or judicial branch. It was limited to the executive branch and the military that serves under it. *That* lacks the feel of freedom!

So would the suspension of the writ of habeas corpus—a drastic step our Constitution authorizes only "when in cases of rebellion or invasion the public safety may require it." If freedom of speech were abrogated and censorship of dissent imposed, that would lack the feel of freedom, as would massive arrests or roundups based on political, religious, ethnic, or racial considerations. So would pervasive monitoring of conversations and tracking of Internet or computer usage.

It is also possible that a combination of restrictions, no one of them by itself determinative, could change the feel of our freedom. We are not close to that situation today. The danger is that, because the "emergency" we find ourselves in following September 11 will endure for a long time, we may become accustomed to so many gradual, incremental compromises that we will not realize when we have crossed the line until we are well beyond it—especially since there is no single bright line separating democracy from tyranny. Moreover, if we gradually compromise the tools of freedom one at a time, we will not have them available when we truly need them to combat tyranny.

Judge Learned Hand once observed that when liberty dies in the hearts of men and women, "no court can save it." He added, "no court can even do much to help it."[30] He may have been right about the first part, but he was probably wrong about the second: by vigorously enforcing basic rights, courts can slow down the process of tyranny—at least under certain circumstances (as American courts did during the McCarthy period). Hand's observation recognizes the importance of the feel of freedom that I have been discussing. If we preserve this feel, no single compromise will turn us into a tyranny. If we lose this feel, no single right will protect us from tyranny.

chapter four

Should the Ticking Bomb Terrorist Be Tortured?

A Case Study in How a Democracy Should Make Tragic Choices

"Authorizing torture is a bad and dangerous idea
that can easily be made to sound plausible. There is a
subtle fallacy embedded in the traditional 'ticking bomb'
argument for torture to save lives."
-—Philip Heymann, former deputy attorney general

In my nearly forty years of teaching at Harvard Law School I have always challenged my students with hypothetical and real-life problems requiring them to choose among evils. The students invariably try to resist these tragic choices by stretching their ingenuity to come up with alternative—and less tragic—options. The classic hypothetical case involves the train engineer whose brakes become inoperative. There is no way he can stop his speeding vehicle of death. Either he can do nothing, in which case he will plow into a busload of schoolchildren, or he can swerve onto another track, where he sees a drunk lying on the rails. (Neither decision will endanger him or his passengers.) There is no third choice. What should he do?

I also present my students with real-life choices from evil cases like the one that occurred in Georgia during the second decade of the twentieth century: A lawyer was told in confidence by his client that another man—a stranger to the lawyer—was about to be executed for a crime that he, the client, rather than the condemned man, had committed. The lawyer had sworn an oath not to reveal any confidential communications given to him by his clients, but to comply with that oath would make him complicit in the death of an innocent stranger. What should the lawyer (or a priest in a comparable situation) do?

Whenever I present these cases to my students, they seek, as any good lawyer should, to avoid the evils of either choice. They desperately try to break out of the rigid constraints of the hypothetical train situation by ascribing to the engineer a supermanlike ability to drive the train off the tracks. I force them back onto the rails of my hypothetical dilemma, and they groan in frustration. Similarly, with the real-life cases, my students come up with clever options by which the lawyer can satisfy both his professional obligation of confidentiality to his client and his moral obligation not to stand idly by as the blood of his neighbor is shed. In the real case described above the lawyer tried to come up with a middle ground—with tragic consequences. He told the governor that he knew for a certainty the condemned man was innocent but that he could not disclose the source of the information. The governor commuted the death sentence to life imprisonment, whereupon the inmate was forcibly removed from the prison by a lynch mob and hanged.

Students love to debate positive choices: good, better, best. They don't mind moderately negative choices: bad, worse, worst. They hate tragic choices: unthinkable versus inconceivable.

Rational decision theory teaches us how to choose among reasonable alternatives—good and bad—on a cost-benefit basis or on the basis of assigning weights to various choices. It does not teach us how to choose among unreasonable alternatives, each so horrible that our mind rebels even at the notion of thinking about the evil options. When I was a child we joked about a hypothetical scenario that, not surprisingly, involved a choice of evils between bodily excretions: If you were up to your neck in a vat of cat vomit and somebody threw a pile of dog poop at your face, would you duck? For those who watch TV shows like *Fear Factor* this might not seem so difficult, but for our preteen minds it was a choice of evils to be debated almost as endlessly as whether it would be worse to have to tell our parents that we (orthodox Jews who were prohibited from eating pig) had contracted trichinosis or syphilis. We actually came up with answers to these absurd hypothetical dramas (no wonder so many of us became lawyers). I will spare you the answer to the vomit-poop dilemma but reveal that the trichinosis-syphilis situation was resolved by the following sexist answer: syphilis was worse if you were a girl, trichinosis if you were a boy.

How the Current Torture Debate Began

Before September 11, 2001, no one thought the issue of torture would ever reemerge as a topic of serious debate in this country. Yet shortly after that watershed event, FBI agents began to leak stories suggesting that they might have to resort to torture to get some detainees, who were suspected of complicity in al-Qaeda terrorism, to provide information necessary to prevent a recurrence. An FBI source told the press that because "we are known for humanitarian treatment" of arrestees, we have been unable to get any terrorist suspects to divulge information about possible future plans. "We're into this thing for 35 days and nobody is talking," he said in obvious frustration. "Basically we're stuck." A senior FBI aide warned that "it could get to the spot where we could go to pressure, . . . where *we won't have a choice,* and we are probably getting there."[1] But in a democracy there is *always* a choice.

In 1978 a terrorist group kidnapped Italy's former prime minister Aldo Moro and threatened to kill him. A summary of the case described the decision not to resort to torture: "During the hunt for the kidnappers of Aldo Moro, an investigator for the Italian security services proposed to General Carlo Della Chiesa [of the State Police] that a prisoner who seemed to have information on the case be tortured. The General rejected the idea, replying, 'Italy can survive the loss of Aldo Moro, but it cannot survive the introduction of torture.'" The terrorists eventually murdered Moro.[2]

The Supreme Court of Israel made the choice to disallow even moderate forms of physical pressure, despite claims that such nonlethal torture was necessary to save lives. Whether to employ any particular form of pressure on a suspect is always a matter of choice. It is the essence of democracy that we always have a choice, and we have appropriate institutional mechanisms for making choices, even—perhaps especially—choices among evils.

Constitutional democracies are, of course, constrained in the choices they may lawfully make. The Fifth Amendment prohibits compelled self-incrimination, which means that statements elicited by means of torture may not be introduced into evidence against the defendant who has been tortured.[3] But if a suspect is given immunity and then tortured into providing information about a future terrorist act, his privilege against self-incrimination has not been violated.[4] (Nor would it be violated if the information were elicited by means of "truth serum," as Judge William Webster, the former head of the FBI and the CIA, has proposed—as long as the information and its fruits were not used against him in a criminal trial.) Nor has his right to be free from "cruel and unusual punishment," since that provision of the Eighth Amendment has been interpreted to apply solely to punishment after conviction.[5] The only constitutional barriers would be the "due process" clauses of the Fifth and Fourteenth Amendments, which are quite general and sufficiently flexible to permit an argument that the only process "due" a terrorist suspected of refusing to disclose information necessary to prevent a terrorist attack is the requirement of probable cause and some degree of judicial supervision.[6]

In addition to possible constitutional constraints, we are also limited by our treaty obligations, which have the force of law. The Geneva Convention Against Torture prohibits all forms of torture and provides for no exceptions. It defines torture so broadly as to include many techniques that are routinely used around the world, including in Western democracies:

> For the purposes of this Convention, the term "torture" means any act by which severe pain or suffering, whether physical or mental, is intentionally inflicted on a person for such purposes as obtaining from him or a third person information or a confession, punishing him for an act he or a third person has committed or is sus-

pected of having committed, or intimidating or coercing
him or a third person, or for any reason based on discrimination of any kind, when such pain or suffering is
inflicted by or at the instigation of or with the consent or
acquiescence of a public official or other person acting
in an official capacity.[7]

Many nations that routinely practice the most brutal forms of
torture are signatories to this convention, but they hypocritically
ignore it. The United States adopted the convention, but with a
reservation: we agreed to be bound by it "only to the extent that it
is consistent with . . . the Eighth Amendment." Decisions by U.S.
courts have suggested that the Eighth Amendment may not pro-
hibit the use of physical force to obtain information needed to save
lives; so if the United States chose to employ nonlethal torture in
such an extreme case it could arguably remain in technical compli-
ance with its treaty obligation. Our courts routinely refuse to apply
the convention to "mental" or "psychological" torture, which is
commonplace.[8]

In any event, there are legal steps we could take, if we chose
to resort to torture, that would make it possible for us to use this
technique for eliciting information in dire circumstances. Neither
the presence nor the absence of legal constraints answers the fundamental moral question: should we? This is a choice that almost
no one wants to have to make. Torture has been off the agenda of
civilized discourse for so many centuries that it is a subject
reserved largely for historians rather than contemporary moralists
(though it remains a staple of abstract philosophers debating the
virtues and vices of absolutism). I have been criticized for even
discussing the issue, on the ground that academic discussion con-
fers legitimacy on a practice that deserves none. I have also been
criticized for raising a red herring, since it is "well known" that torture does not work—it produces many false confessions and use-

less misinformation, because a person will say anything to stop being tortured.[9]

This argument is reminiscent of the ones my students make in desperately seeking to avoid the choice of evils by driving the hypothetical railroad train off the track. The tragic reality is that torture sometimes works, much though many people wish it did not. There are numerous instances in which torture has produced self-proving, truthful information that was necessary to prevent harm to civilians. The *Washington Post* has recounted a case from 1995 in which Philippine authorities tortured a terrorist into disclosing information that may have foiled plots to assassinate the pope and to crash eleven commercial airliners carrying approximately four thousand passengers into the Pacific Ocean, as well as a plan to fly a private Cessna filled with explosives into CIA headquarters. For sixty-seven days, intelligence agents beat the suspect "with a chair and a long piece of wood [breaking most of his ribs], forced water into his mouth, and crushed lighted cigarettes into his private parts"—a procedure that the Philippine intelligence service calls "tactical interrogation." After successfully employing this procedure they turned him over to American authorities, along with the lifesaving information they had beaten out of him.[10]

It is impossible to avoid the difficult moral dilemma of choosing among evils by denying the empirical reality that torture *sometimes* works, even if it does not always work.[11] No technique of crime prevention always works.

It is also sometimes argued that even when torture does produce accurate information that helps to foil a terrorist plot—as the Philippine torture apparently did—there is no hard evidence that the *total amount* of terrorism is thereby reduced. The foiling of any one plot may simply result in the planning of another terrorist act, especially given the unlimited reservoir of potential terrorists. This argument may have some merit in regard to recurring acts of retail terrorism, such as the suicide bombings in Israel. Preventing one bombing may not significantly reduce the total number of civilian deaths, though it does, of course, make a difference to those who would have been killed in the thwarted explosion. But the argument is much weaker when it comes to acts of mega-terrorism, such as those prevented by the Philippine torture or the attacks perpetrated on September 11, 2001. It is the prospect of such mega-acts—and the possibility of preventing them—that raises the stakes in the torture debate.

It is precisely because torture sometimes does work and can sometimes prevent major disasters that it still exists in many parts of the world and has been totally eliminated from none. It also explains why the U.S. government sometimes "renders" terrorist suspects to nations like Egypt and Jordan, "whose intelligence services have close ties to the CIA and where they can be subjected to interrogation tactics—including torture and threats to families—that are illegal in the United States," as the *Washington Post* has reported. "In some cases, U.S. intelligence agents remain closely involved in the interrogation. . . . 'After September 11, these sorts of movements have been occurring all of the time,' a U.S. diplomat said. 'It allows us to get information from terrorists in a way we can't do on U.S. soil.' " As former CIA counterintelligence chief Vincent Cannistraro observed: "Egyptian jails are full of guys who are missing toenails and fingernails." Our government has a "don't ask, don't tell" policy when it comes to obtaining information from other governments that practice torture.[12] All such American complicity in foreign torture violates the plain language of the Geneva Convention Against Torture, which explicitly prohibits torture from being inflicted not only by signatory nations but also "at the instigation of or with the consent or acquiescence of" any person "acting in an official capacity." As we began to come to grips with the horrible evils of mass murder by terrorists, it became inevitable that torture would return to the agenda, and it has. The recent capture of a high-ranking al-Qaeda operative, possibly with information about terrorist "sleeper cells" and future targets, has raised the question of how to compel him to disclose this important information. We must be prepared to think about the alternatives in a rational manner. We cannot evade our responsibility by pretending that torture is not being used or by having others use it for our benefit.

Accordingly, this chapter considers torture as an example of how to think about the kinds of tragic choices we are likely to confront in the age of biological, chemical, and nuclear terrorism.

How I Began Thinking About Torture

In the late 1980s I traveled to Israel to conduct some research and teach a class at Hebrew University on civil liberties during times of crisis. In the course of my research I learned that the Israeli security services were employing what they euphemistically called "moderate physical pressure" on suspected terrorists to obtain information deemed necessary to prevent future terrorist attacks. The method employed by the security services fell somewhere between what many would regard as very rough interrogation (as practiced by the British in Northern Ireland) and outright torture (as practiced by the French in Algeria and by Egypt, the Philippines, and Jordan today). In most cases the suspect would be placed in a dark room with a smelly sack over his head. Loud, unpleasant music or other noise would blare from speakers. The suspect would be seated in an extremely uncomfortable position and then shaken vigorously until he disclosed the information. Statements made under this kind of nonlethal pressure could not be introduced in any court of law, both because they were involuntarily secured and because they were deemed potentially untrustworthy—at least without corroboration. But they were used as leads in the prevention of terrorist acts. Sometimes the leads proved false, other times they proved true. There is little doubt that some acts of terrorism—which would have killed many civilians—were prevented. There is also little doubt that the cost of saving these lives—measured in terms of basic human rights—was extraordinarily high.

In my classes and public lectures in Israel, I strongly condemned these methods as a violation of core civil liberties and human rights. The response that people gave, across the political spectrum from civil libertarians to law-and-order advocates, was essentially the same: but what about the "ticking bomb" case?

The ticking bomb case refers to a scenario that has been discussed by many philosophers, including Michael Walzer, Jean-Paul Sartre, and Jeremy Bentham. Walzer described such a hypothetical case in an article titled "Political Action: The Problem of Dirty Hands." In this case, a decent leader of a nation plagued with terrorism is asked "to authorize the torture of a captured rebel leader who knows or probably knows the location of a number of bombs hidden in apartment buildings across the city, set to go off within the next twenty-four hours. He orders the man tortured, convinced that he must do so for the sake of the people who might otherwise die in the explosions—even though he believes that torture is wrong, indeed abominable, not just sometimes, but always."[13]

In Israel, the use of torture to prevent terrorism was not hypothetical; it was very real and recurring. I soon discovered that virtually no one was willing to take the "purist" position against torture in the ticking bomb case: namely, that the ticking bomb must be permitted to explode and kill dozens of civilians, even if this disaster could be prevented by subjecting the captured terrorist to nonlethal torture and forcing him to disclose its location. I realized that the extraordinarily rare situation of the hypothetical ticking bomb terrorist was serving as a moral, intellectual, and legal justification for a pervasive *system* of coercive interrogation, which, though not the paradigm of torture, certainly bordered on it. It was then that I decided to challenge this system by directly confronting the ticking bomb case. I presented the following challenge to my Israeli audience: If the reason you permit nonlethal torture is based on the ticking bomb case, why not limit it exclusively to that compelling but rare situation? Moreover, if you believe that nonlethal torture is justifiable in the ticking bomb case, why not require advance judicial approval—a "torture warrant"? That was the origin of a controversial proposal that has received much attention, largely critical, from the media. Its goal was, and remains, to reduce the use of torture to the smallest amount and degree possible, while creating public accountability for its rare use. I saw it not as a compromise with civil liberties but rather as an effort to maximize civil liberties in the face of a realistic likelihood that torture would, in fact, take place below the radar screen of accountability.

I am not the only civil libertarian who has been stimulated into thinking about tragic choices by examining the tragic reality in Israel. At about the same time I was investigating civil liberties in Israel, the late Supreme Court justice William J. Brennan—perhaps the most committed civil libertarian in Supreme Court history—visited Israel and wrote the following:

> It may well be Israel, not the United States, that provides the best hope for building a jurisprudence that can protect civil liberties against the demands of national security, for it is Israel that has been facing real and serious threats to its security for the last forty years and seems destined to continue facing such threats in the foreseeable future. . . .
>
> I [would not] be surprised if in the future the protections generally afforded civil liberties during times of world danger owed much to the lessons Israel learns in its struggle to preserve simultaneously the liberties of its

citizens and the security of its nation. For in this crucible of danger lies the opportunity to forge a worldwide jurisprudence of civil liberties that can withstand the turbulences of war and crisis.[14]

It may well be, however, that the United States should be cautious in learning from Israel. What may be right for Israel—or any small country facing terrorism—may be wrong, or not quite as right, for the world's most powerful and influential nation. When Israel takes an action, such as publicly acknowledging that it may be proper to administer nonlethal torture in the ticking bomb case, that action does not immediately become a precedent for other nations. Indeed, Israel is generally condemned, even by nations that have done, and continue to do, far worse. Its actions, even when arguably proper, result in it being characterized as an "outlaw" state. Were the United States, on the other hand, to declare its intention to allow nonlethal torture in the ticking bomb case, that declaration would effectively change international law, since our actions help define the law. Accordingly, the stakes are far higher in the debate now taking place in this country.

The Case for Torturing the Ticking Bomb Terrorist

The arguments in favor of using torture as a last resort to prevent a ticking bomb from exploding and killing many people are both simple and simple-minded. Bentham constructed a compelling hypothetical case to support his utilitarian argument against an absolute prohibition on torture:

Suppose an occasion were to arise, in which a suspicion is entertained, as strong as that which would be received as a sufficient ground for arrest and commitment as for felony—a suspicion that at this very time a considerable number of individuals are actually suffering, by illegal violence inflictions equal in intensity to those which if inflicted by the hand of justice, would universally be spoken of under the name of torture. For the purpose of rescuing from torture these hundred innocents, should any scruple be made of applying equal or superior torture, to extract the requisite information from the mouth of one criminal, who having it in his power to make known the place where at this time the enormity was practising or about to be practised, should refuse to do so? To say nothing of wisdom, could any pretence be made so much as to the praise of blind and vulgar humanity, by the man who to save one criminal, should determine to abandon 100 innocent persons to the same fate?[15]

If the torture of one guilty person would be justified to prevent the torture of a hundred innocent persons, it would seem to follow—certainly to Bentham—that it would also be justified to prevent the murder of thousands of innocent civilians in the ticking bomb case. Consider two hypothetical situations that are not, unfortunately, beyond the realm of possibility. In fact, they are both extrapolations on actual situations we have faced.

Several weeks before September 11, 2001, the Immigration and Naturalization Service detained Zacarias Moussaoui after flight instructors reported suspicious statements he had made while taking flying lessons and paying for them with large amounts of cash.[16] The government decided not to seek a warrant to search his computer. Now imagine that they had, and that they discovered he was part of a plan to destroy large occupied buildings, but without any further details. They interrogated him, gave him immunity from prosecution, and offered him large cash rewards and a new identity. He refused to talk. They then threatened him, tried to trick him, and employed every lawful technique available. He still refused. They even injected him with sodium pentothal and other truth serums, but to no avail. The attack now appeared to be imminent, but the FBI still had no idea what the target was or what means would be used to attack it. We could not simply evacuate all buildings indefinitely. An FBI agent proposes the use of nonlethal torture—say, a sterilized needle inserted under the fingernails to produce unbearable pain without any threat to health or life, or the method used in the film *Marathon Man,* a dental drill through an unanesthetized tooth.

The simple cost-benefit analysis for employing such non-lethal torture seems overwhelming: it is surely better to inflict nonlethal pain on one guilty terrorist who is illegally withholding information needed to prevent an act of terrorism than to permit a large number of innocent victims to die.[17] Pain is a lesser and more remediable harm than death; and the lives of a thousand innocent people should be valued more than the bodily integrity of one guilty person. If the variation on the Moussaoui case is not sufficiently compelling to make this point, we can always raise the stakes. Several weeks after September 11, our government received reports that a ten-kiloton nuclear weapon may have been stolen from Russia and was on its way to New York City, where it would be detonated and kill hundreds of thousands of people. The reliability of the source, code named Dragonfire, was uncertain, but assume for purposes of this hypothetical extension of the actual case that the source was a captured terrorist—like the one tortured by the Philippine authorities—who knew precisely how and where the weapon was being bought into New York and was to be detonated. Again, everything short of torture is tried, but to no avail. It is not absolutely certain torture will work, but it is our last, best hope for preventing a cataclysmic nuclear devastation in a city too large to evacuate in time. Should nonlethal torture be tried? Bentham would certainly have said yes.

The strongest argument against any resort to torture, even in the ticking bomb case, also derives from Bentham's utilitarian calculus. Experience has shown that if torture, which has been deemed illegitimate by the civilized world for more than a century, were now to be legitimated—even for limited use in one extraordinary type of situation—such legitimation would constitute an important symbolic setback in the worldwide campaign against human rights abuses. Inevitably, the legitimation of torture by the world's leading democracy would provide a welcome justification for its more widespread use in other parts of the world. Two Bentham scholars, W. L. Twining and P. E. Twining, have argued that torture is unacceptable even if it is restricted to an extremely limited category of cases:

> There is at least one good practical reason for drawing a distinction between justifying an isolated act of torture in an extreme emergency of the kind postulated above and justifying the *institutionalisation* of torture as a regular practice. The circumstances are so extreme in which most of us would be prepared to justify resort to torture, if at all, the conditions we would impose would be so stringent, the practical problems of devising and enforcing adequate safeguards so difficult and the risks of abuse so great that it would be unwise and dangerous to entrust any government, however enlightened, with such a power. Even an out-and-out utilitarian can support an absolute prohibition against institutionalised torture on the ground that no government in the world can be trusted not to abuse the power and to satisfy in practice the conditions he would impose.[18]

Bentham's own justification was based on *case* or *act* utilitarianism—a demonstration that in a *particular case,* the benefits that would flow from the limited use of torture would outweigh its costs. The argument against any use of torture would derive from *rule* utilitarianism—which considers the implications of establishing a precedent that would inevitably be extended beyond its limited case utilitarian justification to other possible evils of lesser magnitude. Even terrorism itself could be justified by a case utilitarian approach. Surely one could come up with a singular situation in which the targeting of a small number of civilians could be thought necessary to save thousands of other civilians—blowing up a German kindergarten by the relatives of inmates in a Nazi death camp, for example, and threatening to repeat the targeting of German children unless the death camps were shut down.

The reason this kind of single-case utilitarian justification is simple-minded is that it has no inherent limiting principle. If nonlethal torture of one person is justified to prevent the killing of many important people, then what if it were necessary to use lethal torture—or at least torture that posed a substantial risk of death? What if it were necessary to torture the suspect's mother or children to get him to divulge the information? What if it took threatening to kill his family, his friends, his entire village?[19] Under a simple-minded quantitative case utilitarianism, anything goes as long as the number of people tortured or killed does not exceed the number that would be saved. This is morality by numbers, unless there are other constraints on what we can properly do. These other constraints can come from rule utilitarianisms or other principles of morality, such as the prohibition against deliberately punishing the innocent. Unless we are prepared to impose some limits on the use of torture or other barbaric tactics that might be of some use in preventing terrorism, we risk hurtling down a slippery slope into the abyss of amorality and ultimately tyranny. Dostoevsky captured the complexity of this dilemma in

The Brothers Karamazov when he had Ivan pose the following question to Alyosha: "Imagine that you are creating a fabric of human destiny with the object of making men happy in the end, giving them peace at least, but that it was essential and inevitable to torture to death only one tiny creature—that baby beating its breast with its fist, for instance—and to found that edifice on its unavenged tears, would you consent to be the architect on those conditions? Tell me the truth."

A willingness to kill an innocent child suggests a willingness to do anything to achieve a necessary result. Hence the slippery slope.

It does not necessarily follow from this understandable fear of the slippery slope that we can never consider the use of nonlethal infliction of pain, if its use were to be limited by acceptable principles of morality. After all, imprisoning a witness who refuses to testify after being given immunity is designed to be punitive—that is painful. Such imprisonment can, on occasion, produce more pain and greater risk of death than nonlethal torture. Yet we continue to threaten and use the pain of imprisonment to loosen the tongues of reluctant witnesses.[20]

It is commonplace for police and prosecutors to threaten recalcitrant suspects with prison rape. As one prosecutor put it: "You're going to be the boyfriend of a very bad man." The slippery slope is an argument of caution, not a debate stopper, since virtually every compromise with an absolutist approach to rights carries the risk of slipping further. An appropriate response to the slippery slope is to build in a principled break. For example, if nonlethal torture were legally limited to convicted terrorists who had knowledge of future massive terrorist acts, were given immunity, and still refused to provide the information, there might still be objections to the use of torture, but they would have to go beyond the slippery slope argument.[21]

The case utilitarian argument for torturing a ticking bomb terrorist is bolstered by an argument from analogy—an *a fortiori* argument. What moral principle could justify the death penalty for past individual murders and at the same time condemn nonlethal torture to prevent future mass murders? Bentham posed this rhetorical question as support for his argument. The death penalty is, of course, reserved for convicted murderers. But again, what if torture was limited to convicted terrorists who refused to divulge information about future terrorism? Consider as well the analogy to the use of deadly force against suspects fleeing from arrest for dangerous felonies of which they have not yet been convicted. Or military retaliations that produce the predictable and inevitable collateral killing of some innocent civilians. The case against torture, if made by a Quaker who opposes the death penalty, war, self-defense, and the use of lethal force against fleeing felons, is understandable. But for anyone who justifies killing on the basis of a cost-benefit analysis, the case against the use of nonlethal torture to save multiple lives is more difficult to make. In the end, absolute opposition to torture—even nonlethal torture in the ticking bomb case—may rest more on historical and aesthetic considerations than on moral or logical ones.

In debating the issue of torture, the first question I am often asked is, "Do you want to take us back to the Middle Ages?" The association between any form of torture and gruesome death is powerful in the minds of most people knowledgeable of the history of its abuses. This understandable association makes it difficult for many people to think about nonlethal torture as a technique for *saving* lives.

The second question I am asked is, "What kind of torture do you have in mind?" When I respond by describing the sterilized needle being shoved under the fingernails, the reaction is visceral and often visible—a shudder coupled with a facial gesture of disgust. Discussions of the death penalty on the other hand can be conducted without these kinds of reactions, especially now that we literally put the condemned prisoner "to sleep" by laying him out on a gurney and injecting a lethal substance into his body. There is no breaking of the neck, burning of the brain, bursting of internal organs, or gasping for breath that used to accompany hanging, electrocution, shooting, and gassing. The executioner has been replaced by a paramedical technician, as the aesthetics of death have become more acceptable. All this tends to cover up the reality that death is forever while nonlethal pain is temporary. In our modern age death is underrated, while pain is overrated.

I observed a similar phenomenon several years ago during the debate over corporal punishment that was generated by the decision of a court in Singapore to sentence a young American to medically supervised lashing with a cane. Americans who support the death penalty and who express little concern about inner-city prison conditions were outraged by the specter of a few welts on the buttocks of an American. It was an utterly irrational display of hypocrisy and double standards. Given a choice between a medically administered whipping and one month in a typical state lockup or prison, any rational and knowledgeable person would choose the lash. No one dies of welts or pain, but many inmates are raped, beaten, knifed, and otherwise mutilated and tortured in American prisons. The difference is that we don't see—and we don't want to see—what goes on behind their high walls. Nor do we want to think about it. Raising the issue of torture makes Americans think about a brutalizing and unaesthetic phenomenon that has been out of our consciousness for many years.[22]

The Three—or Four—Ways

The debate over the use of torture goes back many years, with Bentham supporting it in a limited category of cases, Kant opposing it as part of his categorical imperative against improperly using people as means for achieving noble ends, and Voltaire's views on the matter being "hopelessly confused."[23] The modern resort to terrorism has renewed the debate over how a rights-based society should respond to the prospect of using nonlethal torture in the ticking bomb situation. In the late 1980s the Israeli government appointed a commission headed by a retired Supreme Court justice to look into precisely that situation. The commission concluded that there are "three ways for solving this grave dilemma between the vital need to preserve the very existence of the state and its citizens, and maintain its character as a law-abiding state." The first is to allow the security services to continue to fight terrorism in "a twilight zone which is outside the realm of law." The second is "the way of the hypocrites: they declare that they abide by the rule of law, but turn a blind eye to what goes on beneath the surface." And the third, "the truthful road of the rule of law," is that the "law itself must insure a proper framework for the activity" of the security services in seeking to prevent terrorist acts.[24]

There is of course a fourth road: namely to forgo any use of torture and simply allow the preventable terrorist act to occur.[25] After the Supreme Court of Israel outlawed the use of physical pressure, the Israeli security services claimed that, as a result of the Supreme Court's decision, at least one preventable act of terrorism had been allowed to take place, one that killed several people when a bus was bombed.[26] Whether this claim is true, false, or somewhere in between is difficult to assess.[27] But it is clear that if the preventable act of terrorism was of the magnitude of the attacks of September 11, there would be a great outcry in any democracy that had deliberately refused to take available preventive action, even if it required the use of torture. During numerous public appearances since September 11, 2001, I have asked audiences for a show of hands as to how many would support the use of nonlethal torture in a ticking bomb case. Virtually every hand is raised. The few that remain down go up when I ask how many believe that torture would actually be used in such a case.

Law enforcement personnel give similar responses. This can be seen in reports of physical abuse directed against some suspects that have been detained following September 11, reports that have been taken quite seriously by at least one federal judge.[28] It is confirmed by the willingness of U.S. law enforcement officials to facilitate the torture of terrorist suspects by repressive regimes allied with our intelligence agencies. As one former CIA operative with thirty years of experience reported: "A lot of people are saying we need someone at the agency who can pull fingernails out. Others are saying, 'Let others use interrogation methods that we don't use.' The only question then is, do you want to have CIA people in the room?" The real issue, therefore, is not whether some torture would or would not be used in the ticking bomb case—it would. The question is whether it would be done openly, pursuant to a previously established legal procedure, or whether it would be done secretly, in violation of existing law.[29]

Several important values are pitted against each other in this conflict. The first is the safety and security of a nation's citizens. Under the ticking bomb scenario this value may require the use of torture, if that is the only way to prevent the bomb from exploding and killing large numbers of civilians. The second value is the preservation of civil liberties and human rights. This value requires that we not accept torture as a legitimate part of our legal system. In my debates with two prominent civil libertarians, Floyd Abrams and Harvey Silverglate, both have acknowledged that they would want nonlethal torture to be used if it could prevent thousands of deaths, but they did not want torture to be officially recognized by our legal system. As Abrams put it: "In a democracy sometimes it is necessary to do things off the books and below the radar screen." Former presidential candidate Alan Keyes took the position that although torture might be *necessary* in a given situation it could never be *right*. He suggested that a president *should* authorize the torturing of a ticking bomb terrorist, but that this act should not be legitimated by the courts or incorporated into our legal system. He argued that wrongful and indeed unlawful acts might sometimes be necessary to preserve the nation, but that no aura of legitimacy should be placed on these actions by judicial imprimatur.

This understandable approach is in conflict with the third important value: namely, open accountability and visibility in a democracy. "Off-the-book actions below the radar screen" are antithetical to the theory and practice of democracy. Citizens cannot approve or disapprove of governmental actions of which they are unaware. We have learned the lesson of history that off-the-book actions can produce terrible consequences. Richard Nixon's creation of a group of "plumbers" led to Watergate, and Ronald Reagan's authorization of an off-the-books foreign policy in Central America led to the Iran-Contra scandal. And these are only the ones we know about!

Perhaps the most extreme example of such a hypocritical approach to torture comes—not surprisingly—from the French experience in Algeria. The French army used torture extensively in seeking to prevent terrorism during a brutal colonial war from 1955 to 1957. An officer who supervised this torture, General Paul Aussaresses, wrote a book recounting what he had done and seen, including the torture of dozens of Algerians. "The best way to make a terrorist talk when he refused to say what he knew was to torture him," he boasted. Although the book was published decades after the war was over, the general was prosecuted—but not for what he had done to the Algerians. Instead, he was prosecuted for *revealing* what he had done, and seeking to justify it.[30]

In a democracy governed by the rule of law, we should never want our soldiers or our president to take any action that we deem wrong or illegal. A good test of whether an action should or should not be done is whether we are prepared to have it disclosed—perhaps not immediately, but certainly after some time has passed.

No legal system operating under the rule of law should ever tolerate an "off-the-books" approach to necessity. Even the defense of necessity must be justified lawfully. The road to tyranny has always been paved with claims of necessity made by those responsible for the security of a nation. Our system of checks and balances requires that all presidential actions, like all legislative or military actions, be consistent with governing law. If it is necessary to torture in the ticking bomb case, then our governing laws must accommodate this practice. If we refuse to change our law to accommodate any particular action, then our government should not take that action.[31]

Only in a democracy committed to civil liberties would a triangular conflict of this kind exist. Totalitarian and authoritarian regimes experience no such conflict, because they subscribe to neither the civil libertarian nor the democratic values that come in conflict with the value of security. The hard question is: which value is to be preferred when an inevitable clash occurs? One or more of these values must inevitably be compromised in making the tragic choice presented by the ticking bomb case. If we do not torture, we compromise the security and safety of our citizens. If we tolerate torture, but keep it off the books and below the radar screen, we compromise principles of democratic accountability. If we create a legal structure for limiting and controlling torture, we compromise our principled opposition to torture in all circumstances and create a potentially dangerous and expandable situation.

In 1678, the French writer François de La Rochefoucauld said that "hypocrisy is the homage that vice renders to virtue." In this case we have two vices: terrorism and torture. We also have two virtues: civil liberties and democratic accountability. Most civil libertarians I know prefer hypocrisy, precisely because it appears to avoid the conflict between security and civil liberties, but by choosing the way of the hypocrite these civil libertarians compromise the value of democratic accountability. Such is the nature of tragic choices in a complex world. As Bentham put it more than two centuries ago: "Government throughout is but a choice of evils." In a democracy, such choices must be made, whenever possible, with openness and democratic accountability, and subject to the rule of law.[32]

Consider another terrible choice of evils that could easily have been presented on September 11, 2001—and may well be presented in the future: a hijacked passenger jet is on a collision course with a densely occupied office building; the only way to prevent the destruction of the building and the killing of its occupants is to shoot down the jet, thereby killing its innocent passengers. This choice now seems easy, because the passengers are certain to die anyway and their somewhat earlier deaths will save numerous lives. The passenger jet must be shot down. But what if it were only *probable*, not certain, that the jet would crash into the building? Say, for example, we know from cell phone transmissions that passengers are struggling to regain control of the hijacked jet, but it is unlikely they will succeed in time. Or say we have no communication with the jet and all we know is that it is off course and heading toward Washington, D.C., or some other densely populated city. Under these more questionable circumstances, the question becomes *who* should make this life and death choice between evils—a decision that may turn out tragically wrong?

No reasonable person would allocate this decision to a fighter jet pilot who happened to be in the area or to a local airbase commander—unless of course there was no time for the matter to be passed up the chain of command to the president or the secretary of defense. A decision of this kind should be made at the highest level possible, with visibility and accountability.

Why is this not also true of the decision to torture a ticking bomb terrorist? Why should that choice of evils be relegated to a local policeman, FBI agent, or CIA operative, rather than to a judge, the attorney general, or the president?

There are, of course, important differences between the decision to shoot down the plane and the decision to torture the ticking bomb terrorist. Having to shoot down an airplane, though tragic, is not likely to be a recurring issue. There is no slope down which to slip.[33] Moreover, the jet to be shot down is filled with our fellow citizens—people with whom we can identify. The suspected terrorist we may choose to torture is a "they"—an enemy with whom we do not identify but with whose potential victims we do identify. The risk of making the wrong decision, or of overdoing the torture, is far greater, since we do not care as much what happens to "them" as to "us."[34] Finally, there is something different about torture—even nonlethal torture—that sets it apart from a quick death. In addition to the horrible history associated with torture, there is also the aesthetic of torture. The very idea of deliberately subjecting a captive human being to excruciating pain violates our sense of what is acceptable. On a purely rational basis, it is far worse to shoot a fleeing felon in the back and kill him, yet every civilized society authorizes shooting such a suspect who poses dangers of committing violent crimes against the police or others. In the United States we execute convicted murderers, despite compelling evidence of the unfairness and ineffectiveness of capital punishment. Yet many of us recoil at the prospect of shoving a sterilized needle under the finger of a suspect who is refusing to divulge information that might prevent multiple deaths. Despite the irrationality of these distinctions, they are understandable, especially in light of the sordid history of torture.

We associate torture with the Inquisition, the Gestapo, the Stalinist purges, and the Argentine colonels responsible for the "dirty war." We recall it as a prelude to death, an integral part of a regime of gratuitous pain leading to a painful demise. We find it difficult to imagine a benign use of nonlethal torture to save lives.

Yet there was a time in the history of Anglo-Saxon law when torture was used to save life, rather than to take it, and when the limited administration of nonlethal torture was supervised by judges, including some who are well remembered in history.[35] This fascinating story has been recounted by Professor John Langbein of Yale Law School, and it is worth summarizing here because it helps inform the debate over whether, if torture would in fact be used in a ticking bomb case, it would be worse to make it part of the legal system, or worse to have it done off the books and below the radar screen.

In his book on legalized torture during the sixteenth and seventeenth centuries, *Torture and the Law of Proof,* Langbein demonstrates the trade-off between torture and other important values. Torture was employed for several purposes. First, it was used to secure the evidence necessary to obtain a guilty verdict under the rigorous criteria for conviction required at the time— either the testimony of two eyewitnesses or the confession of the accused himself. Circumstantial evidence, no matter how compelling, would not do. As Langbein concludes, "no society will long tolerate a legal system in which there is no prospect in convicting unrepentant persons who commit clandestine crimes. Something had to be done to extend the system to those cases. The two-eyewitness rule was hard to compromise or evade, but the confession invited 'subterfuge.'" The subterfuge that was adopted permitted the use of torture to obtain confessions from suspects against whom there was compelling circumstantial evidence of guilt. The circumstantial evidence, alone, could not be used to convict, but it was used to obtain a torture warrant. That torture warrant was in turn used to obtain a confession, which then had to be independently corroborated—at least in most cases (witchcraft and other such cases were exempted from the requirement of corroboration).[36]

Torture was also used against persons already convicted of capital crimes, such as high treason, who were thought to have information necessary to prevent attacks on the state.

Langbein studied eighty-one torture warrants, issued between 1540 and 1640, and found that in many of them, especially in "the higher cases of treasons, torture is used for discovery, and not for evidence." Torture was "used to protect the state" and "mostly that meant preventive torture to identify and forestall plots and plotters." It was only when the legal system loosened its requirement of proof (or introduced the "black box" of the jury system) and when perceived threats against the state diminished that torture was no longer deemed necessary to convict guilty defendants against whom there had previously been insufficient evidence, or to secure preventive information.[37]

The ancient Jewish system of jurisprudence came up with yet another solution to the conundrum of convicting the guilty and preventing harms to the community in the face of difficult evidentiary barriers. Jewish law required two witnesses and a specific advance warning before a guilty person could be convicted. Because confessions were disfavored, torture was not an available option. Instead, the defendant who had been seen killing by one reliable witness, or whose guilt was obvious from the circumstantial evidence, was formally acquitted, but he was then taken to a secure location and fed a concoction of barley and water until his stomach burst and he died. Moreover, Jewish law permitted more flexible forms of self-help against those who were believed to endanger the community.[38]

Every society has insisted on the incapacitation of dangerous criminals regardless of strictures in the formal legal rules. Some use torture, others use informal sanctions, while yet others create the black box of a jury, which need not explain its commonsense verdicts. Similarly, every society insists that, if there are steps that can be taken to prevent effective acts of terrorism, these steps should be taken, even if they require some compromise with other important principles.

In deciding whether the ticking bomb terrorist should be tor-

tured, one important question is whether there would be less torture if it were done as part of the legal system, as it was in sixteenth- and seventeenth-century England, or off the books, as it is
in many countries today. The Langbein study does not definitively
answer this question, but it does provide some suggestive insights.
The English system of torture was more visible and thus more
subject to public accountability, and it is likely that torture was
employed less frequently in England than in France. "During
these years when it appears that torture might have become routinized in English criminal procedure, the Privy Council kept the
torture power under careful control and never allowed it to fall
into the hands of the regular law enforcement officers," as it had
in France. In England "no law enforcement officer . . . acquired
the power to use torture without special warrant." Moreover,
when torture warrants were abolished, "the English experiment
with torture left no traces." Because it was under centralized control, it was easier to abolish than it was in France, where it persisted for many years.[39]

It is always difficult to extrapolate from history, but it seems
logical that a formal, visible, accountable, and centralized system
is somewhat easier to control than an ad hoc, off-the-books, and
under-the-radar-screen nonsystem. I believe, though I certainly
cannot prove, that a formal requirement of a judicial warrant as a
prerequisite to nonlethal torture would decrease the amount of
physical violence directed against suspects. At the most obvious
level, a double check is always more protective than a single
check. In every instance in which a warrant is requested, a field
officer has already decided that torture is justified and, in the
absence of a warrant requirement, would simply proceed with the
torture. Requiring that decision to be approved by a judicial officer will result in fewer instances of torture even if the judge rarely
turns down a request. Moreover, I believe that most judges would
require compelling evidence before they would authorize so

extraordinary a departure from our constitutional norms, and law enforcement officials would be reluctant to seek a warrant unless they had compelling evidence that the suspect had information needed to prevent an imminent terrorist attack. A record would be kept of every warrant granted, and although it is certainly possible that some individual agents might torture without a warrant, they would have no excuse, since a warrant procedure would be available. They could not claim "necessity," because the decision as to whether the torture is indeed necessary has been taken out of their hands and placed in the hands of a judge. In addition, even if torture were deemed totally illegal without any exception, it would still occur, though the public would be less aware of its existence.

I also believe that the rights of the suspect would be better protected with a warrant requirement. He would be granted immunity, told that he was now compelled to testify, threatened with imprisonment if he refused to do so, and given the option of providing the requested information. Only if he refused to do what he was legally compelled to do—provide necessary information, which could not incriminate him because of the immunity—would he be threatened with torture. Knowing that such a threat was authorized by the law, he might well provide the information.[40] If he still refused to, he would be subjected to judicially monitored physical measures designed to cause excruciating pain without leaving any lasting damage.

Let me cite two examples to demonstrate why I think there would be less torture with a warrant requirement than without one. Recall the case of the alleged national security wiretap placed on the phones of Martin Luther King by the Kennedy administration in the early 1960s. This was in the days when the attorney general could authorize a national security wiretap without a warrant. Today no judge would issue a warrant in a case as flimsy as that one. When Zacarias Moussaoui was detained after raising suspicions while trying to learn how to fly an airplane, the government did not even seek a national security wiretap because its lawyers believed that a judge would not have granted one. If Moussaoui's computer could have been searched without a warrant, it almost certainly would have been.

It should be recalled that in the context of searches, our Supreme Court opted for a judicial check on the discretion of the police, by requiring a search warrant in most cases. The Court has explained the reason for the warrant requirement as follows: "The informed and deliberate determinations of magistrates . . . are to be preferred over the hurried action of officers."[41] Justice Robert Jackson elaborated:

> The point of the Fourth Amendment, which often is not grasped by zealous officers, is not that it denies law enforcement the support of the usual inferences which reasonable men draw from evidence. Its protection consists in requiring that those inferences be drawn by a neutral and detached magistrate instead of being judged by the officer engaged in the often competitive enterprise of ferreting out crime. Any assumption that evidence sufficient to support a magistrate's disinterested determination to issue a search warrant will justify the officers in making a search without a warrant would reduce the Amendment to nullity and leave the people's homes secure only in the discretion of police officers.[42]

Although torture is very different from a search, the policies underlying the warrant requirement are relevant to the question whether there is likely to be more torture or less if the decision is left entirely to field officers, or if a judicial officer has to approve a request for a torture warrant. As Abraham Maslow once observed, to a man with a hammer, everything looks like a nail. If the man with the hammer must get judicial approval before he can use it, he will probably use it less often and more carefully.

There are other, somewhat more subtle, considerations that should be factored into any decision regarding torture. There are some who see silence as a virtue when it comes to the choice among such horrible evils as torture and terrorism. It is far better, they argue, not to discuss or write about issues of this sort, lest they become legitimated. And legitimation is an appropriate concern. Justice Jackson, in his opinion in one of the cases concerning the detention of Japanese-Americans during World War II, made the following relevant observation:

> Much is said of the danger to liberty from the Army program for deporting and detaining these citizens of Japanese extraction. But a judicial construction of the due process clause that will sustain this order is a far more subtle blow to liberty than the promulgation of the order itself. A military order, however unconstitutional, is not apt to last longer than the military emergency. Even during that period a succeeding commander may revoke it all. But once a judicial opinion rationalizes such an order to show that it conforms to the Constitution, or rather rationalizes the Constitution to show that the Constitution sanctions such an order, the Court for all time has validated the principle of racial discrimination in criminal procedure and of transplanting American citizens. The principle then lies about like a loaded weapon ready for the hand of any authority that can bring forward a plausible claim of an urgent need. Every repetition imbeds that principle more deeply in our law and thinking and expands it to new purposes. All who observe the work of courts are familiar with what Judge Cardozo described as "the tendency of a principle to

expand itself to the limit of its logic." A military commander may overstep the bounds of constitutionality,
and it is an incident. But if we review and approve, that
passing incident becomes the doctrine of the Constitution. There it has a generative power of its own, and all
that it creates will be in its own image.[43]

A similar argument can be made regarding torture: if an
agent tortures, that is "an incident," but if the courts authorize it, it
becomes a precedent. There is, however, an important difference
between the detention of Japanese-American citizens and torture.
The detentions were done openly and with presidential accountability; torture would be done secretly, with official deniability. Tolerating an off-the-book system of secret torture can also establish a
dangerous precedent.

A variation on this "legitimation" argument would postpone
consideration of the choice between authorizing torture and forgo-
ing a possible tactic necessary to prevent an imminent act of terrorism until after the choice—presumably the choice to torture—has
been made. In that way, the discussion would not, in itself, encourage the use of torture. If it were employed, then we could decide
whether it was justified, excusable, condemnable, or something in
between. The problem with that argument is that no FBI agent
who tortured a suspect into disclosing information that prevented
an act of mass terrorism would be prosecuted—as the policemen
who tortured the kidnapper into disclosing the whereabouts of his
victim were not prosecuted. In the absence of a prosecution, there
would be no occasion to judge the appropriateness of the torture.

I disagree with these more passive approaches and believe
that in a democracy it is always preferable to decide controversial
issues in advance, rather than in the heat of battle. I would apply
this rule to other tragic choices as well, including the possible use

of a nuclear first strike, or retaliatory strikes—so long as the discussion was sufficiently general to avoid giving our potential enemies a strategic advantage by their knowledge of our policy.

Even if government officials decline to discuss such issues, academics have a duty to raise them and submit them to the marketplace of ideas. There may be danger in open discussion, but there is far greater danger in actions based on secret discussion, or no discussion at all.

Whatever option our nation eventually adopts—no torture even to prevent massive terrorism, no torture except with a warrant authorizing nonlethal torture, or no "officially" approved torture but its selective use beneath the radar screen—the choice is ours to make in a democracy. We do have a choice, and we should make it—before local FBI agents make it for us on the basis of a false assumption that we do not really "have a choice." We have other choices to make as well, in balancing security with liberty. It is to these choices that we now turn.

chapter five

Striking the Right Balance

"To those who scare peace-loving people with phantoms of lost liberty, my message is this: Your tactics only aid terrorists, for they erode our national unity and diminish our resolve. They give ammunition to America's enemies and pause to America's friends."
—Attorney General John Ashcroft before the Senate Judiciary Committee, December 6, 2001

Any effective approach to combating terrorism within the rule of law must be multifaceted. It must combine macro and micro approaches and must tailor its actions to the differing objects of terrorist groups over time. Most important, it must remain consistent with core principles of legality and morality.

This chapter accordingly presents macro approaches that address the big-picture aspects of confronting different types of terrorism, and then a number of micro approaches to controlling it at a more retail level. In the process, I will discuss a number of particularly controversial issues that may require some rethinking of the proper balance between security and liberty.

Macro Steps: Making Terrorism a Losing Proposition

The first and most important macro step is eliminating all possible incentives for terrorism by enforcing the principle that terrorists must never be permitted to benefit from it. This step is particularly important with respect to terrorist groups that have specific political goals. These goals, no matter how noble, must never be allowed to advance as a result of terrorism.

Even if the international community were to achieve consensus on the principle of never rewarding terrorism—an unlikely prospect—some terrorist leaders may still believe, at least for a time, that terrorism will advance their cause. It is therefore not enough simply to remove all positive incentives. If the only consequence of a terrorist act is to preserve the status quo, with some possibility of advancing the cause, then the terrorists may still be induced to take their chances, especially because the cost of terrorism is low for groups that have volunteers eager to die for the cause. Accordingly there must always be a deterrent added to the elimination of the incentive. In that way, the message will be clear that the cause not only has nothing to gain, it also has something significant to lose from engaging in terrorism. On top of that, a promise of benefits and rewards must be built into the system, which assures that serious attention will be paid to causes that forgo terrorism and resort to more peaceful tactics of conflict resolution. Any rational terrorist group that operates according to cost-benefit calculation will, at least in theory, be inclined to opt for the tactic or tactics that hold the best prospect for furthering their goals. At the moment, that tactic is terrorism. If terrorism is to be eliminated, other tactics must hold greater promise of reward.

For this rational approach to work in practice, it must have widespread support in the international community. Before September 11, 2001, it not only had no such support, it was being actively undercut by several groups of nations and institutions. The first of these groups included countries that directly supported, financed, and harbored terrorist groups. Leading that list were the former Soviet-bloc countries, which for decades actively trained an array of terrorists and provided them weapons, money, and logistical support; despite the demise of the Soviet Union, this legacy of supporting terrorism is still palpable in many parts of the world. Right behind the former Soviet-bloc states were such nations as Iraq, Iran, Syria, and Libya, which did—and continue to do—the same, but primarily for Palestinian groups. Saudi Arabia also provides financial support to Palestinian terrorists. Afghanistan and Pakistan harbored al-Qaeda and other Islamic terrorist groups.

All these nations were directly abetting terrorism in one way or another. But also undermining the world's rational response to terrorism was a second tier consisting of countries and organizations that, though formally opposed to terrorism, encouraged it by releasing captured terrorists, routinely giving in to their demands, and rewarding terrorism by supporting the causes for which it was undertaken. Leading this list were France, Germany, Italy, the U.N. General Assembly, the Nobel Peace Prize Committee, and several churches.

Following this group were the countries that vigorously fought terrorism when it was directed against themselves, but encouraged, or did nothing to stop, terrorism against others. Egypt and Jordan are representative of this type.

Finally, there are the handful of nations that have generally done everything reasonably within their power to combat and discourage all forms of terrorism. The United States has always led that list, though often imperfectly. Since September 11, 2001, it has taken a more aggressive leadership role in combating terrorism, especially the kind of apocalyptic, religiously inspired global terrorism directed against the free world, of which it is the leader.

If all incentives for terrorism are to be eliminated and meaningful deterrents imposed in their place, the United States will have to go even further and take the lead in imposing *a single standard* of response to all forms of terrorism. It must become a firm pillar of American foreign policy that no nation or international organization be allowed to reward terrorism and that all must punish it. This does require that the United States assume the role, if not of policeman to the world, then at least of police commissioner in regard to terrorism. No other nation can perform this role, and if we refuse to undertake it, it will simply not get done.

If we are serious about combating terrorism, it will not be enough to take action *only* against those terrorist groups that directly target *us*. President Bush has, in fact, declared that it is our policy to combat all forms of terrorism. At the United Nations on November 10, 2001, he said, "We must unite in opposing all terrorists, not just some of them," and went on to say, "any government that rejects this principle, trying to pick and choose its terrorist friends, will know the consequences." A month later he said, "American power will be used against all terrorists of global reach."[1]

The reality, however, has been quite different. We continue to reward Palestinian terrorism by sending mixed messages. For example, Secretary of State Colin Powell stated on April 6, 2002, "any time you incentivize in any way this kind of activity [suicide terrorism] you are contributing to the activity." Yet a few days later, Powell called for "accelerated negotiations to establish a Palestinian state"—a move characterized as "a shift in tactics," but one seen by the Palestinians as a reward for terrorism. He agreed to the Palestinian demand that he meet with Arafat even if Arafat refused to comply with the insistence of the United States that he renounce, in Arabic, all terrorism.

Europe has been even more rewarding of terrorism. Shortly after Powell agreed to meet with Arafat, Middle East expert Michael Rubin wrote in the *Wall Street Journal:*

> France, Belgium and four other European Union members endorsed a U.N. Human Rights Commission resolution condoning "all available means, including armed struggle," to establish a Palestinian state. Hence, six European Union members and the rights commission now join the 57 nations of the Islamic Conference in legitimizing suicide bombers. By their logic of moral equivalence, terror is justifiable because its root cause is Israel's occupation. That Palestinian terror predates occupation, or that suicide bombings became a tactic of choice only after the initiation of the Oslo process, is too inconvenient to mention.
>
> Unfortunately the U.N. goes beyond giving rhetorical support for terrorism. In a variety of ways, its agencies have been complicit in Middle Eastern terror.[2]

The bottom line remains that Palestinian terrorism—which is the paradigm of carefully calculated, cost-benefit terrorism with concrete goals—continues to produce significant dividends for the Palestinian cause. It persists because it is successful, and it is successful because the international community rewards it with important concessions, and decreased support for the country it targets.³

This reaction has put Israel in precisely the dilemma contemplated by the terrorists. If Israel capitulates to terrorism—as it appeared to do when it left southern Lebanon—it is perceived as weak and susceptible to more terrorism. The radical Islamic Palestinian group Hamas has claimed that the terrorist tactics that succeeded in Lebanon should be expanded to the occupied territories and then to Israel proper. In addition to emulating the means used in southern Lebanon, Hamas has also been clear about its ultimate goal. In a *New York Times* interview on April 4, Hamas leader Mahmoud al-Zahar said, "From our ideological point of view, it is not allowed to recognize that Israel controls one square meter of historic Palestine." The spiritual head of Hamas, Sheikh Ahmed Yassin, said, "our equation does not focus on a cease-fire; our equation focuses on an end to the occupation," by which the *Times* said he means "an end to the Jewish occupation of historical Palestine."⁴ If Israel fights back against the terrorists, it is seen as overreacting and loses support among the European nations and even the United States. The Palestinians have learned to exploit the harsh arithmetic of pain; they understand, as the *Times* said, that Palestinian casualties play in their favor, and Israeli casualties play in their favor. Thomas Friedman has put it this way:

> As Ismail Haniya, a Hamas leader, said in The Washington Post, Palestinians have Israelis on the run now because they have found their weak spot. Jews, he said, "love life more than any other people, and they prefer not to die." So suicide bombers are ideal for dealing with them. That is really sick. . . . The Palestinians are so blinded by their narcissistic rage that they have lost sight of the basic truth civilization is built on: the sacredness of every human life, starting with your own. If America,

the only reality check left, doesn't use every ounce of
energy to halt this madness and call it by its real name,
then it will spread.[5]

But America is not doing enough to halt this madness. And much
of the rest of the world is actively rewarding it. Why then should
the Palestinians stop their terrorism? They have every incentive,
and few disincentives, to continue. And continue they will, unless
and until their tactic proves counterproductive—by their own
standards.

Moreover, since their standard of cost and benefit values the
life of the terrorist, especially the suicide terrorist, very differently
than traditional deterrence theory values a life, the threat of killing
terrorists—either in the course of terrorist action or as subsequent
punishment—is ineffective. So is the threat of imprisonment, since
the terrorists believe, quite rightly, that they will be quickly freed.
Indeed, the expectation of martyrdom, whether religious or political, makes the prospect of death or brief imprisonment, followed by
a hero's welcome, a positive incentive rather than a disincentive.[6]

It is not "racism," as the PLO representative to the United
States has charged, to observe that some Palestinians place a lower
value on life than other people do. Hamas leaders boast of the fact
that their suicide bombers are eager to kill and die. It is outra-
geous, moreover, to compare suicide bombers to American patriots,
like Nathan Hale, who were willing to give up their lives for our
independence. They were not willing to kill innocent British children in the process. Nor were they willing to sacrifice their own
children. Friedman wrote angrily after it was disclosed that one of
the suicide bombers was a teenage girl: "I have a teenage daughter. There is no teenager capable of making the political decision to
commit suicide. You can bet it was older men who encouraged her
to do this and who wrapped her in dynamite. That is not martyrdom, that is ritual sacrifice." Dr. Fadel Abu Heen, director of the

community Training and Crisis Management Center in Gaza, has confirmed this conclusion: "The martyrs in their eyes are heroes. Thousands of people participate in their funerals. Their pictures are posted on school walls, medals, and copybooks. They are talked about in the mosques and the alleys. Political parties publish special leaflets eulogizing them." Abu Heen "conducted a recent poll of Palestinian schoolboys ages 8 to 15 in which 700 out of the 1,000 boys questioned said they wanted to be martyrs for the Palestinian cause."[7]

Deterring Those Who Benefit from Terrorism

Because of the difficulty of bringing disincentives to bear against the terrorists themselves, it is important to direct deterrence not at them but rather at those who send them, those who benefit from their actions, and those who can have some influence over them. Whenever a deterrent is directed against anyone other than the immediately culpable actor, it can be deemed a form of collective punishment. Although collective punishment is prohibited by international law, it is widely practiced throughout the world, including by the most democratic and liberty-minded countries. Indeed, no system of international deterrence can be effective without some reliance on collective punishment. Every time one nation retaliates against another it collectively punishes citizens of that country. The American and British bombings of German cities punished the residents of those cities. The atomic bombings of Hiroshima and Nagasaki killed thousands of innocent Japanese for the crimes of their leaders. The bombing of primarily military targets inevitably kills civilians. Even the killing of soldiers—especially those drafted against their will—is a form of collective punishment.

Beyond the killing and wounding of nonculpable individuals, there is collective economic punishment, such as U.N.-approved sanctions and the bankrupting of an enemy nation's economy, which is a common weapon of both hot and cold wars. Nations that wage aggressive war and are defeated often lose territory, and such punishment may well have a negative impact on innocent residents of that territory. Many ethnic Germans—some of whom did not support Hitler—were forced to relocate following Germany's defeat in World War II.[8] The point is that collective punishment is very much a matter of degree, with Sippenhaft—the deliberate murder of kin or townsfolk—at one end of the continuum, and economic consequences of aggression at the other. Calling something collective punishment is often a political or public relations tactic calculated to confuse rather than to clarify. There is much wrong with certain types and degrees of collective punishment. But there is little wrong—and often something very right and noble—about some kinds and degrees of collective accountability for the actions of popular leaders.

As an example of this kind, it was right for the entire German people to suffer for what their elected leader had unleashed on the world.[9] The few Germans who fought against Hitler should have been rewarded, but the vast majority of Germans should have been held accountable for their complicity with evil. In a perfect world, the accountability should have been imposed in direct proportion to the complicity, with those most directly involved being imprisoned and those less directly involved being made to suffer economic deprivation. Since the German people were promised that they would benefit from a Nazi victory—that is part of the reason so many supported Hitler—it was just for them to suffer from a Nazi defeat, even though some among the sufferers were less culpable than others. That is part of what it means to be a nation or a people. Those who start wars and lose them often—not often enough—bring suffering to their people. That is rough justice. It is also a useful deterrent to unjust wars.

Applying this principle of collective accountability to terrorism committed on behalf of a cause, it is not unjust to make the cause suffer for terrorist actions committed on its behalf, especially if there is widespread support for the terrorism within the cause. In this context, recall the poll described earlier, taken in March 2002, that found 87 percent of Palestinians in favor of continuing terrorist attacks.[10] Recall as well that Palestinians claim that Yasser Arafat, who has been instrumental in fomenting and organizing terrorism, is the *elected* leader of the Palestinian Authority, supported by an overwhelming majority of Palestinians. (The vast majority of those who oppose him do so because they want even more terrorism of the kind practiced by Hamas, Hezbollah, and Islamic Jihad.) Since the cause hopes and expects to benefit collectively from the terrorism, it is just (albeit imperfectly just) to hold it collectively accountable for the murderous acts perpetrated in its name and under its ultimate control. If this benign form of collective accountability can effectively save innocent lives by deterring terrorism, the balance of justice weighs heavily in its favor.

The kind of suicide terrorism practiced by the Palestinians—mass murder of perfectly innocent civilians with the widespread logistical, financial, religious, political, and emotional support of a large majority of the civilian population—challenges us to rethink the classic bright-line distinction between combatants and noncombatants. This line, which lies at the core of the international law of war, has been exploited in the interest of terrorism. Palestinian terrorists have learned how to use civilians as both swords and shields: they target Israeli and Jewish civilians, and then hide behind Palestinian civilians when the Israeli military comes after them. They use "noncombatants" as an aide to combatants. The result is that Israel must choose between employing wholesale self-defense tactics, such as air strikes, that risk killing large numbers of noncombatants among whom the combatants are hiding, or employing retail tactics, such as house-to-house combat, that risk the lives of Israeli soldiers. There is no precise formula for calculating the appropriate combatant/noncombatant ratio even in conventional warfare. A moral nation must be prepared to place *some* of its own soldiers at risk to prevent the collateral killing of enemy civilians, but it need not risk the lives of *many* of its own combatants to achieve this salutary aim. The proper moral ratio should depend, at least in part, on the complicity of the noncombatants. If many of them willingly allow combatants to hide among them, if they provide support for the combatants, if they make martyrs of the murderers, their own complicity increases and they move closer to combatant status on what has become a continuum, rather than a bright line separating civilians from combatants.

How far, then, along the continuum of collective accountability would it be just to move in order to combat terrorism? Certainly not to the point of deliberately targeting completely innocent people for murder. Indeed, that is precisely what the terrorists do. But economic sanctions imposed on supporters of terrorism are fair and may be effective. Even if some people who do not support terrorism feel some economic impact, that seems a small moral price to pay—especially since they expect to reap the benefits of the terrorism—for saving many innocent lives. Whenever collective economic punishment is imposed on those who support terrorism, I am always flabbergasted to hear the protestations made in high moral dudgeon against it by those—such as Yasser Arafat—who themselves support lethal terrorism against civilians.

The situation here reminds me of the infamous Fall River rape case (fictionalized in the film *The Accused*), in which there were several categories of morally and legally complicit individuals: those who actually raped the woman; those who held her down; those who blocked her escape route; those who cheered and encouraged the rapists; and those who could have called the police but did not. No rational person would suggest that any of these people were entirely free of moral guilt, although reasonable peo-

ple might disagree about the legal guilt of those in the last two categories. The objection to imposing legal responsibility on people in
these two categories would be diminished if the only sanction on
them were economic—a fine, say, or civil liability. Their accountability for rape is surely a matter of degree, as is the accountability
for terrorism of those who cheer the terrorists, make martyrs of
them, encourage their own children to become terrorists, or expect
to benefit from terrorism. There is nothing morally wrong with
holding such complicitors accountable, so long as the consequences
imposed on them are proportional to their complicity. Consequence, like complicity, is a matter of degree, and it is the relation-
ship between them that determines morality.

The U.S.-led economic sanctions against Iraq, Libya, and
Cuba are collective punishments imposed on large populations for
the deeds of their leaders. So were the sanctions and boycotts
imposed against Israel by the Arab League. Israel's policy of
demolishing the homes of terrorists or those who harbor them is a
soft form of collective punishment directed against the property of
those who are deemed somewhat complicit. That it occasionally
has an impact on innocent people detracts from its moral purity,
but to a considerably lesser degree than widespread economic
sanctions direct against entire nations. Yet the United Nations has
supported such economic sanctions even as it has condemned
Israel's policy on punishing those who support terrorists.

In March 2002, as the cycle of Middle East violence escalated
frighteningly and began to seem unstoppable, I proposed a way of
revising Israel's policy of demolishing homes that would be more
effective in stopping the killing than what Israel was then doing.
The idea was to apply the principle of collective accountability
using a targeted economic sanction that focused on individuals
who are at least somewhat complicit in terrorism and spared people who were innocent. The key was to make the reprisal pre-

dictable in a way that would increase its deterrent effect and would remove any reasonable moral objections to the policy. The mechanism was to announce clearly, in advance, exactly what the response to future terrorist attacks would be.

Israel's first step in implementing this policy would be to completely stop all retaliation against terrorist attacks for five days. It would then publicly declare precisely how it will respond in the event of another terrorist act, such as by destroying empty houses in a particular village that has been used as a base for terrorists, and naming that village in advance. The next time terrorists attack, the village's residents would be given twenty-four hours to leave, and then Israeli troops would bulldoze the houses.

The point is to make the destruction the fault of the terrorists, who will have received plain advance warning of the specific consequences of their actions. The Israeli soldiers would act automatically, carrying out a previously announced policy. Any more attacks would put into motion the destruction of other previously announced locations—a list of which Israel would make public to all Palestinians. The policy and its implications will be perfectly clear to all the Palestinian people: whenever terrorists blow themselves up and kill Israeli civilians, they also blow up houses in one of their own villages. The destruction is entirely their fault, and it is entirely preventable by them—which gives the villagers a good reason to blame them when homes are destroyed, and an incentive to pressure the terrorists to prevent it.

There is something seriously troubling, of course, about bulldozing an entire village, even if its residents have been evacuated. Not all those whose homes will be destroyed are equally complicit in terrorism. But Palestinian terrorism does, in fact, enjoy widespread support in the area controlled by the Palestinian Authority; by encouraging suicide bombers in this way, Palestinians share culpability for the murder of civilians. Terrorists kill people; Israel would be destroying empty buildings, and only after giving advance warning and a chance for Palestinians to prevent the terrorist acts.

Along with this proposal, I also suggested an alternative policy. Israel could announce that, in the event of peace, it will give the Palestinians what they say they want: their own state in the occupied territories. But, if terrorist attacks continue, every such act will automatically result in a permanent decrease in the amount of land that will constitute the Palestinian state, with these portions being annexed to Israel. This policy can work only if the U.S. government approves it in advance. Israel should not be criticized for the policy if it gives full notice to the Palestinians and maintains a moratorium on all retaliation for a designated period. If the world community understands that this policy will be enacted automatically, and that the terrorists themselves will trigger it should they attack, additional pressure will be brought to bear on the terrorists to discontinue their activities. Genuine efforts must also be made to restart the peace talks with the Palestinian Authority if this policy is to work. This policy will further two noble causes: the reduction of terrorism and the promotion of peace.[11]

Although the thrust of my proposal was to step *down* the Israeli responses to terrorism by limiting them to destruction of empty houses and the annexation of unpopulated land—all announced in advance to maximize the deterrent impact—the outcry against the proposal was immediate and confrontational. My classes were picketed by Palestinian groups calling me a "war criminal," a "racist," and a "violator of human rights." At least some of the people using this rhetoric have supported terrorism. As one woman said of the Palestinians: "They have no choice. They have been driven to terrorism." To the charge that I am advocating "collective punishment," I replied that collective economic and geographic sanctions were justified against those who would benefit from terrorism and without whose support it would be far more difficult to carry out. I challenged the group to debate my approach in a public forum, but they declined.

The major problem with the first part of my proposal, as with Israel's more retail approach to the destruction of houses involved in terrorism, is not with its morality. A nonlethal approach like this is among the most moral and calibrated responses to terrorism, far more so than massive military retaliation, which inevitably produces collateral deaths of noncombatants (especially when combatants blend in with noncombatants, and when noncombatancy is often a matter of degree). The problem with destruction of houses is how the world literally sees it. Indeed, in some Muslim countries television viewers are led to believe that the houses are destroyed with *people still in them!* Even when it is clear that no one is inside, the inevitable picture of the crying woman bemoaning the loss of her home creates sympathy, even if that same woman was yesterday cheering at the news of an Israeli restaurant being blown up with a dozen teenagers inside. (If the terrorists would agree to give advance warning that they were going to blow up a building, the way the Israelis do, then there might be some argument for moral equivalency.) House destruction is also ineffective because Hamas pays people whose houses are destroyed enough money to build a bigger house. Saddam Hussein announced in April 2002 that he would pay the family of any suicide bomber who killed Jews $25,000 in cash. Under U.S. law, this makes him, and anyone else who agrees in advance to pay the family of suicide bombers, a conspirator in terrorism.

The international community must come to accept the justice of directing proportionate, nonlethal deterrents against those who support and benefit from terrorism, rather than threatening meaningless sanctions against the suicide terrorists themselves. This is both fair and, if widely practiced and approved, potentially effective as a deterrent against many types of terrorism, especially those that rely on suicide volunteers.

At the macro level, we should, of course, try to resolve the political conflicts that generate terrorism, but we must do so *without actually rewarding,* or even being *perceived* as rewarding, terrorism. We must resist the temptation to find a quick fix that provides the short-term solution to one particular source of terrorism only to encourage other potential terrorists to pursue that "successful" tactic. As we have seen, almost 90 percent of Palestinians polled in March 2002 favored both terrorism and "liberating all of Palestine"—which includes all of Israel. If terrorism succeeds in securing a Palestinian state in the West Bank and the Gaza Strip, why should it not continue to be used to secure what the vast majority of Palestinians say they want? As Friedman put it in a column shortly after the poll: "The Palestinians cannot yet be trusted to control these areas of their own if Israel withdraws. Would you trust Yasir Arafat to police your neighborhood?" Friedman has also aptly observed: "Palestinians who use suicide bombers to blow up Israelis at a Passover meal and then declare 'Just end the occupation and everything will be fine' are not believable. No Israeli in his right mind would trust Yasir Arafat, who has used suicide bombers when it suited his purposes, not to do the same thing if he got the West Bank back and some of his people started demanding Tel Aviv."[12]

It will not be easy to resolve the political conflicts that generate terrorism without being seen as rewarding it, since we may view what we are doing one way and the terrorists may view it quite differently. As an example, when the General Assembly granted observer status to the PLO in the wake of numerous airplane hijackings, some of those voting for the resolution may not have thought of their country as rewarding terrorism, but the terrorist organizations expressed the clear view that it was their terrorism that brought about the desired result—a result that they honestly believe would not have come about without using terrorism. The consequence, of course, was to encourage ever greater reliance on terrorism as a tactic, a reliance that continues to this day.

Similarly, if the Palestinians were now to be granted statehood while they continued to rely on the tactic of terrorism, they would believe—correctly in my view—that it has been a reward for their renewed terrorism. The message will be clear to them and others: that future terrorism will get them more than they now have. The *New York Times* quoted an unnamed diplomat observing the March 2002 Arab League meeting in Beirut who was critical of the Bush administration's "holding out national statehood as a reward." The effect, he said, "has been to raise Palestinian expectations and increase their impatience by legitimating their demands." He continued: "If they think it's going to buy off the militancy of the Palestinians, it's mistaken. It's going to increase it, because it gives it legitimacy."[13]

Any effective attack calculated to reduce terrorism—especially suicide bombers—*must* include an element of collective accountability and punishment for those supporting terrorism. Rewarding terrorism, instead of punishing it, is a sure path to more terrorism.

Incapacitating the Apocalyptic Terrorist

The apocalyptic terrorist who is inspired by religious zealotry and seeks no realistic political goals will be far more difficult to deter or disincentivize. For such terrorists, the emphasis must be placed on massive incapacitation—the imprisonment or death of those who would organize or implement such terrorist acts, the interdiction of their weapon supply lines, and the destruction of their organizational infrastructure, communication system, and financial network. The prevention of terrorism by such groups cannot rely on a model of rational cost-benefit calculation. Unlike politically motivated, calculating terrorists, apocalyptic religious terrorists cannot be dissuaded by the fear of adverse public reaction or international condemnation. They *know* they are right and they believe that God knows they are right, and that is all that matters to them. Their reward and punishment is not in this world, and hence we cannot influence it, since we cannot get God to tell them they are wrong.[14] We must assume, therefore, that they will proceed—if they are physically able to—regardless of the perceived consequences. In this respect, they are like cunning beasts of prey: we cannot reason with them, but we can—if we work at it—outsmart them, set traps for them, cage them, or kill them. The difference is, of course, that they are much smarter than the most cunning of beasts. Indeed, we must operate on the assumption that they are as smart as we are, but more determined, more single-minded, more ruthless, and less constrained by morality, decency, and legality. The fact that they are prepared to sacrifice their own children—and that their children are eager to be sacrificed for a cause they may not even understand—shows how daunting this task will be.

The macro approaches to apocalyptic terrorism must be unrelenting. They will never be completely successful so long as terrorist groups retain the capacity to carry out acts of terrorism. The events of September 11, 2001, demonstrate how much "bang" can be achieved for how little "buck." It cost the al-Qaeda terrorists approximately $300,000 to murder three thousand people, destroy billions of dollars worth of property (directly and indirectly), and shatter the confidence of the world.[15] Moreover, it took no hard-to-get weapons or direct support from governments. (It could have been planned as easily in Germany as in Afghanistan.) But it did take years of careful planning and many man-hours of dedicated preparation. The real problem is that a comparable catastrophic attack could be carried out in the future for even less money, with even fewer people, from almost any country in the world. If the apocalyptic terrorists seek to escalate the damage they cause to include nuclear, chemical, or biological disaster, it will probably cost more money and may well require some state support. Such a mega-plot would also be more likely to be foiled, since it could not be carried out without the knowledge of some who arc outside the very closely knit group that apparently carried out the September 11 terrorist attack.

Tight control over actual sources of nuclear, biological, and chemical weapons is, of course, essential, coupled with the easy *apparent* availability of such weapons from undercover intelligence sources, whose job it is to set traps for potential terrorists. Terrorist organizations must be infiltrated by our agents, while at the same time their agents are extorted and bribed to report to us. This will not be easy with regard to apocalyptic groups composed of religious zealots who are not easily susceptible to financial or other material inducement, or threats. For that reason, we will also need to rely on technological intercepts, disruptions of their communications, and surveillance of their movements, money transfers, and weapon acquisitions. We must stop the teenage suicide killer before he or she is given the means to commit mass murder, by interdicting training, delivery of bombs, and necessary logistical support.

The most controversial means of incapacitating terrorists is targeted assassination. Although it is the opposite of collective punishment, it raises difficult questions because whoever authorizes the hit is prosecutor, judge, and jury. There is no defense counsel and no appeal. Moreover, the act is deliberate, premeditated, and cold-blooded. Legally, it constitutes murder in the first degree—unless it is justified by a law that trumps the prohibition against willful killing. The execution of guilty murderers is one such exception to laws against murder, as are shooting a fleeing felon, killing in self-defense, or the use of lethal force by a soldier in combat. The last of these provides the closest analogy to targeted assassination. A soldier is permitted to ambush (or bomb) an enemy soldier and kill him in cold blood, before the enemy has an opportunity to surrender—or to shoot first.[16] The enemy soldier need not be guilty of anything. Terrorists are combatants who are preparing to kill civilians.[17] We need not wait until they succeed—or even until they are ready to act. If there is a high level of proof that a given person is actually engaged in planning or carrying out an act of terrorism, and he is not reasonably subject to apprehension or arrest, it is appropriate to stop him by the use of lethal force, just as it is proper to use such force against a dangerous felon who cannot otherwise be apprehended.

If a major terrorist leader, like Osama bin Laden, were harbored in a country beyond our political and military reach—say Iran—and we had reliable information that he was plotting further terrorist actions, what options would be available to us? We could try diplomatic, economic, or military pressure. If these failed we would have three basic options: (1) do nothing; (2) try to bomb his enclave; or (3) send in a hit squad to assassinate him.

The first option is unacceptable if the threat he poses is high. The second option would probably result in many people, some innocent, being killed, especially if the terrorist leader were ensconced among civilians. The third option would pose risks to our agents, but it would probably be more morally acceptable than the bombing option. Yet there would surely be an outcry against our "mafia tactics," as there has been against Israel. Nevertheless, it might be the right—or the least wrong—option to pursue.

There are, of course, grave risks that this extraordinary power could be misused, as it clearly has been throughout history. But all techniques of incapacitation are capable of being misused. Before targeted assassination is authorized, a process must be in place for assuring that it is employed only in extreme cases where the threat is great, the certainty high, and the unavailability of other mechanisms of incapacitation certain. This combination will be rare. It presumably existed when President Clinton reportedly authorized the targeted assassination of Osama bin Laden following the East African embassy bombings in 1998.[18]

A more questionable use of targeted assassination is against terrorists who have participated in mass murder and gotten away with it and are now beyond the jurisdiction of the victim state. Israel assassinated several participants in the Munich Olympics massacre, after they were freed and treated as heroes. It justified its actions by arguing that allowing these terrorists to live the good life after what they had done would make it easier for terrorist groups to recruit new killers. Assassinating them constituted general deterrence directed against other potential killers. It was also justified as incapacitating terrorists who were likely to engage in future acts of terrorism.[19] Israel continues to use targeted assassination against terrorist organizers and facilitators, such as "the Engineer" who planned suicide bombings and helped devise the weapons. The Israelis consider these actions preemptive self-defense (as the United States did when it authorized the hit on bin Laden), but it is difficult to assess their justification in each case.

These incapacitory tactics may help to prevent many acts of terrorism, but determined terrorists, driven by zealous religious or nationalistic beliefs for which they are prepared to die, will always manage to succeed some of the time. In this age of easily available nuclear, biological, and chemical weapons, even once may be too much. We simply cannot count on the preventive approaches always working. That is why it is so important that we change our policy toward the macro issues of deterring and disincentivizing potential terrorists from choosing this course of action. And if we are to be successful in changing our policy, we cannot distinguish among terrorist groups. We must never reward any terrorists, whether they are targeting us or someone else. That is the mistake made by several European countries when they formed their diabolical pact with Palestinian terrorists: if you do not direct your terrorism toward us, we will not hinder your terrorism toward Israel and the United States. Now the United States appears to be doing something similar: it is tolerating Palestinian terrorism toward

Israel in the hope that it will reduce the risk of terrorism against its citizens and enhance its influence in the Arab and Muslim world. It won't work. The success of terrorism anywhere breeds terrorism everywhere. Friedman got it exactly right when he said: "Palestinians have adopted suicide bombings as a strategic choice, not out of desperation. This threatens all civilization because if suicide bombing is allowed to work in Israel, then, like hijacking and airplane bombing, it will be copied and will eventually lead to a bomber strapped with a nuclear device threatening entire nations. That is why the whole world must see this Palestinian suicide strategy defeated."[20]

For that reason, we must adopt a far more aggressive policy against every nation—friend and foe alike—that lends any support to terrorism. We have been soft on the suppliers, encouragers, and harborers of terrorists. Without the assistance of these nations, terrorist groups would lose much of their power. If our foreign policy is to be directed against terrorism, then its primary focus must be on nations with return addresses, rather than on shadowy groups that can easily dissolve and reconstitute themselves. We took a positive first step with Pakistan. Now we must extend that step to other countries that make terrorism possible. We must implement Secretary of State Powell's astute observation that "any time you incentivize in any way this kind of activity [suicide terrorism] you are contributing to the activity."[21]

Even if we do implement all of these, and other, macro measures, we will still have to rely on micro measures. It is these micro measures—many of which will take place within our shores and be directed against our citizens, residents, and visitors—that will raise the most daunting constitutional issues and require us to strike an appropriate balance between security and liberty, in the face of these new and different dangers.

Micro Steps: Striking a New Balance

Before considering specific micro steps—such as tightening controls over our borders, requiring national ID cards, authorizing military tribunals, infiltrating domestic groups, expanding electronic monitoring authority, permitting more exchanges of information among prosecutorial and intelligence agencies, and imposing some restrictions on freedom of speech—it is important to think about whether the new threat of massive terrorism by nonstate actors requires us to rethink our general approach to balancing security and liberty.

Every American schoolchild learns a basic maxim of our system of criminal justice: "It is better for ten guilty criminals to go free than for even one innocent person to be wrongfully convicted." It should surprise no one to learn that this maxim predates our Constitution. Contemporary law books credit it to William Blackstone and other English legal commentators, but centuries before they lived a Jewish philosopher and doctor named Maimonides wrote: "If we do not punish on very strong probabilities, nothing can happen other than that a sinner be freed; but if punishment be done on probability and opinion it is possible that one day we might kill an innocent man and it is better and more desirable to free a thousand sinners, than ever to kill one innocent."[22] The principle underlying the maxim can be traced even farther back in time, to the Biblical account of Abraham's argument with God over the sinners of Sodom and Gomorrah when God informed Abraham of his plan to destroy these evil cities. Abraham objected on the ground that these cities of sinners might include too many innocent people.[23]

Although our Constitution contains no specific reference to this maxim, the Supreme Court has repeatedly interpreted the due process clause to require that the prosecution must prove guilt beyond a reasonable doubt. In support of that interpretation, the justices have invoked the maxim and explained its underlying rationale.

The maxim was first articulated in the context of the death penalty, which was once the routine punishment for all serious felonies. Indeed, its early foundations sometimes explicitly referenced the irreversible nature of the capital sentence.[24] But over time the maxim was applied to imprisonment as well. This should not be surprising, since imprisonment was often tantamount to death in an age of "gaol fever" and other harsh, often lethal consequences of confinement.

Although many Americans (and many jurors) probably disagree with the maxim—they would probably not prefer to see ten murderers go free to prevent the false imprisonment of one wrongly accused defendant—it has become enshrined among the principles that distinguish nations governed by the rule of law from nations governed by the passion of persons.

In addition to its original provenance during an age when a wrongful conviction could mean almost certain death, the maxim emerged from a criminal justice system that dealt with crime as a retail rather than wholesale phenomenon. The guilty murderer who might go free as a result of its application was not likely to engage in future mass murders. The cost of applying the maxim could be measured in individual deaths, terrible as any preventable murder might be.

Now, with the advent of terrorists using weapons of mass destruction, the calculus may have changed. It remains true, in my view, that it is better for ten guilty criminals (even murderers) to go free (and perhaps recidivate on a retail basis) than for even one innocent person to be wrongfully convicted. But it does not necessarily follow from this salutary principle that it is also better for ten potential mass terrorists to go free (and perhaps recidivate on a *wholesale* basis) than for even one innocent person to be detained for a limited period of time, sufficient to determine that he is not a potential terrorist. (Nor does it necessarily follow that it is better for ten acts of terrorism to occur than for the home of one innocent supporter of terrorism to be destroyed.)

Numbers do matter, even in principled decisions. It is clearly right to shoot down a commercial jet with hundreds of innocent passengers in it, if the jet is being flown toward a fully occupied large building that cannot be evacuated. It is less clearly right to shoot down that same jet if it is being flown toward the Washington Monument at midnight when only a night watchman is in it. By the same reasoning, it is proper to bomb a military target close to a small number of civilians, but less proper to bomb a similar target adjacent to a large and fully occupied civilian hospital. It is also less unjust to destroy a house in a village in which 95 percent of the residents actively support terrorism than in a village where there is far less support.

There are several variables in the application of the maxim to suspected terrorists. The first is the number of potential victims if a mistake of Type I is made—that is, if an actual terrorist is wrongly released. Consider the case of Mohamed Atta, who was allowed into the United States despite information linking him to terrorism. If he had been detained, it is certainly possible that the catastrophe of September 11 might have been prevented. We will, of course, never know.

The failure to detain Atta was a failure of information coordination, rather than a refusal to apply the maxim. But what if the relevant information had been known to those who did not detain him? To detain a suspect on the basis of the kind of vague and general information known to American officials would be to invite many Type II errors—that is, the detention of many people suspected of association with terrorism who, in fact, have no such association.[25]

This brings us to the second variable. If the consequence of a Type II error were to be the execution of an innocent person, that would raise the stakes considerably. But if the only consequence were a few weeks of erroneous detention, unaccompanied by the risk of death or injury, the stakes are considerably reduced. They do not, however, vanish. It is still costly, in moral as well as material currency, to wrongfully detain an innocent person for a matter of weeks. The costs increase when those wrongly detained belong to a disfavored minority group. And these costs must be weighed against the costs of a Type I error (the erroneous release of an actual terrorist). But who should be doing the weighing, and who should be striking the appropriate balance? This becomes a daunting challenge, especially when those who traditionally do the balancing represent the potential victims of a Type I, rather than a Type II, error.

These are the kinds of issues we will have to begin worrying about, if potential terrorists with weapons of mass destruction pass through our legal system, as some inevitably will. We will have to determine how many false positives (Type II errors) we should be willing to tolerate in order to prevent how many false negatives (Type I errors). In order to implement any policy decisions we make in this regard, we will also have to assess the accuracy of our predictive resources—accuracy both in terms of correctly *spotting* potential terrorists and in terms of *not incorrectly including* innocent people in that target category. Although the maxim that prefers the acquittal of multiple criminals to the acquittal of one innocent is rooted specifically in the criminal trial, it has become a metaphor for the appropriate balance to be struck whenever security and liberty come into conflict. Whether or not the ratio should remain identical when different values are at stake, surely we must maintain our preference for liberty even in the face of the most pressing claims of security. But liberty, like security, is a matter of degree. It is also a matter of feel, as I previously argued. Preserving both the feel and the reality of freedom, when confronted with serious threats to security, is the true test of a democracy committed to the rule of law. Although freedom is more than the sum of individual restrictions and liberties, the specifics do matter, and our Constitution does impose constraints on some specific actions that a nation without a Constitution might choose to take. It is to these issues that we now turn.

The "Constitution is not a suicide pact," Justice Robert Jackson once observed. But neither is it merely a list of hortatory aspirations. It represents our commitment to the rule of law and recognizes the need to balance security and liberty. "Law" and "order" may not always be perfectly compatible. Complying with the law may make it more difficult to maintain order, especially against terrorists who do not care about law and whose goal is disorder.

One of the goals of terrorism is to frighten citizens into surrendering their civil liberties and welcoming a police state. This goal is often achieved because many citizens prefer security to liberty even during times of tranquillity, and many governments are all too willing to use the fear of terrorism as a justification for asserting more control over their citizens. And frightened citizens generally go along, as evidenced by public opinion polls that strongly suggest a willingness—even, among some, an apparent eagerness—to give up civil liberties at the first sign of danger in the name of unity and safety.

The suicide terrorism of September 11 illustrates the dangers of this phenomenon even in a nation as steeped in historical traditions of liberty as ours is. Although these terrorist acts were the result primarily of *human errors*—intelligence and security failures—rather than *inadequate laws*, the first reaction of the government was to urge a massive overhaul of our legal system, especially of our rights. Some conservative politicians immediately called for Americans to compromise civil liberties in the name of security. They introduced legislation expanding wiretapping authority, extending the time during which suspects could be detained,

enhancing the penalties for terrorists and their accessories, allowing the seizure of assets, and authorizing secret searches of e-mail.
Liberal politicians (along with some right-wing libertarians) sought
compromises, including sunset provisions specifying when these
new powers would expire. In the end, Congress enacted a typically
political law—unsubtly named the "USA Patriot Act" of 2001—
which gave a little bit to each side without doing very much to protect the safety of Americans.

   In addition to changes in the law, law enforcement authorities
detained hundreds of Arab and Muslim Americans on the basis of
little more than suspicion coupled with ethnic profiling. Nor was
such profiling limited to government officials. Private security
guards, airline personnel, and ordinary citizens have become
understandably suspicious of foreign-looking people, especially
young men, who fit the stereotype of the terrorist. Attorney General John Ashcroft has announced an "aggressive detention" policy
under which anyone suspected of association with terrorists will be
arrested for even minor offenses—he mentioned spitting on the
street—and held until it could be determined that they had no
involvement with terrorist acts or plans. Although there have been
protests from the American Civil Liberties Union and other
groups, the general public and most politicians seem to be accept-
ing all this without much protest.

   The easiest first step a government can take in response to an
emergency is to curtail the civil liberties of its enemies, its noncitizens, and other "theys." It is far less controversial to go after
"them" than "us." This is precisely what the Bush administration
did in the wake of September 11, 2001. Most of the restrictions
were directed against noncitizens. Citizens of Arab or Muslim
background were subjected to more frequent identity checks and
other forms of selective intrusions. To be sure, there were random
checks at airports, which included "grandmas from Idaho," but
they were done more to make a point than to enhance security and

constituted little more than an inconvenience for most people who were subjected to the symbolic searches.

Although our civics books and Fourth of July orations are filled with the rhetoric of liberty, our actual history is one of quick surrender to the forces of authority during perceived emergencies. Times of crisis—wars, insurrections, even labor strikes—have provoked calls for extraordinary restrictions on liberty, even including the declaration of martial law and the suspension of the writ of habeas corpus.

The great emancipator, Abraham Lincoln, was also the great incarcerator. He suspended the writ of habeas corpus during the Civil War, thus allowing many civilians to be tried by courts-martial, with no judicial review. In the early part of the twentieth century, martial law was declared by several state governors seeking to break strikes by unpopular labor unions. During World War I political dissenters and draft resisters were imprisoned. It was in that context that even the great Oliver Wendell Holmes affirmed the imprisonment of draft protesters who were employing entirely lawful means to criticize the war and the draft. His inept analogy to "falsely shouting fire in a crowded theater" became a metaphor for repression. Following the war, the Palmer raids resulted in the imprisonment and deportation of many left-wing immigrants who were merely exercising their freedom of speech to protest capitalism and advocate socialism.

Perhaps the worst example of surrender of our civil liberties occurred after our entry into World War II, when a liberal president, Franklin Delano Roosevelt, urged on by a moderate attorney general of California, Earl Warren, authorized the detention of 110,000 Japanese-Americans, many of them citizens, in camps far away from the Pacific coast. The FBI's records show that there was not a single case of espionage or sabotage by an American resident of Japanese ancestry before, during, or after the war, yet the absence of such activity did not satisfy a hysterical population with

deep-rooted racial antagonisms. Warren even expressed the Alice
in Wonderland view that it was the very absence of sabotage that
was "the most ominous sign in our whole situation," convincing
him that "the sabotage . . . the fifth column activities that we are to
get are timed just like Pearl Harbor," and that the inaction of
Japanese-Americans was deliberately designed to lull us "into a
false sense of security."[26]

During the Cold War, McCarthyism trampled on our liberties, as even liberal senators demanded the detention of communists and the declaration of a national state of emergency. The
Kennedy administration authorized J. Edgar Hoover to install a
"national security" wiretap and bug in Martin Luther King's hotel
room, which picked up conversations between the civil rights
leader and a white woman with whom he was having an affair. In
the late 1960s, student demonstrations provoked a call for qualified
martial law by then assistant attorney general William Rehnquist,
subsequently the chief justice of the United States.

It is a credit to our nation that we seem to learn from our
most serious mistakes. In the wake of the September 11 disaster,
no responsible politicians have called for the mass detention of
Arab or Muslim Americans or the suspension of the writ of habeas
corpus, or severe restrictions on freedom of speech. Most of the
demands have been for calibrated compromises of existing rights,
and the governmental response has been relatively mild, at least
when compared with the past. To be sure, the people whose rights
have been compromised the most have been, as usual, "them,"
rather than "us."

In 1986 I wrote an article about what I hoped would be "an
unlikely hypothetical scenario." I postulated the possibility that
someday an evil terrorist mastermind might "unleash suicide terrorists on innocent civilians in the United States." The article
spelled out some possibilities: "What if bombs were planted in
Boston movie theaters? What if machine-gun-toting fanatics

started shooting up the La Guardia and O'Hare airport terminals? What if terrorists poisoned the Los Angeles drinking water? What if a team of assassins killed several high-ranking executive, legislative, and judicial officials in Washington?"[27]

I then asked, "How would American law enforcement authorities respond to massive threats of terrorism?" I tried to answer this question by reference to our past history, cataloging "some of the more moderate emergency measures we could realistically expect" if suicide squads began to operate in the cities and towns of this country. These measures included:

- Substantial restrictions on immigration and on the rights of aliens, especially from certain parts of the world
- The instituting of mandatory internal passports or some other form of identification papers to be carried by all individuals in the United States
- FBI infiltration of political organizations sympathetic to terrorist goals
- Extensive wiretapping, bugging, and surveillance of suspected terrorists and their associates
- Detention of suspected terrorists
- Governmental controls over the dissemination of information about terrorist activities
- Increased security checks, roadblocks, and searches near theaters, restaurants, and other public gathering places

My predictions have proved generally correct—at least so far! The restrictions imposed on civil liberties, though controversial, are generally consistent with the rule of law. But what if matters were to get considerably worse? What if bioterrorism were to expand from sporadic outbreaks of anthrax to systematic spreading of lethal diseases? What if a nuclear or chemical explosion seemed imminent? What if suicide bombers began to blow up our schools, shopping centers, restaurants, and government buildings?

One of the first responses might well be to exercise far greater control over the movement of potentially dangerous people into, out of, and within our country. Already we are hearing calls for massive restrictions on immigration and on visas, especially for people of Muslim and Arab backgrounds. In the pages to come, I will outline some steps we should consider taking in order to improve our security without losing either the feel or the reality of freedom.

Controlling the Movement of People

Every nation has the authority, under international law and the accepted norms of state action, to exercise reasonable control over who enters, remains in, and leaves its territory. Under our Constitution, there are limits even to the exercise of that broad power. For almost a hundred years, beginning as early as 1870, we restricted immigration and citizenship on the basis of race, religion, political beliefs, and national origin. It is doubtful we could do that today, at least in so blatant a manner.[28] But we do retain virtually unlimited power to protect our borders from potential terrorists. The problem is that the agencies charged with the responsibility of protecting us from foreign terrorists are doing an incompetent job. Whether because they lack the technical resources, the personnel, or the institutional determination to control our vast and porous borders against those planning to harm us, the reality is that they are not doing so. The disaster of September 11 reflected a massive failure of personnel, priorities, and institutions far more than it did a failure of existing laws. Although the terrifying attacks of that day made clear the need for some legal changes, these will not be effective unless they are accompanied by even more important institutional changes. We must keep terrorists out of the country, off our airplanes, and away from our vulnerable targets. This will require a massive new effort that our anachronistic Immigration and Naturalization Service is simply incapable of mounting and implementing. We need an effective border control system adapted to the new threats we now face.

Any such border control system should be coordinated with an airport security system both outside and inside the country. It must also be coordinated, though this will be far more difficult, with other means of traveling across our borders and within our territory. Such coordination will require sophisticated computer hookups among all relevant agencies, to avoid the lack of communication that may have permitted some of the September 11 terrorists to enter and remain in this country. On June 3, 2000, Mohamed Atta entered the United States on a visitor visa. Although his visa expired on December 2, 2000, Atta remained in the country until January 3, 2001. He then left the United States, but returned one week later. He was allowed back into the country because a computer check indicated that the student visa for which he had applied was pending. Six months after September 11, the INS finished processing Atta's visa request and mailed his student visa approval to the flight school in Florida. We must also close the information gap that resulted in top officials not receiving timely information about Zacarias Moussaoui's connections to terrorist operatives in Malaysia or to payments from an al-Qaeda co-conspirator—allegations that now form part of the indictment against him.[29]

Information is power, and we rightly worry about the government having too much information and too great an ability to coordinate it. We keep the Internal Revenue Service—which has more private information about Americans than any other governmental agency—from sharing its information with other agencies. Until recently we prevented disclosure to the Central Intelligence Agency of information secured by grand jury subpoenas. Some of this deliberate compartmentalization is reasonable, even essential. But in other areas coordination and need for information sharing must trump our concern about the government having too much data.

Wisely distinguishing between *when it is important to compartmentalize* and *when it is important to coordinate* is necessary for striking the appropriate balance between security and liberty. Scant attention was paid to this issue before September 11. With few exceptions, the pervasive lack of coordination did not reflect any carefully thought through policy seeking to strike appropriate balances. It reflected anachronistic computer systems with inadequate linkage, institutional jealousies between competing agencies unwilling to share "their" proprietary information, and just plain incompetence. It also reflected, and continues to reflect, partisan, political agendas. A good example of this is the Justice Department's refusal to allow the FBI to check the gun purchase records of noncitizens who were detained in the days and weeks following the attacks in September. The National Rifle Association was, and remains, adamantly opposed to the FBI having access to the information once the background check has been completed. When Attorney General Ashcroft was a senator, he tried to amend the law to require destruction of all background information used to check gun purchasers upon completion of the check. The NRA supported this amendment, but it failed. Notwithstanding its rejection by Congress, this policy has now effectively been adopted by the current administration. Despite the FBI's understandable desire to secure highly relevant information regarding gun purchases by detained suspects, the NRA's highly partisan position has denied the FBI this information.[30]

This kind of politicized agenda-driven barrier to information sharing must be ended. The battle against terrorism may have to be fought with one hand behind our back, because the Constitution properly precludes us from taking every action we might deem effective, but we cannot afford to have our other hand gratuitously disabled by partisan ideological constraints.

In addition to these legal and intelligence changes, we must upgrade the personnel responsible for protecting our borders. This should be a law enforcement job, performed by highly trained agents. Retired FBI, CIA, police, and military personnel should be recruited for supervisory roles. The pay must reflect the importance of the job to the security of our country. An agency can be no better than the people in it, and today many of the people responsible for our security are simply not up to the job.

National ID Cards

An important adjunct to any system that seeks to control the flow of people is a mechanism for correctly identifying them. We have the technical capacity to create a near foolproof system of identification using fingerprints or, for even greater accuracy, DNA information or retinal scans. We could create a data bank that begins at birth and ends at death. We could theoretically go even further and implant chips in everyone in this country, enabling the government to track each person's movements—and more. Big Brother is not beyond our current technical capacity, but he would surely deny us both the feel and the reality of freedom.

At the other end of the continuum would be an absolute right to anonymity, denying government the power ever to ask people who they are. This Thoreauvian model has long since been abandoned in this country and most others. The Internal Revenue Service, registration for the draft (if you are a male), Social Security, driver's licenses, airport identity checks, Medicare, and hundreds of other requirements or everyday intrusions have moved us quite far along the continuum away from Walden Pond and closer to Big Brother, without losing our feel of freedom.

The observation cuts both ways, of course. Because we are already so close to Big Brother, one might argue, we have very little "anonymity" to lose by moving a little closer. The proper response to this is, precisely because we are already so close to Big Brother, we must protect against any step that threatens to bring us even closer. The reality, however, is that not every step is qualitatively or even quantitatively the same. Some should be vigorously resisted. Others should be welcomed. And still others should be carefully considered. An example of the first kind would be the implanting of a chip into every American so that all movements could be monitored. An example of the second is the routine toe-printing of every baby, to avoid mixups and to maintain a source of identification in the event of death. Toe prints—as distinguished from the far more definitive, and therefore more accurate, DNA "prints"—tell us nothing about a person except the pattern of whorls on one toe. An example of the third category would be the creation of a DNA print bank that could help solve crimes, free wrongly convicted inmates, and help identify people who have lost their memories or their lives. But DNA prints can also disclose information about genetic dispositions and other private matters. The creation of a universal DNA bank, or even a more limited "criminal" DNA bank, would require trade-offs among important values.[31]

Another example of a step that would require trade-offs would be the requirement (or even option) of a national identity card. For some, such a card would lack the feel of freedom and would risk moving us too close to the slippery slope leading to Big Brother. To others, it is a logical extension of the easily faked driver's license or Social Security card, but with a positive protection against fraud, identity theft, and circumvention. For me, it is an issue that deserves careful consideration. It requires us to think hard about the difference between privacy and anonymity. Privacy involves information that an individual should be allowed to keep to him or herself—information such as medical records, sexual preferences, religious views. Anonymity involves something quite different: the right not to be known to the government—in effect, to be able to wear a bag over your head. No such general right is even hinted at in the Constitution, although there is a more limited right to publish anonymously or join organizations without having one's identity disclosed. But what one willingly discloses to public view—one's face, name, and so on—is protected neither by the right to privacy nor by the limited right to anonymity. It is also useful to distinguish among different kinds of identification systems and different aspects of any such system.

Before September 11, 2001, I had not thought much about national identity cards. My knee-jerk opposition to any such intrusion grew primarily out of the misuse of ID cards by the apartheid regime in South Africa and the totalitarian regimes in the Soviet Union and China. But the ease with which several of the September 11 hijackers managed to hide in open view and fall between the bureaucratic cracks made it clear to me that a foolproof national ID card had some real virtues. Then I started to think about its vices. I was hard pressed to come up with any compelling civil libertarian arguments against a simple card, which would contain only five elements: the bearer's name, address, Social Security number, and photograph, and a finger or retinal print matching a chip in the card. This chip would make it virtually impossible for anyone to use a card that was not his or hers, and it would allow appropriate authorities under appropriate circumstances to check the identity of all people properly in this country.

No ID card can be more accurate than its source of information. If an applicant for such a card presented an existing ID—say a passport or a driver's license—with a false name, his national ID card will also have a false name. For the system to work, there would have to be some background identity check before the card was issued.

There are, of course, grave dangers inherent in any system of information gathering by government officials. Anyone who lived through J. Edgar Hoover's tenure as FBI director understands this danger. That is why there should be a national debate over what kind of information is appropriate for the government to collect in its databases. But that is a different debate from the one about national ID cards. We already have the databases. Whenever you return from a trip abroad, you must show your passport, and the authorities can match it with an existing database. The ID card would not add anything to the database except the finger or retinal print. There is, of course, the danger that a limited ID card could expand into something far more invasive of privacy. Justice Benjamin Cardozo wrote of "the tendency of a principle to expand itself to the limit of its logic." Once the government was empowered to require every person to have a card, the pressures would increase to expand the uses that could be made of the card and the information that could be accessed from it. That is why the debate about ID cards should be a stimulus to the more important debates about the content of government databases and the circumstances under which authorities should be entitled to ask anyone to identify him or herself. The understandable fear of the slippery slope is a reason for setting clear limits and drawing reasonable distinctions, not an excuse for inaction. Yet both the liberal ACLU and the conservative Eagle Forum oppose not only a national ID card but even a nationally standardized driver's license, on the ground that it "would diminish privacy in America and do nothing to prevent further acts of terrorism on our soil." These conclusions seem overstated, even in the face of concerns about the vulnerability of current smart cards.[32]

An alternative to a mandatory national ID card would be an optional one. Since the vast majority of Americans already carry several forms of identification, including at least one photo ID, I believe that most Americans would sign up for the national card, especially because its bearer would be able to pass through appropriate checkpoints—such as airports, high-rise buildings, government offices—more expeditiously than those who opted out of the national ID system.

Another virtue of the national ID card is that it would eliminate much of the justification now offered for racial or ethnic profiling. When African-American students first started to attend Harvard in significant numbers, many of them were routinely hassled by security officers and others, since they didn't "look" as if they "belonged" on or around the Harvard campus. When ID cards were issued to all students, it became easier for African-American students to avoid harassment by simply showing their cards. To be sure, they were asked to show their cards more often than white students—and that clearly is inappropriate. But the net result of the ID cards was to reduce the amount of inappropriate hassling of minority students. I think the same thing would be true for Arab-Americans. Under current conditions, Arab-American men would probably be asked for their IDs more often, but by showing the card, they could avoid the kind of harassment that many have recently experienced on airplanes.

As a general proposition, I think it is far better for everybody to be deprived of a little bit of anonymity than for one specific ethnic group to bear a disproportionate part of the burden. I prefer "we-we" compromises over "we-they" compromises. "We-we" intrusions provide a more effective check on abuses, since those whose rights are being compromised have more political power than the "theys." An optional national ID card is a "we-we" intrusion, since those who deliberately opt out of the national ID system have made a decision to endure more intrusive searches in exchange for not having to carry the card. In some respects, this is a little like the trade-off people make when they agree to have their automobile identified by a radio computer when crossing bridges and going through tunnels, rather than stopping and paying an anonymous toll.

I would certainly require foolproof ID cards for anyone visiting the United States. Today foreign visitors are required to have passports and other immigration documents, and the additional requirements of a card with a print would not be onerous and would reduce the opportunity for circumvention.

For reasons similar to those for which I favor a national ID card, I also favor limited use of face recognition technology in public buildings, airports, or other places where identification is now required. Face recognition machines—to the extent that they can be made to work more effectively than they now do—are certainly preferable to ethnic stereotyping, which is simply a primitive, human method of face identification. Civil libertarians need not fear technology, so long as we control it, rather than allowing it to control us.

An issue closely related to the national ID card is the authority to require a person to identify him or herself and the criteria for when such a request for identification is proper. Again there is a continuum. At the Big Brother end is the system of frequent checkpoints, random demands for "your papers, please," and even electronic monitoring of movement. At the softer end would be a system in which no one was required to carry a national ID card— as no one today is required to carry a driver's license when not driving—but if anyone wanted to go to a place where ID was properly required, like an airport or a government building, the only acceptable ID would be the national card (or the only ID that would get you into the quick lane would be the national one).

Following September 11, identification requests have moved from airports and government buildings into the private arena. An

ID is now required to enter virtually any high-rise building. We have not reached the point of having to show an ID on the street, and I hope it will not come to that, but for anyone who does more than just stay at home or walk in the streets identification requests are becoming routine. It feels somewhat uncomfortable and is sometimes inconvenient, but it does not feel tyrannical, perhaps because the requesters are not wearing government badges and carrying guns. The source of the request matters. Indeed, many citizens seem willing to accept massive intrusions on their privacy from the private sector, which seeks purely private financial gain for itself. Robert Kuttner has pointedly observed:

> In a sense, we Americans have the worst of both worlds. Business has found new ways to violate our privacy, but we don't trust government to rein in business. And terrorism has given government an excuse to expand its police powers, well beyond what the national emergency requires. No wonder we are uncertain where to turn.
>
> Conservatives and liberals both distrust a national ID card. Yet the data that would be contained in an identity card already reposes in countless private credit files and public Social Security, passport, and motor vehicle records. It would be far more rational to have a national ID card, but then strictly limit its use. We could be more secure that terrorists were not boarding flights and criminals not using guns and also that confidential data would not be abused.[33]

We should not institute checkpoints or authorize random ID checks. We should, however, consider a system under which visitors to this country are required to check in telephonically (from a land-line phone) on a regular basis, say every ten or fifteen days.

We have the technology available to do this, and it would help us track visitors who have overstayed their visas or are otherwise out of status. Recently many long-term illegal immigrants who had remained out of trouble and productively employed were granted amnesty and may now apply to become lawful residents or citizens. That is a positive development for at least two reasons. First, it recognizes that some of our citizens who have contributed so much to this country are descended from immigrants who came here under questionable circumstances.[34] Second, it moves us toward a system under which "illegal immigrant" status really means something. We can no longer accept a situation in which millions of people are de facto accepted as residents while de jure being illegally here. That twilight-zone status makes it nearly impossible to enforce our immigration laws in a way that protects us from potential terrorists. We must move toward a time when people who are in this country illegally are tracked down and detained or deported. If they have no right to be here, they should not be here. If we want them to be here, their status should be changed to that of lawful residents or visitors. The need for security in this age of terrorism demands that the legal status of everyone in this country be unambiguously clear.

One place where virtually all Americans want more security is at our airports. The events of September 11 *would*—not might—have been prevented by decent airport security. Two of the hijacked planes originated at Logan Airport in Boston, out of which I have regularly flown for many years. Security there was notoriously lax, and those planning the hijacking obviously knew that. Boston is a hotbed of nepotism, cronyism, and political patronage—from its public schools to its police force to its airport security. As *Boston Globe* columnist Derrick Z. Jackson put it, "patronage still comes before passengers."

The sad reality is that thousands of citizens died in part because other citizens failed to do their jobs well. Unless the people who were at fault are quickly identified and fired and the procedures at fault are pinpointed and fixed, we risk repetition. Our understandable wish to present a united front against terrorism should not deter us from pointing an accusatory finger at those Americans who were responsible for allowing the terrorists to inflict so much damage on so many innocent people. To place some of the blame on our own citizens is not in any way to diminish the moral culpability of the terrorists, who are the only criminals. But we may not be able to get at the terrorists. We can do something about our own failures.

The other sad reality is that too many of the people responsible for our security are simply not smart enough, not knowledgeable enough, and not experienced enough to do the job. We must do better. Airport security should be the job of retired FBI agents and others with extensive law enforcement experience.

Nor should we resist technological support for airport security. When tests began at the Orlando airport for some cutting-edge devices capable of detecting explosives and other dangerous items, the ACLU immediately complained because one of the machines could see through clothing. Although this machine would be operated by guards of the same sex as the scanned person, prudish concerns were raised, comparing the intrusiveness of this electronic scan with a "virtual strip search."[35] The analogy is absurd, as anyone who has been poked and groped during a strip search can attest. Such an unwillingness to distinguish between degrees and kinds of intrusion will make it far more difficult to strike the proper balance.

Another proposal for increasing airport security is racial profiling. The term itself is among the most misunderstood and emotionally laden terms in the modern vocabulary of law enforcement and politics. There is of course nothing wrong with profiling as such. Profiles of certain types of criminals, such as child molesters and serial murderers, are effectively used by local and federal law enforcement. The profile of the Unabomber bore an uncanny resemblance to Theodore Kaczynski, the man ultimately convicted of the Unabomber's crimes. Most profiling involves factors unique to certain individuals and does not touch on the volatile issues of race, ethnicity, or religion. It is when profiling does involve these factors that it becomes understandably suspect, especially in a society, like ours, with so terrible a racial history. But even race may sometimes be relevant and permissible in certain kinds of profiling. Consider a situation in which a victim describes his assailant as a young black man. When color pigmentation is one of the major identifying factors, it may be permissible to limit the investigation to persons of that race (and age and gender) as much as it would be to limit the inquiry to one-legged men if that were a salient identifying characteristic.[36]

A second area where race or ethnicity may be relevant is where the crime has a racial or religious component. For example, in looking for Klansmen who may have lynched an African-American, it would be foolish to look beyond the white community, since we know that all such racially motivated lynchings were committed by whites (although we also know that the vast majority of whites never committed a racial lynching). The same would be true of people of Islamic background. We know that all al-Qaeda members, and certainly all al-Qaeda suicide bombers, are Muslims. It is foolish, therefore, to misallocate our resources in the fight against suicide bombers by devoting equal attention to searching an eighty-year-old Christian woman from Maine and a twenty-two-year-old Muslim man from Saudi Arabia. It certainly does not follow from this that it would be permissible to arrest or detain or harass a twenty-two-year-old male just because he is a Muslim—even a Muslim from Saudi Arabia. The vast majority of Muslims from Saudi Arabia have nothing to do with terrorism, and it would be foolish to misallocate our resources by focusing on the many innocent Muslims from Saudi Arabia. More should be required before law enforcement authorities can arrest, detain, or even search a Muslim from Saudi Arabia.

The same is true of racial profiling for ordinary crimes. Even if there were a type of crime which only black people committed (and I can think of none), the sole fact that a person is black should never be enough for arrest, detention, or search even in situations where no whites are suspected. That should be true even if the assailant has been identified as black. Limiting the inquiry to blacks or Muslims does not mean that all Muslims or blacks can properly be subject to the inquiry.

True racial profiling of an impermissible nature occurs when all members of a particular race become suspect because of their race, ethnicity, or nationality alone. The most extreme example of racial profiling in American history was the mass detention of Japanese-Americans during the Second World War. It did not work, and it made our nation guilty of inexcusable racism.[37]

We must think not only about current threats to liberty raised by our need to control the movement of people, but about potential future threats as well. For example, if there were to be a bioterrorist attack involving a contagious disease—such as viral smallpox, as distinguished from bacterial anthrax—one immediate response would be to seek to quarantine contagious people to prevent or control the spread of the disease. This may sound relatively simple from a legal or constitutional perspective, since most contagious people would want to be quarantined. But if history is a guide, there will be some allegedly contagious people who may resist being isolated. The laws of quarantine, which go back to the time of tuberculosis and other "natural" epidemics, are inadequate to deal with bioterrorism, especially if the weapons of mass infection include suicide carriers sent by terrorist organizations to spread disease as widely as possible. The quarantine laws now on our books provide few protections, even for those who have plausible claims of misdiagnosis.

A leading scholar of quarantine laws has concluded that "both law and science have changed since the time when quarantine was a standard tool against infectious disease. A court giving unquestioning approval to quarantine in modern circumstances would be utilizing an anachronistic rationale." But this was written in 1985, in the context of an AIDS epidemic. It did not take into account the weaponization of contagious disease. The time has come for experts to rewrite the laws of quarantine, making them both more responsive to current needs and more protective of civil liberties.[38]

These are some of the issues concerning control of people's movement that may be required to preserve our security but that impinge on our liberty. The balances I favor striking may tilt too heavily in favor of security for some reasonable people, and too far in favor of liberty for others. The important thing is to begin a debate now about how to strike a proper balance. No one of the proposals suggested above will, by itself, turn us from a democracy into a tyranny, and no one of them will offer complete protection from the threats of terrorism. That is the nature of balances that must be struck under the rule of law. An appropriate balance increases security considerably without diminishing liberty unduly. That is the true meaning of due process. I believe that the combination of micro steps I have proposed for restricting the movement of people and ascertaining their identity strikes an appropriate balance.

Controlling the Flow of Information

There are no rights more essential to democracy than the free flow of information and the untrammeled exercise of freedom of speech, press, assembly, and dissent. These are the lubricants that keep the "channel of democracy"—to borrow Professor John

Hart Ely's elegant phrase—open and free-flowing. Freedom of expression comprises many elements. Paramount among them is the freedom of individual citizens and of the media to express dissenting views without fear of governmental censorship. Also essential is the right of citizens and the media to have access to sources of truthful information about what the government is doing.

It should not be surprising that the first casualty of war has often been truth, since the paradigm of the military is control, including control of information. Propaganda, disinformation, and secrecy are important weapons of the military, and journalists are often willing to subordinate truth to patriotism. This is understandable, if such subordination takes the form of briefly withholding information about troop movements or other battle plans when immediate disclosure might endanger our soldiers or the success of our attack. But when journalistic patriotism results in refusal to report critically on the performance of government officials—from the president to military commanders—our system of checks and balances can be harmed.

During times of national emergency, our governmental system of checks and balances often breaks down, as the legislative and judicial branches defer to the executive branch, and especially to the military. Claims of national security generally trump assertions of individual rights. This has certainly been the lesson of history. It is precisely during such times that the nongovernmental "checks" on government become essential if the proper "balance" is to be maintained. Among the most important of these nongovernmental checks are a free press, a zealous defense bar, an independent religious leadership, and a critical professoriate and student body. No emergency requires any compromise with the right to dissent. Attorney General Ashcroft was way out of line when he suggested that those who disagree with the administration's approach to terrorism give aid and comfort to the terrorists.

There is an important difference between dissent and incitement, but it is a distinction that has been difficult to draw, especially during times of national emergency. There are, of course, clear cases at both ends of the continuum. All statements of opposition to government policy—no matter how "unpatriotic" or unpopular—must be accorded complete constitutional protection, even if they are thought to hinder the war effort. On the other hand, an order from a terrorist leader to a suicide bomber exhorting him to destroy his target is not protected, even though it takes the form of speech. Between these "easy" cases lies a wide range of hard cases, including the ones discussed in Chapter 3, involving religious leaders who answer questions and give blessings to terrorists. These hard cases will make new law, and if history is a guide they will probably make bad law. In my view, all reasonable doubts should always be resolved in favor of freedom of speech, even in situations where the goals of the First Amendment are not directly furthered by the speech at issue. The temptations toward censorship are simply too great, especially during times of crisis, when any form of unpopular speech seems to pose a "clear and present danger" and can be analogized to "shouting fire in a crowded theater."

Even though the imam telling a follower that terrorism is permitted or required does not fit within the paradigm of protected expression, it may be difficult to draw a bright line that isolates that genre of speech without also leaving other, more borderline, situations unprotected. The greatest danger lies in official governmental censorship and prior restraint, but self-censorship resulting from the "chilling" impact of feared governmental censorship may damage the feel of freedom. For that and other reasons it is better for some unprotected speech to be tolerated than for even a small amount of protected speech to be censored.

To argue in favor of resolving doubts in favor of more speech does not deny that some speech can be dangerous. We pay a price—sometimes a high one—for freedom of expression. In the context of terrorism, the price we would have to pay for not curtailing questionable speech may not be so high. Even if we were to criminalize the speech of the religious leaders who encourage terrorism by answering questions and giving blessings, these leaders would quickly learn to speak in vague and metaphorical terms, understandable to their followers but capable of evading the constitutional tests for unprotected incitement. We would devote many resources to any effort to criminalize such incitement, make much bad law, and not get any real return on these expensive investments. We are better advised to devote our resources to proactive undercover and intelligence gathering activities that take advantage of the willingness of religious leaders to talk, and thereby to provide information that may be useful in preventing future terrorism. Here is one instance where maximizing the protection of free expression may—at least in some instances—also enhance our security.

We can also try to implement the classic civil libertarian alternative to censorship—more and better speech. Rather than making futile efforts to silence radical imams who declare terrorism a religious duty, we can publicize the contrary statements of moderate Islamic religious leaders who regard the killing of innocent civilians as a violation of the Koran and the Sharia. We have not done enough to elicit the support of such Islamic leaders in the battle against terrorism and to bring their views to the attention of potential suicide bombers. This will not be easy to do, because these potential murderers live in closed societies where the flow of information to them is carefully controlled by those determined to use these vulnerable people as human weapons. But we can do more—and so can those moderate religious leaders who oppose suicide bombings.

Military Tribunals, Due Process, and the
Right to Zealous Defense Counsel

Another important check on governmental overreaching is trial by jury and open trials. That check was substantially undercut by President George W. Bush's authorization of military tribunals to try noncitizens suspected of ties to terrorism. A long-term resident of the United States who President Bush believes may have aided a terrorist can now be tried in secret by a military commission and be sentenced to death on the basis of hearsay and rumor with no appeal to any civilian court, even the Supreme Court. This is the upshot of the "military order" President Bush issued in November 2001. And that is not all. Noncitizens suspected of membership in al-Qaeda, or of harboring an "aim to cause injury or adverse effects on the United States," can be rounded up and "detained at an appropriate location" for an indefinite time without access to the courts.

This is the kind of "military justice" now in effect for our alleged enemies, both foreign and domestic. No wonder so many experts on wartime tribunals believe that "military justice is to justice as military music is to music." The role of the military is to win wars, to protect citizens, and to follow the orders of the commander in chief. Under our constitutional system of civilian control over the military, it is not the role of military subordinates to question or challenge determinations made by the president, and, in every case coming before a military commission pursuant to this new order, the president will have already "determined" that there is reason to believe that the suspect is a terrorist. Command influence over terrorist military tribunals will be inevitable—far more so than when our own soldiers are tried by court-martial.

Nor will the suspect have an adequate opportunity to defend himself, since the ordinary rules of evidence will not be followed. The military commission will be allowed to base its decision on any evidence that would "have probative value to a reasonable person." Translated from the legalese, this means that hearsay, coerced confessions, and the fruits of illegal searches can be considered, and that cross-examinations will not always be allowed. It also means that the prosecution need not even disclose the sources of its hearsay if such disclosure would reveal a "state secret"—a broad term that is nowhere specifically defined.

It's one thing to subject prisoners of war who are captured on foreign battlefields to military tribunals. Although secret military trials of bin Laden and his foreign associates may be unwise, they would probably be constitutional. It is quite another thing to treat American residents, some with long ties to this country, as if they had no rights under our Constitution. There are no Supreme Court precedents justifying secret military trials of American residents who are not citizens and who are accused of domestic crimes. The nonresidents who tried to blow up the World Trade Center back in 1993 were tried in a federal court and convicted, after being accorded the full panoply of constitutional rights. So were the al-Qaeda terrorists who blew up American embassies in Africa. The independent jury in the latter case refused to do the government's bidding on sentencing, declining to impose the death penalty. That is the proper function of a jury—to follow its own lights on sentencing within the bounds of law. And it is precisely this independence that President Bush is determined to avoid—as was President Roosevelt before him—by placing "justice" against suspected terrorists within the chain of military command. In a post–Civil War case, the Supreme Court ruled that as long as civilian courts remain open, trials of civilians must be tried in such courts, rather than in military tribunals. That case involved an American citizen, but the Court suggested no distinction between citizens and residents. In a case from World War II, the Supreme Court upheld a military tribunal's conviction and execution of Nazi spies who had landed in the United States, but they were German soldiers out of uniform, and a long tradition of military justice makes such spies subject to military tribunals. This tradition does not apply to long-term American residents suspected of aiding terrorists.

As the result of widespread opposition to President Bush's plan—opposition that came from the right as well as the left—the proposal was modified somewhat in March 2002. Although the evidentiary rules have not been changed, the right to counsel has been somewhat amplified to include paid counsel of the defendant's choosing. A unanimous vote will be required to impose the death penalty, and there will be a review panel appointed by the secretary of defense. The presumption will be in favor of open trials but the commission would have the power to close them. Although these changes are significant, they are still a far cry from the due process accorded in civilian courts or in military courts-martial.

I was not surprised to read an editorial in the *Wall Street Journal* favoring Bush's original order. The *Journal*'s editors don't much like our constitutional system of justice, with its emphasis on procedural safeguards, exclusionary rules, and the right to a vigorous defense. They see terrorism as a justification—an excuse—for ridding us of "the excesses of the modern U.S. criminal justice system," with its rigorous "standards of evidence," its "exclusionary rule," and "the legal artifice of Johnnie Cochran."[39]

The real danger is that many Americans, not only the editors of the *Wall Street Journal,* have always distrusted our constitutional system of justice, with its historical preference for the acquittal of the guilty over the conviction of the innocent. They prefer a more streamlined system, with fewer safeguards and fewer acquittals. They trust the government to bring only the guilty to trial. And they distrust zealous defense attorneys who are willing to challenge the government at every turn.

Because the war against terrorism—unlike previous wars—will not end on a specific date, the military approach to justice reflected in the Bush order may well persist indefinitely, and perhaps even expand in its scope. Its visible successes, undiscounted by its less visible failures, will encourage many Americans to view the military approach to trials—which favors efficiency and certainty over fairness and the resolution of doubts in favor of the accused—as the norm rather than the exception. This must never be allowed to happen, if our liberties are to be preserved. As the Supreme Court said, in ruling that Abraham Lincoln had violated the Constitution by subjecting Confederate sympathizers to military tribunals:

> [Our Constitution] foresaw that troublous times would arise, when rulers and people would become restive under restraint and seek by sharp and decisive measures to accomplish ends deemed just and proper; and that the principles of constitutional liberty would be in peril, unless established by irrepealable law. . . .
>
> This nation . . . has no right to expect that it will always have wise and humane rulers, sincerely attached to the principles of the Constitution. Wicked men, ambitious of power, with hatred of liberty and contempt of law, may fill the place once occupied by Washington and Lincoln, and if this right [to suspend provisions of the Constitution during the great exigencies of government] is conceded, and the calamities of war again befall us, the dangers to human liberty are frightful to contemplate.[40]

We must begin to contemplate these dangers *now,* in the face of President Bush's frightening order.

One alternative to military tribunals that has been proposed is some kind of international court under the auspices of the United Nations, modeled on the one now sitting in The Hague and exercising jurisdiction over war crimes allegedly committed in the former Yugoslavia.

Our own courts have at least one distinct advantage over international tribunals. Every defendant in an American court has the right to trial by jury, whereas international trials are generally conducted in front of judges. And in highly political cases—and any international trial of an alleged global terrorist would be distinctly political—judges are likely to be far less independent than jurors, and more likely to do the bidding of the governments that selected them for the tribunal. Many judges have future judicial and political aspirations, and all judges want to be well regarded among their patriotic peers.

A jury, on the other hand, disperses after completing its singular job of administering justice in a particular case, and the individual jurors return to the anonymity their lives had previously. Government officials can (and do) whisper to judges, but they cannot whisper to jurors, because anything communicated to a juror must be a matter of record. Jurors often refuse to do the bidding of the government, as evidenced by the refusal of a jury in New York to impose the death penalty on the terrorists who blew up an American embassy. Juries do, of course, make mistakes—perhaps even more often than judges do, but jury mistakes are less likely to be a function of political pressures. Emotions, of course, are extremely high throughout the United States, and a fair jury trial will be much more difficult to ensure, but so will a fair trial before judges. Were I defending an accused terrorist—even after the recent disaster—I would almost certainly prefer a jury trial to a trial before a judge.

The issue of who would actually defend an accused terrorist in front of an American jury raises the most daunting questions regarding the possibility of a fair trial in this country. Within hours of the terrible events of September 11, 2001, my telephone began to ring off the hook. The second question invariably put to me—the first was, "Is your family okay?"—was whether I would defend the people who did this. It was not so much a question as a plea: "You're not going to defend these bastards, are you?" Even today, people stop me on the street to urge me not to defend accused terrorists. It seems as if most Americans believe in the right of every defendant to be represented by a zealous lawyer—as an abstract matter. But when it comes to the hard cases—the cases of defendants accused of the most despicable crimes—attitudes change. Americans want to be sure that every accused murderer is represented by a lawyer, as long as that lawyer isn't very good or doesn't try too hard to win! I have received threats in regard to the World Trade Center case, even before there is a case, and despite the fact that I am not a trial lawyer and have expressed no interest in defending any accused terrorist. But threats of this kind will have an impact on those lawyers who may be asked to perform the patriotic duty of defending anyone accused of destroying the World Trade Center. Yes, it would be a patriotic duty, comparable to the duty performed by prosecutors—or doctors who ministered to the wounded victims. But the defense lawyer's job is far more difficult, controversial and in some respects hazardous. The lawyers who end up representing accused terrorists—even bin Laden, if we are fortunate enough to bring him to trial—will be vilified and threatened, especially if they provide the kind of zealous advocacy demanded by the Constitution. They will be providing a constitutional service to clients they detest and fear. They will receive no praise for doing their job, especially if they do it well.

This is the great paradox of our legal system. We boast of a process in which the most despised are treated fairly and represented zealously, and yet we condemn those who provide this constitutionally required zealous representation. Unless we begin to understand how inconsistent we are, we will not be true to our claim of providing the fairest trials of any nation in the world.

The zealous defense counsel standing between the prosecutor and the defendant suspected of terrorism-related crimes serves as another important check on government, especially during times of emergency. Our history in this regard is decidedly mixed. At law day ceremonies, we recall John Adams defending the British soldiers accused of perpetrating the Boston Massacre, but we conveniently forget the way the bar performed—or failed to perform—during the McCarthyite witch-hunts of the 1950s. Most establishment lawyers were so terrified of any association with communists that they refused to represent anyone even accused of having been a communist. We recall the few—very few—brave exceptions, but we tend not to remember the large majority who constituted the rule.

Now the attorney general has announced that lawyers who represent accused terrorists may be subject to having their conversations with their clients monitored. The flimsy justification offered for this violation of the lawyer-client privilege—a privilege rooted in the Sixth Amendment—is that terrorists might use their lawyers as conduits for information to other terrorists. The lawyers might be dupes or co-conspirators. In other words, they would be either fools or felons. As a Justice Department spokesman put it, law enforcement officials "may have substantial reason to believe that certain inmates that have been involved in terrorist activities will pass messages through their attorneys [or the attorney's legal assistant or interpreter] to individuals on the outside for the purpose of continuing terrorist activities." If the government had probable cause for suspecting that a terrorist was using his lawyer in this way—as it has alleged with regard to Sheikh Omar Abdel Rahman—it could obtain a warrant. But the policy announced by the administration would be for situations in which there was no probable cause. This is an unacceptable compromise with an important constitutional right. If lawyers are to serve as an effective check on prosecutorial abuse, the confidentiality of their conversations should not be subject to the whim of the very prosecutors they are checking. Nor should their patriotism be questioned.

Adapting the Old Laws of War to the New Terrorism

The international law of war has evolved over time and reflects the experiences of earlier wars. The war against terrorism is a new phenomenon, not adequately addressed by current law. Traditional wars were fought by combatants in uniform, representing nations with return addresses and accountability. Even "civil" or "revolutionary" forms of warfare generally distinguished between combatants and civilians. The current terrorist wars are different. The terrorists are themselves "civilians," their targets are civilians, they hide among civilians, and they are supported and financed by civilians. They exploit the traditional international law of war, especially the Geneva Accords, to their advantage and place those who seek to protect their civilian populations on the defensive. Since these terrorists ignore the law of war, they are free to target civilians with impunity. If they are captured, they demand "prisoner of war" status. If the nations they target try to defend themselves by going after terrorists hiding among civilians, the terrorists invariably complain that these nations are violating the Geneva Accords by endangering "civilians." It is a win-win situation for the terrorists and a lose-lose situation for the victims— because of the inadequacy of current law. Victim nations are constantly put on the defensive for failing to comply with the letter of international law, even if their conduct is moral and proportional.

The time has come for the United States to insist that the international law of war be changed to reflect the new realities of fighting terrorism. We should not be in the position of trying to fit our acts of self-defense into anachronistic formulations that give the terrorists an undue advantage in the courts of public opinion and international law. To remain credible and effective, laws must change with experience, and the laws of war must now be changed so that they can no longer be hypocritically exploited, as both sword and shield, by the terrorists.

It is important in this time of danger that those who are in charge of our safety and those who see their role as defending our liberty work together as much as possible to avoid unnecessary conflict. When the Canadian government invoked the War Measures Act in response to terrorism in the early 1970s, its attorney general invited leading civil libertarians to work together with government officials. This worked tolerably well. Now is the time for our government to invite civil libertarians into the tent to consult with law enforcement officials. We can work together to avoid lawsuits and recriminations. Civil libertarians need not fear every change or technological innovation. Indeed, there are technologies that have the potential to maximize both safety and civil liberties.

Any change in our fundamental civil liberties should be debated. A civil liberties impact statement should accompany every compromise, as should a sunset provision. New measures will not ensure our safety with absolute certainty. The balances we ultimately strike will contain trade-offs between our liberties and our safety that will not satisfy absolutists in either the law enforcement or the civil libertarian camps. But if we work together—if civil libertarians are brought into the tent in advance, rather than playing their traditional role of criticizing from outside afterward—the beneficiaries will be all Americans who rightly demand both safety and freedom.

Conclusion

Are We Overreacting?

In the wake of September 11, I am frequently asked the following question: are we overreacting or underreacting to the threats of terrorism? In trying to answer that difficult question, I think of how I might have answered the same question in Hitler's Germany in the mid-1930s. At that time, no one could have known how matters would turn out. The Nazis' mass slaughter of the Jews, Gypsies, and other civilians was unpredictable, despite Hitler's own statements of intention. Now that we know what the Nazis eventually did, almost anything that was done in the 1930s seems underreactive. But if Hitler had failed—if he had been assassinated and his replacement had not been as brutal—we might see some of the steps taken by anti-Nazi activists as overreactive. The same can be said for the crisis we now face. If the tragic events of September 11 turn out to be the last major terrorist attack, perhaps we will be accused of overreacting. But if these attacks are merely the harbinger of much worse and more extensive mass attacks that endanger our very existence, then we may ultimately be charged with underreaction.

Future critics, armed with the benefit of hindsight, would point to the explicit warnings given by the terrorists of their intentions, much as post-Holocaust critics point to the words of Hitler prior to the genocidal actions against Jews and Gypsies. There are indeed haunting and frightening similarities between what Hitler said he would do to the Jews and what many Islamic leaders are now saying they intend to do to the Jews, the Americans, and the heathens. Listen to their words: Dr. Atallah Abu al-Sabh, a columnist for the Hamas newspaper, wrote, discussing anthrax, "If I may give you a word of advice, enter the air of those 'symbols' [America and Israel], the water faucets from which they drink, and the pens with which they draft their traps and conspiracies against the wretched peoples. . . . Turn the bodies of the tyrants into matches burning slowly and gradually." Sheikh Omar Bakri Muhammad, the London-based founder of the Hizb al-Tahrir (Islamic Liberation Party), said in an interview: "American people must reconsider their foreign policy or their children will be sent back to them in coffins [especially because of the stationing of troops in the Middle East]. . . . [The existence of Israel] is a crime. Israel must be removed. . . . Our duty is to work to establish an Islamic state anywhere in the world, even in Britain." Muhammad Mustagab, in his column for the Egyptian newspaper *Al-Usbu',* described his reaction to watching the World Trade Center towers fall: "[Those moments of] exquisite, incandescent hell were the most beautiful and precious moments of my life. . . . The generations of the past, and, with Allah's help, the generations to come, will envy us for having witnessed [these images]." There is more, much more, easily accessible to those who want to read these threats.[1]

Evil people do not always do what they threaten. Many statements similar to those quoted above have ended up in the waste bin of history, but we cannot be certain, now, whether the statements made by radical Islamic leaders fall into the "Hitler" or the "waste bin" category. We know that these statements reflect the views of millions of radical Muslims—perhaps even tens of millions. We also know that they do not reflect the views of hundreds of millions of other Muslims. We also know that some radical Islamic leaders and followers are capable of slaughtering large civilian populations, including children, women, and elderly, as they have done in Algeria, and other places.

I believe there is a small but significant possibility that Islamic radicals could succeed in killing hundreds of thousands—perhaps even more—Americans and Israelis. If they manage to secure access to weapons of mass destruction, I have little doubt there will be some who would try to use them against New York, Los Angeles, Washington, D.C., or Tel Aviv. They have told us as much, and we should take them at their word.[2] Whether they succeed or fail will depend on many factors, including our preparedness to prevent such an attack. It may also depend somewhat on dumb luck. We can do little about the latter, but we can do much about the former.

Since we are not prophets, we must try our best to strike the appropriate balances without knowing what the future holds. In striking these balances, we must never forget our deep commitment to liberty, equality, and the rule of law. We must not allow the terrorists to win either by destroying us or by destroying what we stand for. It will not be easy.

Although we are not prophets, we can do a far better job of protecting ourselves against potential future attacks by considerably expanding and diversifying the base of the people now working on this issue. The Bush administration has limited the personnel assigned to terrorism prevention to a close-knit in-house team. President Bush appointed a family friend, who lacks relevant experience, to be in charge of domestic security. Others in the inner circle reflect a relatively narrow range of backgrounds. At least two additional groups of individuals should be added to the mix.

First, we need to have a better understanding of exactly what went wrong before September 11 that allowed terrorists to wreak so much damage with so few people, such primitive weapons, and so little money. How did these determined zealots make it through our multilayered security system without a single one of them getting caught? Or, if one did get caught, why did his detention not trigger action that might have foiled the plot?[3] Why did we not take seriously the warnings from Philippine security agents that al-Qaeda was planning to crash airplanes into buildings? Why was there no adequate coordination of the Philippine warning with the CIA warning in August 2001 about possible airline hijackings by Osama bin Laden, with the FBI warning in July 2001 about a possible bin Laden plan to train Middle Eastern terrorists at American flight schools, with the earlier French information about a terrorist plot to fly a plane into the Eiffel Tower, and with the detention of a man with al-Qaeda connections who was trying to learn how to fly, but not land, a commercial airliner? Who in our intelligence community, our immigration service, our airport security network, and our other institutions was at fault? Are these people still responsible for protecting us? The time has come, indeed it is long past, for finger-pointing and blame-assessing, not for purposes of recrimination, but rather for purposes of avoiding recurrence.

For this reason we urgently need a blue-ribbon commission of inquiry, composed of distinguished citizens outside politics, to assess blame and recommend change. We convened the Roberts Commission following Pearl Harbor; the British had royal commissions of inquiry following preventable disasters in their country; the Israelis set up such a commission following the surprise attack on Yom Kippur in 1973. Now we must do the same. The Roberts Commission concluded that a general and an admiral were guilty of dereliction of duty and recommended their discharge and replacement. These conclusions did not undercut our united front against the Axis powers. Comparable conclusions regarding September 11 would be no more likely to undermine our efforts. We need to know everything that went wrong in the past in order to avoid repetition—or worse.

Second, we can also borrow from our successful experience in World War II by recruiting the nation's—indeed the world's— smartest and most experienced scientists, technicians, weapons experts, and others to develop longer-range approaches to dealing with global terrorism, especially regarding its potential use of nuclear, biological, and chemical weapons. After Pearl Harbor we brought together some of the world's most distinguished scientists for the Manhattan Project, which culminated in the development of the atomic bomb by our country before Germany, which already had a superior delivery system, could develop its own. We took advantage of the expertise we had as the result of so many brilliant scientists having left Nazi Germany. We also organized some of the nation's brightest people to crack the enemy's codes and to make our own less subject to enemy interception.

We must do the same today. We cannot limit the intelligence

being deployed in our effort to combat terrorism to one adminis-tration, one party, or one group of people. This is a critical national and international problem, with grave potential for many more deaths and serious damage to our nation. We must expand the base of those working on it to include people from the universities and from the private business sector, both in this country and among our allies.

This administration seems to distrust outsiders, especially academics, scientists, and intellectuals. It seems to lack the self-confidence to acknowledge that it could benefit from the wisdom, intelligence, and experience of people who may not have voted for it. But this must truly be a *non*-partisan—as distinguished from a bipartisan—effort. It must extend beyond Republican and Democratic politicians and include anyone who can contribute to the antiterrorism effort.

We have seen that politics and security as usual did not pre-vent the most massive terrorist attack in history, but we do not seem to have learned much from this lesson. We need to start thinking outside the boxes that failed us, but without becoming like those who attacked us.

Notes

Introduction

1. Philip B. Heymann, *Terrorism and America* (Cambridge: MIT Press, 2000), p. 2. Most notes have been condensed at the ends of paragraphs.
2. On capturing media attention, Heymann writes: "Terrorism is best understood as an effort to speak to audiences with a greatly amplified voice. Duration is as important as volume for conveying a message and creating the public concerns that can move the government. Holding hostages keeps the story in the lead of television news and on the front pages of newspapers throughout the country for a far more sustained period of time than any terrorist action except a far more difficult extended campaign of bombings. The holding of American hostages in Lebanon following the hijacking of TWA Flight 847 in 1985 captured the headlines for weeks. Even our largest corporations could not have afforded to buy similar access to the American people. Speaking of this hijacking, the State Department Legal Advisor Abraham Sofaer said, 'The hijackers sought publicity, and they got it. The world was treated to a media extravaganza that gave irresponsibility and tastelessness a new meaning.' Tom Brokaw, NBC News anchor, and his ABC counterpart, Peter Jennings, agreed that the press had served the terrorists' purposes too well." Ibid., p. 37.

   "Propaganda by the deed" is from David Rapoport, "Fear and Trembling: Terrorism in Three Religious Traditions," *American Political Science Review,* vol. 78, no. 3 (1984), p. 660.
3. It *is* necessary to articulate unambiguous definitions when the word is used in legislation or other formal contexts in which serious consequences may flow from designating persons or acts as "terrorist." In creating any such definition, it is important to recognize several different components, each of which operates along a continuum and overlaps the others. These may include:

   a. the *nature of the group* engaging in, or supporting, the violence—is it a government, an army, a movement (with or without government backing), a religious group, a small group (gang, drug cartel), or even an individual (the Unabomber)?

   b. the *nature of the targets and victims*—are they military, diplomatic, police, occupiers, citizens of an enemy nation, co-religionists, children, randomly selected? Are the targets relatively small (a bus, a restaurant) or large (a building or an entire city)?

   c. the *means* selected—are those who carry out the violence trying to survive or are they suicide bombers?

   d. the *goals* to be achieved by the violence—is the goal specific and limited (the freeing of prisoners), broad (the establishment of a state or the recognition of a movement), or unspecified and unlimited (the end of Western domination over Islam)? Is the goal religious, political, or some combination?

e. the *mechanism* for achieving the goals—are the victims expected to respond by giving in to specific demands, by overreacting and denying civil liberties, by taking military action, by becoming terrorized and frightened, by destabilizing the economy, or by a combination of the above?

It may also be important to acknowledge that not all terrorism is a matter of degree. Certain genres of terrorism are so far along the continuum as to warrant universal condemnation. These include deliberate targeting of innocent noncombatants based on their religion, race, or nationality, as well as targeting random civilians who happen to be in a given place at a given time. These genres of terrorism can be distinguished from the targeting of military personnel, collateral killing of noncombatants during a legitimate military operation, and other uses of violence that may belong on a continuum of terrorism, but closer to the end that may not warrant universal condemnation. The most difficult genre of violence to distinguish is the deliberate *military* targeting of entirely civilian population centers, such as the dropping of atomic bombs on Hiroshima and Nagasaki, as well as the firebombing of Dresden. These military actions were undertaken in an effort to end aggressive wars and in response to the targeting of civilians by the enemy, but the intent and result—the deliberate targeting of many innocent noncombatants—is essentially the same.

4. Several Palestinian groups have worked closely with neo-Nazi groups over the years. It is widely believed that the destruction of a Jewish community center in Buenos Aires in 1994 was the work of such a combination. Conversation with Argentine law enforcement official, February 2002. See also Peter Ford, "Israel Blames Hizbullah for Argentine Bombing; With Nazi Investigation Files Located in Bombed Building, Israelis also Consider Possibility of Nazi Role," *Christian Science Monitor,* 7/20/1994.

5. The ancient Israelites, according to the Book of Joshua, "utterly destroyed all that was in [Jericho, which had already fallen to a siege], both man and woman, young and old, and ox, and sheep, and ass, with the edge of a sword." Roman rulers used terrorism to bring stability to their empire, including the gruesome public executions of Christians. The Mongols, infamous for their terror tactics in warfare, were known to annihilate the entire populations of cities.

6. A brilliant study of three religious traditions by Professor David Rapoport of UCLA compared three early terrorist groups. The first was a Hindu

group called the Thugs, or Thugees. This group, which operated for centuries, may have killed hundreds of thousands of victims, one at a time. They used strangulation and focused on specific categories of victims while exempting others. They seem to have had no political agenda. Murder for them was a cleansing activity inspired by somewhat bizarre religious beliefs. A second group, known as the Assassins, was an Islamic group whose name is rooted in the word "hashish." They were called "hashashin," which literally means hashish eaters. They too assassinated specific targeted leaders by planting loyal followers in their midst who waited years for the proper opportunity to strike. They were suicide killers whose use of the dagger "seems designed to make certain that he will be captured and killed." And there is even a suggestion that "to survive a mission was shameful." The third group, called the Zealots-Sicarii, was of Jewish origin and lasted only twenty-five years during the Roman occupation of Judea. Rapoport discusses the primitive nature of the weapons used—the noose, the dagger, and the sword—and points out that even such retail, one-on-one killing could add up over the centuries. Each Thug averaged three murders annually, but one claimed to have helped strangle nine hundred victims. Rapoport, "Fear and Trembling," pp. 658–75.

7. Massimo Calabresi and Romesh Ratnesar, "Can We Stop the Next Attack?" *Time,* 3/11/2002, pp. 25–28. Diagrams of U.S. nuclear facilities were also found in al-Qaeda camps.

Heymann points out: "Nor is political violence new to the United States. We have lost four presidents and two senators to assassination. We have also had our share of famous bombings, including the Haymarket Square bombing in 1886; the *Los Angeles Times* bombing in 1910; the San Francisco Preparedness Day bombing in 1916; and the Wall Street bombing in 1920. And we have had groups such as the Ku Klux Klan dedicated for decades to terrorizing an important segment of our population—black Americans." Heymann, *Terrorism and America,* p. 3.

8. Ehud Sprinzak, "The Lone Gunmen: The Global War on Terrorism Faces a New Brand of Enemy," *Foreign Policy,* Nov.–Dec. 2001, pp. 72–73.

9. Two examples of brilliant experts who have reconsidered some earlier views regarding terrorism are Ehud Sprinzak and Philip Heymann. Sprinzak has found the old model inadequate, with its premise that leaders use terrorism ultimately to achieve political goals. Now, Sprinzak has said experts also must look at the "megalomaniac terrorist." Heymann had previously focused primarily on the retail, tactical use of terrorism to achieve specific political goals, rather than on global, apocalyptic terrorism. He argued that the priority in confronting terrorism is to preserve social unity and individual liberty. Benjamin Netanyahu's book *Fighting Terrorism* (New York: Farrar, Straus and Giroux, 1995) focused on state sponsorship, the anti-Western motives of radical Islamic groups, and the need

to move swiftly to close down terror networks. His prescient strategy is the one being adopted in the current war on terror. For other examples of pre–September 11 scholarship see *Western Responses to Terrorism,* edited by Alex P. Schmid and Ronald D. Crelinsten (London: Frank Cass, 1993); Paul Wilkinson, *Terrorism and the Liberal State,* 2d edition (New York: New York University Press, 1986); *The Terrorism Reader: A Historical Anthology,* rev. edition, edited by Walter Laqueur and Yonah Alexander (New York: NAL Penguin, 1987); Paul Wilkinson, *Terrorism Versus Democracy: The Liberal State Response* (London: Frank Cass, 2000).

Chapter 1: Deterring Terrorism

1. Inevitably, incapacitation generally does change behavior. Animals may become more docile in cages, whereas some human beings become more violent in prison.
2. See Dick Lehr and Gerard O'Neill, *Black Mass: The Irish Mob, the FBI, and a Devil's Deal* (New York: Public Affairs, 2000).
3. "In Bush's Words: 'Break Free of Old Patterns,'" *New York Times,* 4/5/2002.
4. In this age of sophisticated instant communication, exile—even imprisonment—does not always assure total incapacitation.
5. Sometimes it may be the self-interest of individuals acting on behalf of the state. Businesses, like states, are also thought to act based on rational self-interest. Thus, the decision whether to prosecute companies like Arthur Andersen or Enron and their executives is based at least in part on the expected impact on other businesses and executives. It is no coincidence that high-profile indictments of tax violators are often announced around April 15.
6. Quoted in Oriana Fallaci, "A Leader of the Fedayeen: 'We Want a War Like Vietnam,'" *Life,* 6/12/1970, p. 34.
7. Heymann, *Terrorism and America,* pp. 7–8.
8. The failure of the Jewish Defense League was largely a function of its inability ever to generate support among Jews, even those who supported the causes of Soviet Jewry, for its use of anti-Soviet terrorism. See Alan M. Dershowitz, *The Best Defense* (New York: Random House, 1982), chapter 1.
9. Quoted in Bruce Hoffmann, *Inside Terrorism* (New York: Columbia University Press, 1998), p. 68.
10. To argue that terrorism has worked in particular situations is not necessarily to conclude that other means would not have been more successful.

The Palestinian resort to terrorism has worked in that it has attracted world attention to its cause and made it inevitable that a Palestinian state of some kind will eventually become a reality. But I believe that had the Palestinians resorted instead to nonviolent civil disobedience tactics, such as those of Mohandas Gandhi and Martin Luther King, they would have achieved statehood sooner. The critical point, for purposes of deterring and disincentivizing terrorism, is not what I (or Thomas Friedman) may believe, but rather what those who opt for terrorism believe. And there can be little doubt that Palestinians who have opted for terrorism believe that it has made a Palestinian state inevitable.

11. Benjamin Netanyahu has written: "It is instructive to note, for example, that the French Resistance during World War II did not resort to the systematic killing of German women and children, although these were well within reach in occupied France. But in Cambodia, the Khmer Rouge showed no such restraint in their war against what they saw as the American-supported occupation. France, of course, is today a democracy; Cambodia is merely another one of the many despotisms where terrorists have come to power—and where they proceeded to carry out some of the most ghoulish crimes committed against humanity since World War II." Netanyahu, *Fighting Terrorism,* pp. 9–10, 52.

12. The vast majority of groups with just causes have not resorted to terrorism. Nor have poverty-stricken groups historically turned to terrorism. Indeed, terrorism has been more closely associated with elite groups promoting questionable causes. In the minds of many, the terrorism itself is what has elevated the cause.

13. "'Please let me go. I am looking forward to face the enemy to avenge the blood of my people and to satisfy Allah,' a Palestinian militant wrote to his leaders, begging to be sent on a suicide bombing mission to Israel. . . . 'I cannot wait to go,' another militant told Reuters this week at an Islamic Jihad rally where would-be suicide bombers, dressed in white, vowed attacks against the Jewish state." Nidal al-Mughrabi, "Palestine: Analysis—Israeli Drive Seen Spurring Suicide," Reuters, 4/3/2002.

"Nasser is every Israeli's nightmare: a man who wants nothing more than to strap explosives on his chest, slip into the Jewish state and blow himself up, taking with him as many of the enemy as possible. . . . 'I am ready now, tomorrow and every time because we have territory occupied by Israel,' he said in a telephone interview arranged by Hezbollah. 'We are believers, deep believers.'" Michael Slackman, "Islamic Debate Surrounds Mideast Suicide Bombers Violence: Some Militant Groups Use Religion as a Rationale," *Los Angeles Times,* 5/27/01.

14. According to Netanyahu, the kind of terrorism we are talking about is always state supported. "There is *no* international terrorism without the support of sovereign states. International terrorism simply cannot be sustained

for long without the regimes that aid and abet it. Terrorists are not suspended in midair. They train, arm, and indoctrinate their killers from within safe havens on territory provided by terrorist states. Often these regimes provide the terrorists with intelligence, money, and operational assistance, dispatching them to serve as deadly proxies to wage a hidden war against more powerful enemies." Netanyahu, *Fighting Terrorism,* p. xiii.

15. Hoffman, *Inside Terrorism,* p. 74.

16. Philip Heymann sees the paradox a bit differently: "There is an inherent potential for conflict between efforts to reduce people's willingness to support a terrorist group and efforts to avoid making concessions that might make terrorism look like a useful tactic. Dealing constructively with the grievances of those who would form the natural allies of the terrorist group, because they would be most sympathetic to its cause, discourages support within the broader population of potential allies. But any action of this sort may also appear to be prompted by the terrorist attacks. If so, the credit and loyalty may go to the terrorist group, creating the least desired effect." Heymann, *Terrorism and America,* p. 103.

Chapter 2: The Internationalization of Terrorism

1. Hoffman, *Inside Terrorism,* p. 67.

2. Zehdi Labib Terzi, quoted ibid., p. 68. Whether this was the ultimate or penultimate goal is not essential to this analysis.

3. Hoffman, *Inside Terrorism,* p. 68.

4. Even before 1948, Palestinians had used violence as a tactic against the British and the Jews in 1920, 1921, 1929, and 1936–38. In 1929, for example, a Palestinian mob killed fifty-nine Jews in Hebron, where Jews had lived for centuries, long before even the Zionist movement. Many of the victims were beaten and stabbed to death.

5. Quoted in Hoffman, *Inside Terrorism,* p. 70.

6. Web site of al-Shindagah, Dubai, "Woman of Distinction: The Leila Khaled Story," July–Aug. 2001, http://alshindagah.com/july2001/.

7. Fallaci, "A Leader of the Fedayeen," p. 34.

8. Associated Press, "Germany Pursues Palestinian Guerrilla," *Toronto Star,* 6/12/1999; al-Shameli quoted in Hoffman, *Inside Terrorism,* p. 71.

9. Ariel Merari and Shlomi Elad, *The International Dimension of Palestinian Terrorism,* JCSS Study no. 6 (Boulder, Colo.: Westview, 1986), pp. 86–87.

10. Simon Reeve, *One Day in September* (New York: Arcade, 2000), pp. 228, 236, 238. A detailed analysis of the botched rescue effort appears at pp. 105–24.

11. See ibid., p. 158, citing Jamal al-Gashey, one of the terrorists responsible for the Munich massacre, and Ulrich Wagener, the founder of the elite German antiterrorist unit GSG-9 (p. 59).
12. The Israelis also assassinated several terrorists responsible for planning the Munich massacre. They also mistook an innocent waiter for one of the terrorists and killed him. Several Israelis served prison sentences for that killing.
13. Reeve, *One Day in September,* p. 158. Several years later France captured but quickly released the mastermind of the Munich massacre (p. 210).
14. Hoffman, *Inside Terrorism,* p. 73.
15. Ibid., p. 74.
16. George Jonas, "Murder Plot Haunts Arafat; Veil of Secrecy Finally Lifts on Tapes Linking Him to Slayings of U.S. Diplomats," *Chicago Sun-Times,* 1/29/2002.
17. Debbie Schlussel, "Arafat's Congressman Buddy," TownHall.com, 4/3/2002; Ion Mihai Pacepa, "The Arafat I Know," *Wall Street Journal,* 1/20/2002.
18. Hoffman, *Inside Terrorism,* p. 75.
19. Palestinian advocates of international terrorism argue that before they resorted to hijackings and mass murder of civilians "world opinion had been neither for nor against the Palestinians." Palestinian claims did not enjoy the high status they currently enjoy on the hierarchy of international grievances. What Palestinian advocates of terrorism do not acknowledge is that, on any objective scale of victimization, the Palestinian cause was just about where it belonged on its merits and demerits. It certainly was not more serious than the plight of numerous other groups that were suffering greater deprivations, such as the Kurds, the Armenians, the Basques, and the Tartars. The Palestinians leapfrogged all the other groups in having their grievances placed at the forefront of international concerns *largely* because they were the first to resort to international terrorism on a large scale. The success of their terrorist tactic is proved by the fact that many readers of this book will be incredulous at my claim that, by any objectively reasonable standard of ranking grievances, the Palestinians' does not deserve to be ranked at a high level. We have become so accustomed to hearing—from the United Nations, religious leaders, prominent academics, and diplomats—that the moral claims of the Palestinians dwarf those of other groups, that we have come to accept this exaggeration as part of the conventional wisdom.

    Other groups with claims comparable to or even greater than those of the Palestinians have considered resorting to terrorism because they have seen how it helped the Palestinian cause. Bruce Hoffman has observed:

> In recent years, for example, Kurds fighting for autonomy in south-eastern Turkey have debated whether to adopt the Palestinian model for their own struggle. To date, the Kurdish Workers Party (PKK) has for the most part eschewed *international* terrorism as means to advance its nationalist claims, concentrating instead on an internal campaign of rural guerrilla warfare coupled with occasional acts of urban terrorism inside Turkey only. But their failure to win the international attention and stature that other, similar movements such as the PLO enjoy has reportedly led to increasing discontent among younger Kurdish militants. "Proponents of terrorism," one account noted, argue that "the Palestinians have embassies in more than 100 countries while the Kurds, a far larger minority, have none." Accordingly, they press for the adoption of an aggressive campaign of international terrorism—against the advice of their more moderate elders, who argue that such a strategy would ultimately deprive their cause of both credibility and international sympathy. The debate has yet to be resolved.

Hoffman, *Inside Terrorism,* p. 79.

An assessment of the comparative justice of the Palestinian cause and the causes of those who have not resorted to global terrorism is beyond the scope of this book, but one can be found in Alan M. Dershowitz, *Chutzpah* (Boston: Little, Brown, 1991), chapter 7.

20. One person, peripherally involved, was captured in international waters and was tried and convicted by the United States. Another was tried and convicted in Germany. Heymann, *Terrorism and America,* p. 37.

21. Ibid., pp. 21, 23, 33.

22. John F. Burns, "Palestinian Summer Camps Offer the Games of War," *New York Times,* 8/3/2000; Jeff Jacoby, "Summer Camps Full of Hate. A Web Site Calling for Nonstop Terrorism. And More Than That: Schoolbooks That Preach Violence Against Jews. Kids' TV Shows That Glorify Suicide Bombers," *Boston Globe,* 8/13/1998; Ariel Jerozolimiski, "Islamic Jihad Is Running Four Camps in the Gaza Strip at Which Eight- to 12-Year-Olds Learn the Importance of Becoming a Suicide Bomber," *Jerusalem Post,* 7/20/2001.

23. Fallaci, "A Leader of the Fedayeen," p. 34.

24. Alan M. Dershowitz, "Let the PLO Hold an Inquiry on Anti-Jewish Terrorism," *International Herald Tribune,* 10/19/1982.

25. Victor L. Simpson, "John Paul Visits Refugee Camp with Arafat," *St. Louis Post-Dispatch,* 3/23/2000.

26. Editorial, "A Poor Change of Subject," *Washington Post,* 3/29/2002.

27. Hoffman, *Inside Terrorism,* pp. 74–75.
28. Seumas Milne, "Hijacker Back in Britain on Campaign Trail," *Guardian* (London), 1/25/2001.
29. *Al-Ayyam* (Palestinian Authority), 12/6/2000, translated by and quoted in Middle East Media Research Institute, Special Dispatch Series, no. 194, 3/9/2001, http://memri.info/.
30. Thomas L. Friedman, "Suicidal Lies," *New York Times,* 3/31/2002.
31. Judith Miller, "In Interview, Arafat's Wife Praises Suicide Bombing," *New York Times,* 4/15/2002.
32. Ibid.
33. Charles Krauthammer, "Arafat's Harvest of Hate," *Washington Post,* 3/26/2002; Tovah Lazaroff, "PA Violating Children's Rights Covenant," *Jerusalem Post,* 3/12/2002.

    A Saudi daily newspaper published the following story, written by a professor at a Saudi university, which claims that Jews make pastries out of Arab and Christian blood for their celebration of Purim, in March 2002.

> For this holiday, the Jewish people must obtain human blood so that their clerics can prepare the holiday pastries. In other words, the practice cannot be carried out as required if human blood is not spilled!!
>
> Before I go into the details, I would like to clarify that the Jews' spilling human blood to prepare pastry for their holidays is a well-established fact, historically and legally, all throughout history. This was one of the main reasons for the persecution and exile that were their lot in Europe and Asia at various times. . . .
>
> For this holiday, the victim must be a mature adolescent who is, of course, a non-Jew—that is, a Christian or a Muslim. His blood is taken and dried into granules. The cleric blends these granules into the pastry dough; they can also be saved for the next holiday. In contrast, for the Passover slaughtering, about which I intend to write one of these days, the blood of Christian and Muslim children under the age of 10 must be used, and the cleric can mix the blood [into the dough] before or after dehydration.
>
> Let us now examine how the victims' blood is spilled. For this, a needle-studded barrel is used; this is a kind of barrel, about the size of the human body, with extremely sharp needles set in it on all sides. [These needles] pierce the victim's body, from the moment he is placed in the barrel.

These needles do the job, and the victim's blood drips from him very slowly. Thus, the victim suffers dreadful torment—torment that affords the Jewish vampires great delight as they carefully monitor every detail of the bloodshedding with pleasure and love that are difficult to comprehend.

After this barbaric display, the Jews take the spilled blood, in the bottle set in the bottom [of the needle-studded barrel], and the Jewish cleric makes his coreligionists completely happy on their holiday when he serves them the pastries in which human blood is mixed.

There is another way to spill the blood: The victim can be slaughtered as a sheep is slaughtered, and his blood collected in a container. Or, the victim's veins can be slit in several places, letting his blood drain from his body.

This blood is very carefully collected—as I have already noted—by the "rabbi," the Jewish cleric, the chef who specializes in preparing these kinds of pastries.

Dr. Umayma Ahmad al-Jalahma, *Al-Riyadh* (Saudi Arabia), 3/10/2002, translated and quoted in the Middle East Media Research Institute, Special Dispatch Series, no. 354, 3/13/2002, http://memri.org/.

34. Joel Brinkley, "Arabs' Grief in Bethlehem, Bombers' Gloating in Gaza: Hamas Spirits Soar," *New York Times,* 4/4/2002.
35. James Bennet, "U.N. Chief Tells Israel It Must End 'Illegal Occupation,'" *New York Times,* 3/13/2002. For an analysis of why the occupation is not illegal, see George Fletcher, "Annan's Careless Language," *New York Times,* 3/21/2002.
36. James Bennet, "Arafat's Edge: Violence and Time on His Side," *New York Times,* 3/18/2002; Serge Schmemann, "Hope Rises for a Mideast Truce, Despite Attacks," *New York Times,* 3/18/2002.
37. A particularly egregious example of false moral equivalency is the speech of the Syrian representative to the U.N. Security Council on January 18, 2002, comparing the Israel demolition of empty houses in Gaza to the murder of nearly three thousand innocent people in the terrorist attacks of September 11, 2001. Serge Schmemann, "Syrian at U.N. Compares Israeli Actions to the Sept. 11 Attack," *New York Times,* 1/19/2002.
38. Hoffman, *Inside Terrorism,* p. 36.
39. A diplomat observing the Arab League meeting in Beirut on March 28, 2002, quoted in James Bennet, "Two-Edged Diplomacy," *New York Times,* 3/29/2002; Thomas L. Friedman, "The Hard Truth," *New York Times,* 4/3/2002.

40. Hoffman, *Inside Terrorism,* p. 174.

41. "U.S. Names Briton as Suspect in Pearl's Kidnapping," *Independent* (London), 2/7/2002; al-Shindagah, "Woman of Distinction: The Leila Khaled Story."

42. Michael R. Gordon, "U.S. Is Given Papers That Israelis Assert Tie Arafat to Terror," *New York Times,* 4/12/2002.

43. Quoted in Matthew Kalman, "Terrorist Says Orders Come from Arafat," *USA Today,* 3/14/2002.

44. Thomas L. Friedman, "The Core of Muslim Rage," *New York Times,* 3/6/2002.

45. The Basques, who live primarily along the Spanish-French border in the western Pyrenees mountains, have long struggled to achieve some measure of autonomy. They enjoyed a degree of independence during the Spanish Civil War, but suffered brutal repression during Francisco Franco's reign. It was also under Franco that the Basque terrorist group ETA was created, after a group of college students decided, in July 1959, that more dramatic action was necessary. Initial terrorist acts—including the murder of a Spanish police chief—brought swift reprisal from Franco's government, yet the ETA survived, and in December 1973 it had its greatest success with the assassination of Luis Carrero Blanco, the Spanish prime minister and Franco's designated successor. Once Franco died and democracy started to take hold in Spain, support for the ETA dropped: it was viewed less as a band of freedom fighters struggling against Franco's repression and more as a terrorist organization opposing a democratic government. The Spanish government, meanwhile, gradually moved to grant the Basques more autonomy. In 1979 it offered, and the Basque people accepted, the establishment of a Basque legislature that would have significant governing authority over the region. At the same time, the government (joined at last by the French government) cracked down on the ETA, imprisoning hundreds of its members. Terrorist attacks nonetheless continue, including the bombing of a Barcelona store in 1994, which killed twenty-one people; the bombing of the car of José María Aznar, who was then opposition leader and later became prime minister, in 1995; and the assassination of a Socialist Party leader in 1996. Meanwhile, ETA's political front, Herri Batasuna—which at one point garnered enough support to earn a seat in the European Parliament—continues to advocate the creation of an independent Basque state.

46. The offer of a Palestinian state in 1948 was made despite the fact that the Palestinian leadership supported Nazi Germany during World War II, and groups that support the losing side generally do not get rewarded with statehood.

    Palestinians did, of course, complain about the refugees that had left their homes during the Arab-initiated war of 1948. But there were millions of other refugees with equal or more pressing claims who did not resort to terrorism: "For example, following the end of World War II, approximately fifteen million ethnic Germans were forcibly expelled from their homes in Poland, Czechoslovakia, Hungary, Romania, Yugoslavia, and other Central Eastern European areas where their families had lived for centuries. Two million died during this forced expulsion. Czechoslovakia alone expelled nearly three million Sudeten Germans, turning them into displaced persons. The United States, Great Britain, and the international community in general approved these expulsions, as necessary to secure a more lasting peace." Dershowitz, *Chutzpah*, pp. 215–17.

For a useful analysis of the Palestinians' history between 1948 and 1967, see David Harris, "Questions for Arabs to Answer Israel," *International Herald Tribune*, 3/22/2002.

47. Friedman, "The Core of Muslim Rage"; Fallaci, "A Leader of the Fedayeen," p. 33.

48. Hoffman, *Inside Terrorism*, p. 78.

49. Ibid., p. 79.

50. Another terrorist group that had difficulty even gaining substantial attention (certainly in the United States) was the Free South Moluccan Organization (FSMO). On behalf of some fifteen thousand South Moluccans who had immigrated to the Netherlands after the Republic of the South Moluccas was absorbed by Indonesia in the early 1960s, the FSMO carried out attacks on a Dutch train and schoolhouse. While the incidents garnered more attention for the Moluccan cause that it would have had without them, "in the end this exposure did nothing to advance their cause or bring them any closer to obtaining their nationalist goals." Ibid.

51. Heymann, *Terrorism and America*, p. xix.

52. Brinkley, "Arabs' Grief in Bethlehem, Bombers' Gloating in Gaza: Hamas Spirits Soar."

53. Shibley Telhami, "Why Suicide Terrorism Takes Root," *New York Times*, 4/4/2002.

54. A detailed description and discussion of the prisoner's dilemma can be found in the on-line Stanford Encyclopedia of Philosophy, http://plato.stanford.edu/entries/prisoner-dilemma/.

55. The reason organized-crime conspiracies have traditionally been harder to prosecute than white-collar conspiracies is that in the former there are self-serving reasons not to cooperate, even if cooperation is rewarded by a shorter sentence. It may also be punished by a bullet in the head.

Chapter 3: How an Amoral Society Could Fight Terrorism

1. For an example of how China has succeeded in suppressing information about terrorism within its borders, see "International Data Reference on Terrorist, Guerilla, and Insurgent Groups: Asia, Indo China, and the Pacific Rim," http://www.dialog.com/fastways/terrorism_in_china.htm. Successful suppression of such information is, of course, generally impossible to document—at least contemporaneously. See also Paul Wilkinson, "The Media and Terrorism: A Reassessment," http://www.st-and.ac.uk/academic/intrel/research/cstpv/publications1c.htm.

2. On February 27, 1933, the German Parliament building (the Reichstag) burned down. Marinus van der Lubbe, a Dutchman, was arrested and charged with arson. (Later, he was found guilty and executed.)

    Some historians believe that van der Lubbe was not actually responsible for the Reichstag fire. Rather, such writers as Klaus P. Fischer believe that the Nazis were most likely involved in setting the fire to create an incident that would justify limiting citizens' rights, while Walter Hofer of Bern suggests that the fire was set by the SA/SS Sondergruppe under the leadership of Reinhard Heydrich and an official of the Prussian Ministry of the Interior, Kurt Daluege.

    Historians concur, however, that regardless of who set the fire, the Nazis "took advantage of the situation to advance their cause at the expense of civil rights." Orville R. Weyrich, Jr., "Reichstag Fire," http://www.weyrich.com/political_issues/. By dawn the morning after the fire, "over 4,000 communists and a miscellany of intellectuals and professional men who had incurred the wrath of the Nazi Party were arrested. A shaken President Hindenburg, 86 years old, was easily convinced that the nation was on the verge of a communist revolution, [and] was induced by Hitler to sign an emergency decree suspending the basic rights of the citizens for the duration of the emergency." Soren Swigart, "The Reichstag Fire," The World at War, http://worldatwar.net/event/reichstagsbrand/.

    The Decree on the Protection of People and State abrogated free expression of opinion, freedom of the press, the right of assembly and association, the right to privacy of postal and electronic communications, protection against unlawful searches and seizures, individual property rights, and states' right of self-government. A supplemental decree also made the SA (Storm Troops) and SS (Special Security) federal police agencies. The decree "also authorized the Reich government to assume full powers in any federal state whose government proved unable to restore public order, [and] ordered death or imprisonment for a number of crimes including some newly invented such as resistance to the decree itself. The decree did not include any provision guaranteeing an arrested person a quick hearing, access to legal counsel, or redress for false arrest.

Those arrested often found their detention extended indefinitely without legal proceedings of any kind....

"[T]he decree of February 28th established what would become the normal order of things under National Socialism—arrest on suspicion, imprisonment without trial, the horrors of the concentration camps. This condition ... persist[ed] until the end of the Third Reich." Swigart, "The Reichstag Fire."

3. The FBI's domestic counterintelligence program was code named COIN-TELPRO. Its purpose, in the words of then–FBI director J. Edgar Hoover, was to "expose, disrupt, misdirect, discredit and otherwise neutralize" specific groups and individuals. A history of the program by Mike Cassidy and Will Miller goes on: "Its targets in this period included the American Indian Movement, the Communist Party, the Socialist Worker's Party, Black Nationalist groups, and many members of the New Left (SDS, and a broad range of anti-war, anti-racist, feminist, lesbian and gay, environmentalist and other groups). Many other groups and individuals seeking racial, gender and class justice were targets who came under attack, including Martin Luther King, Cesar Chavez, the NAACP, the National Lawyer's Guild, SANE-Freeze, American Friends Service Committee, and many, many others." Frequently, COINTELPRO relied on psychological warfare as a way to discredit and pressure local groups. "They planted false media stories and published bogus leaflets and other publications in the name of targeted groups. They forged correspondence, sent anonymous letters, and made anonymous telephone calls. They spread misinformation about meetings and events, set up pseudo movement groups run by agents, and manipulated or strong-armed parents, employers, landlords, school officials and others to cause trouble for activists." Mike Cassidy and Will Miller, "A Short History of FBI COINTELPRO," http://www.monitor.net/monitor/9905a/jbcointelpro.html.

COINTELPRO was not the only disinformation program the United States was involved in. In 1986, journalist Bob Woodward reported that the Reagan administration had conducted a disinformation program "designed to unnerve Libyan leader Moammar Gadhafi." Woodward based his claim on a memo by National Security Adviser John Poindexter "outlining a strategy that 'combines real and illusionary events—through a disinformation program—with the basic goal of making Gadhafi think there is a high degree of internal opposition to him within Libya, that his key trusted aides were disloyal, that the United States is about to move against him militarily.'" This disinformation plan included having "a Poindexter aide [talk] to a Wall Street Journal reporter and the result was a front-page story falsely reporting that the administration was completing plans for 'a new and larger bombing of Libya,' after finding new evidence that Gadhafi had again 'begun plotting terrorist attacks.' The day it was published, [Reagan's press spokesman Larry] Speakes told reporters the Journal report was 'authoritative' and other media, including the Post and the major networks, carried similarly inaccurate stories." David S. Broder, "How Press Secrecy Backfired on Reagan," *Washington Post,* 3/22/87.

4. An article in the *Washington Post* described the FBI's actions in the Moussaoui case:

> FBI investigators in Minneapolis wanted to seek a criminal search warrant to inspect the laptop. But during often heated debates from Aug. 18 to 20, officials at headquarters opposed the request, arguing that investigators could not show probable cause that a crime had been committed.
>
> The FBI counsel in the Minneapolis office concurred, according to one senior official, arguing that the U.S. attorney's office there would be unlikely to grant approval.
>
> The investigator's other option was a Foreign Intelligence Surveillance Authority warrant, which allows the FBI to conduct surveillance and searches on people who are believed to be agents of a foreign power or of a recognized terrorist group such as al-Qaida.
>
> The problem, senior U.S. law enforcement officials said, was that investigators had no reliable evidence that Moussaoui was connected to any group designated a terrorist organization by the State Department. Requests for information from Britain, where Moussaoui had lived for years, came up empty, authorities said.

Dan Eggen, "Moussaoui Probe Pushed U.S. Limits; FBI Wanted to Deport Suspect to France to Access His Computer," *Washington Post,* 1/31/2002.
It turns out, however, that *ten days before* the attacks on the World Trade Center and the Pentagon, French authorities—Moussaoui is a French citizen—told American authorities that he was associated with al-Qaeda.

5. See Alan M. Dershowitz, *Shouting Fire* (New York: Little, Brown, 2002), pp. 142–47; Dershowitz, *The Best Defense,* chapter 6.

6. *Gitlow v. New York,* 268 U.S. 652, 673 (1925) (Holmes, J., dissenting).

7. The imam could also claim protection under the free exercise of religion provision of the First Amendment, but the courts have generally held that "religiously neutral" criminal statutes not directed specifically against a particular religion (or religion in general) are constitutional, so long as they are consistent with other provisions of the Constitution—in this case freedom of speech.

8. See *United States v. Ham,* 998 F.2d 1247, 1250 (4th Circuit 1993), which describes how the leader of a Hare Krishna community instructed a follower that under Krishna scriptures he was permitted to kill a man who had raped his wife.

9. "Eskin Gets Four Months for Curse on Rabin," *Jerusalem Post,* 7/21/1997.

10. Geoff Winestock, "Seeds of Change: For Egypt's Terrorists, Fertile Ground Lay in Widespread Poverty," *Wall Street Journal,* 1/18/2002; Peter Beinart, "Out of Egypt," *New Republic,* 11/5/2001, p. 8. In Winestock's account, "Egypt tried tackling terrorism with head-on confrontation and brute force." In response to the massacre at Luxor, the government imprisoned and exiled the leaders of the Gama'at al-Islamiyya, or Islamic Group (IG), the group responsible for the attack. In an attempt to combat terrorism in general, Egypt focused on the countryside where terrorists generally lived. The police burned cane fields about a hundred yards back from the roads to reduce the risk of ambush and to discover terrorists in hiding. Thousands of suspects nationwide were jailed, with many facing torture and execution. The government also established special military courts and implemented emergency law (this law has been in place since 1981).

    Beinart's article, however, goes on to say that Egypt's attempts to crack down on terrorism have not come without a cost: "When a government abandons the rule of law in its fight against fundamentalists, it usually abandons it altogether. So while it's true that Egypt's crackdown has crippled Islamic terrorism, it has also crippled Egypt's civil society. . . . [S]ome local NGOs, which had relied on foreign funding, have shut down. And as a result there was no effective independent monitoring of last year's parliamentary elections. Under the emergency law, the government has also detained labor activists critical of working conditions at state-owned companies. As Fouad Ajami has written, 'The terror had given [President Hosni] Mubarak a splendid alibi and an escape from the demands put forth by segments of the middle class and its organizations in the professional syndicates—the lawyers, the engineers, and the journalists—for a measure of political participation.' And, of course, the lack of political participation means greater corruption, which means greater poverty, which plays into the Islamists' hands."

11. *60 Minutes,* 3/10/2002.

12. Editorial, "The Cancer of Suicide Bombing," *New York Times,* 4/3/2002 (emphasis added); David Rohde, "Passions Inflamed, Teenagers Are Killed in Suicidal Raids," *New York Times,* 4/25/2002. This use of children is comparable to the use of children by drug kingpins. As a result, the profile of the drug smuggler has been expanded to cover young boys and girls.

13. Dareh Gregorian, "City Is Now a Police State," *New York Post*, 9/27/2001.
14. In Lidice, 173 men were shot, 196 women were sent to Ravensbrück, 105 children were sent to Chelmno (only 17 survived), and the village was burned to the ground.
15. Fallaci, "A Leader of the Fedayeen," p. 33.
16. Haim Maas, "A Leaf Out of Islamic Law to Combat Terrorism," *Jerusalem Post*, 3/21/1991.
17. Tim Weiner, "Making Rules in the World Between War and Peace," *New York Times*, 8/19/2001; William Blum, "Killing Hope: U.S. Military and CIA Interventions Since World War II," http://members.aol.com/bblum6/assass.htm.
18. Mary Curtius and Tracy Wilkinson, "Demonstrators Vow to Avenge Hamas Official," *Los Angeles Times*, 11/25/2001.
19. Security Council Resolution 487, which passed unanimously, read in part: "Deeply concerned about the danger to international peace and security created by the premeditated Israeli air attack on Iraqi nuclear installations on 7 June 1981."
20. Aleksandr Solzhenitsyn, *The Gulag Archipelago*, translated by Thomas P. Whitney (New York: Harper & Row, 1974–78).
21. But see William Bradford Huie, *The Execution of Private Slovak* (New York: Delacorte, 1970).
22. Joseph E. Persico, *Roosevelt's Secret War* (New York: Random House, 2001), p. 208.
23. See Dershowitz, *Shouting Fire*, pp. 418–30.
24. *Leon v. State of Florida* 410 So.2d 201 (Fla.3d DCA 1982); *Leon v. Wainwright* 734 F.2d 770, 772–73 (11th Circuit 1984).The state judge's dissent elaborated: "For the first time in history, and the majority concedes as much, there is articulated a distinction between violent police conduct, the purpose of which is to gain information which might save a life, and such conduct employed for the purpose of obtaining evidence to be used in a court of law. The majority holds that where the illegal conduct is motivated by the first consideration no coercive taint will attach so as to render inadmissible evidence subsequently obtained for the purpose of securing a conviction. In essence, evidence of the whereabouts of a victim may be obtained using 'rack and pinion' techniques if the officer on the scene determines the situation life-threatening, and after the information sought has been extracted the status is 'deemed' as if the illegality had never occurred—an eerie proposition which should be rejected outright for all too obvious reasons." *Leon v. Florida* 206.
25. As Justice Potter Stewart once observed about hard-core pornography: "I know it when I see it." A word of appreciation to Harvey Silverglate for suggesting the term "feel of freedom" to me.

26. The occasional trials of prominent Palestinian leaders, such as Azmi Bishara, the member of the Israeli Knesset who was accused of advocating terrorism, marks the outer limit of this freedom, especially because it involves the issue of parliamentary immunity. Bishara's trial is ongoing. See Joel Greenberg, "Israel Tries Legislator for Praising Hezbollah," *New York Times*, 2/28/2002; David Rudge, "Sheetrit: Bishara Backed Terrorism," *Jerusalem Post*, 3/1/2002.

27. On March 20, 2002, the Israeli Supreme Court ruled that Palestinians who were injured as a result of negligence by the Israeli army must be compensated. "Israeli Army Ruled Liable in '88 Raid," *Toronto Star*, 3/21/2002.

28. Dershowitz, *Shouting Fire*, pp. 418–30.

29. See Anthony Lewis, "Taking Our Liberties," *New York Times*, 3/9/2002.

30. Learned Hand, *The Spirit of Liberty* (New York: Knopf, 1960), p. 190.

Chapter 4: Should the Ticking Bomb Terrorist Be Tortured?

1. Walter Pincus, "Silence of 4 Terror Probe Suspects Poses a Dilemma for FBI," *Washington Post*, 10/21/2001 (emphasis added).

2. Elizabeth Fox, "A Prosecution in Trouble," *Atlantic Monthly*, 3/1985, p. 38.

3. But see the case of *Leon v. Wainwright* 734 F.2d 770 (11th Circuit 1984), holding that a *subsequent* statement made by a man who had been *previously* tortured into revealing the whereabouts of a kidnap victim could be introduced into evidence.

4. *Kastigar v. United States*, 406 U.S. 441 (1972).

5. The relevant portion of the Supreme Court decision in *Ingraham v. Wright* 430 U.S. 651, 664 (1977) reads: "An examination of the history of the [Eighth] Amendment and the decisions of this Court construing the proscription against cruel and unusual punishment confirms that it was designed to protect those convicted of crimes. We adhere to this long-standing limitation."

6. See *Leon v. Wainwright*. I have written previously on how the due process clauses could allow torture in certain circumstances. The following analysis is from Alan M. Dershowitz, "Is There a Torturous Road to Justice?" *Los Angeles Times*, 11/8/2001.

> The constitutional answer to this question may surprise people who are not familiar with the current Supreme Court interpretation of the 5th Amendment privilege against self-incrimination, which does not prohibit *any* interrogation techniques including the use of truth serum or even torture. The

privilege only prohibits the *introduction into evidence* of *the fruits* of such techniques in a criminal trial against the person on whom the techniques were used. Thus, if a confession were elicited from a suspect by the use of truth serum or torture, that confession—and its fruits—could not be used against that suspect. But it could be used against *another* suspect, or against *that* suspect in a non-criminal case, such as a deportation hearing.

If a suspect is given "use immunity"—a judicial decree announcing in advance that nothing the defendant says (or its fruits) can be used against him in a criminal case—he can be *compelled* to answer all proper questions. The question then becomes what sorts of pressures can constitutionally be used to implement that compulsion. We know that he can be imprisoned until he talks. But what if imprisonment is insufficient to compel him to do what he has a legal obligation to do? Can other techniques of compulsion be attempted?

Let's start with truth serum. What right would be violated if an immunized suspect who refused to comply with his legal obligation to answer questions truthfully were compelled to submit to an injection which made him do so? Not his privilege against self-incrimination, since he has no such privilege now that he has been given immunity. What about his right of bodily integrity? The involuntariness of the injection itself does not pose a constitutional barrier. No less a civil libertarian than Justice William J. Brennan rendered a decision that permitted an allegedly drunken driver to be involuntarily injected in order to remove blood for alcohol testing. Certainly there can be no constitutional distinction between an injection that *removes* a liquid and one that *injects* a liquid. What about the nature of the substance injected? If it is relatively benign and creates no significant health risk, the only issue would be that it compels the recipient to do something he doesn't want to do. But he has a legal obligation to do precisely what the serum compels him to do: answer all questions truthfully.

What if the truth serum doesn't work? Could the judge issue a "torture warrant," authorizing the FBI to employ specified forms of nonlethal physical pressure in order to compel the immunized suspect to talk? Here we run into another provision of the Constitution—the "due process" clause, which may include a general "shock the conscience" test. And torture in general certainly shocks the conscience of most civilized nations. But what if it were limited to the rare "ticking bomb" case—the situation in which a captured terrorist who knows of an imminent large-scale threat but refuses to disclose it?

7. "Convention Against Torture and Other Cruel, Inhuman or Degrading Treatment or Punishment," adopted by the U.N. General Assembly, 12/10/1984, and in effect since 6/26/1987, after it was ratified by twenty nations.

8. Samuel Francis, "Son of New World Order," *Washington Times,* 10/24/1990; *USA v. Cobb* 1 S.C.R. 587 (2001). Relevant decisions include the above-cited *Ingraham v. Wright* and *Leon v. Wainwright.*

9. William F. Buckley, among others, points to the case of the person who was tortured by Philippine authorities and confessed to having taken part in the Oklahoma City bombing, but of course no one believed him. Compare this to the account described in the next paragraph of the tortured suspect whose information may have prevented a serious act of terrorism.

10. Matthem Brzezinski, "Bust and Boom: Six Years Before the September 11 Attacks, Philippine Police Took Down an al Qaeda Cell That Had Been Plotting, Among Other Things, to Fly Explosives-Laden Planes into the Pentagon—and Possibly Some Skyscrapers," *Washington Post,* 12/30/2001. See also Alexander Cockburn, "The Wide World of Torture," *Nation,* 11/26/2001; Doug Struck, Howard Schneider, Karl Vick, and Peter Baker, "Bin Laden Followers Reach Across the Globe," *Washington Post,* 9/23/2001.

11. There can be no doubt that torture sometimes works. Jordan apparently broke the most notorious terrorist of the 1980s, Abu Nidal, by threatening his mother. Philippine police reportedly helped crack the 1993 World Trade Center bombings by torturing a suspect. Steve Chapman, "No Tortured Dilemma," *Washington Times,* 11/5/2001. It is, of course, possible that judicially supervised torture will work less effectively than unsupervised torture, since the torturee will know that there are limits to the torture being inflicted. At this point in time, any empirical resolution of this issue seems speculative.

12. Rajiv Chandrasekaran and Peter Finn, "U.S. Behind Secret Transfer of Terror Suspects," *Washington Post,* 3/11/2002; Kevin Johnson and Richard Willing, "Ex-CIA Chief Revitalizes 'Truth Serum' Debate," *USA Today,* 4/26/2002.

13. Michael Walzer, "Political Action: The Problem of Dirty Hands," *Philosophy and Public Affairs,* 1973.

14. William J. Brennan, "The Quest to Develop a Jurisprudence of Civil Liberties in Times of Security Crisis," paper delivered in Jerusalem, Decem-

ber 22, 1987. Thanks to Einer Elhauge for bringing this to my attention.

15. Quoted in W. L. Twining and P. E. Twining, "Bentham on Torture," *Northern Ireland Legal Quarterly,* Autumn 1973, p. 347. Bentham's hypothetical question does not distinguish between torture inflicted by private persons and by governments.

16. David Johnston and Philip Shenon, "F.B.I. Curbed Scrutiny of Man Now a Suspect in the Attacks," *New York Times,* 10/6/2001.

17. It is illegal to withhold relevant information from a grand jury after receiving immunity. See *Kastigar v. U.S.* 406 U.S. 441 (1972).

18. Twining and Twining, "Bentham on Torture," pp. 348–49. The argument for the limited use of torture in the ticking bomb case falls into a category of argument known as "argument from the extreme case," which is a useful heuristic to counter arguments for absolute principles.

19. To demonstrate that this is not just in the realm of the hypothetical: "The former CIA officer said he also suggested the agency begin targeting close relatives of known terrorists and use them to obtain intelligence. 'You get their mothers and their brothers and their sisters under your complete control, and then you make that known to the target,' he said. 'You imply or you directly threaten [that] his family is going to pay the price if he makes the wrong decision.'" Bob Drogin and Greg Miller, "Spy Agencies Facing Questions of Tactics," *Los Angeles Times,* 10/28/2001.

20. One of my clients, who refused to testify against the mafia, was threatened by the government that if he persisted in his refusal the government would "leak" false information that he was cooperating, thus exposing him to mob retaliation.

21. *USA v. Cobb.*

22. On conditions in American prisons, see Alan M. Dershowitz, "Supreme Court Acknowledges Country's Other Rape Epidemic," *Boston Herald,* 6/12/1994.

The United States may already be guilty of violating at least the spirit of the prohibition against torture. In a recent case the Canadian Supreme Court refused to extradite an accused person to the United States because of threats made by a judge and a prosecutor regarding the treatment of those who did not voluntarily surrender themselves to the jurisdiction of the U.S. court. First, as he was sentencing a co-conspirator in the scheme, the American judge assigned to their trial commented that those fugitives who did not cooperate would get the "absolute maximum jail sentence." Then, the prosecuting attorney hinted during a television interview that uncooperative fugitives would be subject to homosexual rape in prison:

Zubrod [prosecutor]: I have told some of these individuals, "Look, you can come down and you can put this behind you by serving your time in prison and making restitution to the victims, or you can wind up serving a great deal longer sentence under much more stringent conditions," and describe those conditions to them.

MacIntyre [reporter]: How would you describe those conditions?

Zubrod: *You're going to be the boyfriend of a very bad man if you wait out your extradition.*

MacIntyre: And does that have much of an impact on these people?

Zubrod: Well, out of the 89 people we've indicted so far, approximately 55 of them have said, "We give up."

After reading the transcripts, the Supreme Court of Canada held: "The pressures were not only inappropriate but also, in the case of the statements made by the prosecutor on the eve of the opening of the judicial hearing in Canada, unequivocally amounted to an abuse of the process of the court. We do not condone the threat of sexual violence as a means for one party before the court to persuade any opponent to abandon his or her right to a hearing. Nor should we expect litigants to overcome well-founded fears of violent reprisals in order to be participants in a judicial process. Aside from such intimidation itself, it is plain that a committal order requiring a fugitive to return to face such an ominous climate—which was created by those who would play a large, if not decisive role in determining the fugitive's ultimate fate—would not be consistent with the principles of fundamental justice." *USA v. Cobb* 1 S.C.R. 587 (2001). (Thanks to Craig Jones, a student, for bringing this matter to my attention.)

23. John Langbein, *Torture and the Law of Proof* (Chicago: University of Chicago Press, 1977), p. 68. Voltaire generally opposed torture but favored it in some cases.

24. A special edition of the *Israel Law Review* in 1989 presented a written symposium on the report on the Landau Commission, which investigated interrogation practices of Israel's General Security Services from 1987 to 1989.

25. A fifth approach would be simply to never discuss the issue of torture—or to postpone any such discussion until after we actually experience a ticking bomb case—but I have always believed that it is preferable to consider and discuss tragic choices before we confront them, so that the issue can be debated without recriminatory emotions and after-the-fact finger-pointing.

26. "The Supreme Court of Israel left the security services a tiny window of opportunity in extreme cases. Citing the traditional common-law defense

of necessity, the Supreme Court left open the possibility that a member of the security service who honestly believed that rough interrogation was the only means available to save lives in imminent danger could raise this defense. This leaves each individual member of the security services in the position of having to guess how a court would ultimately resolve his case. That is extremely unfair to such investigators. It would have been far better had the court required any investigator who believed that torture was necessary in order to save lives to apply to a judge. The judge would then be in a position either to authorize or refuse to authorize a 'torture warrant.' Such a procedure would require judges to dirty their hands by authorizing torture warrants or bear the responsibility for failing to do so. Individual interrogators should not have to place their liberty at risk by guessing how a court might ultimately decide a close case. They should be able to get an advance ruling based on the evidence available at the time.

"Perhaps the legislature will create a procedure for advance judicial scrutiny. This would be akin to the warrant requirement in the Fourth Amendment to the United States Constitution. It is a traditional role for judges to play, since it is the job of the judiciary to balance the needs for security against the imperatives of liberty. Interrogators from the security service are not trained to strike such a delicate balance. Their mission is single-minded: to prevent terrorism. Similarly, the mission of civil liberties lawyers who oppose torture is single-minded: to vindicate the individual rights of suspected terrorists. It is the role of the court to strike the appropriate balance. The Supreme Court of Israel took a giant step in the direction of striking that balance. But it—or the legislature—should take the further step of requiring the judiciary to assume responsibility in individual cases. The essence of a democracy is placing responsibility for difficult choices in a visible and neutral institution like the judiciary." Dershowitz, *Shouting Fire,* pp. 476–77.

27. Charles M. Sennott, "Israeli High Court Bans Torture in Questioning; 10,000 Palestinians Subjected to Tactics," *Boston Globe,* 9/7/1999.

28. Osama Awadallah, a green-card holder living in San Diego, has made various charges of torture, abuse, and denial of access to a lawyer. Shira Scheindlin, a federal district court judge in New York, has confirmed the seriousness and credibility of the charges, saying Awadallah may have been "unlawfully arrested, unlawfully searched, abused by law enforcement officials, denied access to his lawyer and family." Lewis, "Taking Our Liberties."

29. Drogin and Miller, "Spy Agencies Facing Questions of Tactics." Philip Heymann is the only person I have debated thus far who is willing to take the position that no form of torture should ever be permitted—or used—even if thousands of lives could be saved by its use. Philip B. Heymann,

"Torture Should Not Be Authorized," *Boston Globe*, 2/16/2002. Whether he would act on that principled view if he were the responsible government official who was authorized to make this life and death choice—as distinguished from an academic with the luxury of expressing views without being accountable for their consequences—is a more difficult question. He has told me that he probably would authorize torture in an actual ticking bomb case, but that it would be wrong and he would expect to be punished for it.

30. Suzanne Daley, "France Is Seeking a Fine in Trial of Algerian War General," *New York Times*, 11/29/2001.

31. The necessity defense is designed to allow interstitial action to be taken in the absence of any governing law and in the absence of time to change the law. It is for the nonrecurring situation that was never anticipated by the law. The use of torture in the ticking bomb case has been debated for decades. It can surely be anticipated. See Dershowitz, *Shouting Fire*, pp. 474–76.

   Indeed, there is already one case in our jurisprudence in which this has occurred and the courts have considered it. In the 1984 case of *Leon v. Wainwright*, Jean Leon and an accomplice kidnapped a taxicab driver and held him for ransom. Leon was arrested while trying collect the ransom but refused to disclose where he was holding the victim. At this point, several police officers threatened him and then twisted his arm behind his back and choked him until he told them the victim's whereabouts. Although the federal appellate court disclaimed any wish to "sanction the use of force and coercion, by police officers" the judges went out of their way to state that this was not the act of "brutal law enforcement agents trying to obtain a confession." "This was instead a group of concerned officers acting in a reasonable manner to obtain information they needed in order to protect another individual from bodily harm or death." Although the court did not find it necessary to invoke the "necessity defense," since no charges were brought against the policemen who tortured the kidnapper, it described the torture as having been "motivated by the immediate *necessity* to find the victim and save his life." *Leon v. Wainwright* 734 F.2d 770, 772–73 (11th Circuit 1984) (emphasis added). If an appellate court would so regard the use of police brutality—torture—in a case involving one kidnap victim, it is not difficult to extrapolate to a situation in which hundreds or thousands of lives might hang in the balance.

32. Quoted in Twining and Twining, "Bentham on Torture," p. 345.

33. For an elaboration of this view, see Dershowitz, *Shouting Fire*, pp. 97–99.

34. The pilot who would have been responsible for shooting down the hijacked plane heading from Pennsylvania to Washington, D.C., on September 11, 2001, has praised the passengers who apparently struggled

with the hijackers, causing the plane to crash. These brave passengers spared him the dreadful task of shooting down a plane full of fellow Americans. The stakes are different when it comes to torturing enemy terrorists.

35. Sir Edward Coke was "designated in commissions to examine particular suspects under torture." Langbein, *Torture and the Law of Proof,* p. 73.

36. Ibid., p. 7.

37. Ibid., p. 90, quoting Bacon.

38. Din Rodef, or Law of the Pursuer, refers to the halachic principle that one may kill a person who is threatening someone else's life. This rule was set forth in the twelfth century by Moses Maimonides, a great Talmudic scholar.

39. Langbein, *Torture and the Law of Proof,* pp. 136–37, 139.

40. When it is known that torture is a possible option, terrorists sometimes provide the information and then claim they have been tortured, in order to be able to justify their complicity to their colleagues.

41. *U.S. v. Lefkowitz,* 285 U.S. 452, 464 (1932).

   The Fourth Amendment provides that "The right of the people to be secure in their persons, houses, papers, and effects, against unreasonable searches and seizures, shall not be violated, and no Warrants shall issue, but upon probable cause, supported by Oath or affirmation, and particularly describing the place to be searched, and the persons or things to be seized." There are numerous exceptions to the warrant requirement. When there are exigent circumstances, for example, or when a person with authority consents to the search, the police do not need a warrant. Also, police officers can search someone without a warrant if they have lawfully arrested the person. If the police arrest someone inside a car, they can also search the interior of the car and any containers inside the car.

42. *Johnson v. U.S.* 333 U.S. 10, 13–14 (1948).

43. *Korematsu v. U.S.* 323 U.S. 214, 245–46 (1944) (Jackson, J., dissenting).

Chapter 5: Striking the Right Balance

1. Sonya Ross, "Bush Says All U.N. Nations Must Fight Terrorism," Associated Press, 11/10/2001; Presidential comments, Department of State Transcript, 12/20/2001.

2. Michael Rubin, "The UN's Refugees," *Wall Street Journal,* 4/18/2002.

3. *Meet the Press,* 4/6/2002; Barry Schweid, "EU, UN, Russia endorse Powell Mission," *Jerusalem Post,* 4/11/2002.

4. Brinkley, "Arabs' Grief in Bethlehem, Bombers' Gloating in Gaza: Hamas Spirits Soar." Hezbollah has made an argument similar to that of Hamas

regarding Lebanon, according to Friedman: "Ever since the unilateral Israeli withdrawal from Lebanon, Palestinians have watched too much Hezbollah TV from Lebanon, which had peddled the notion that Israel had become just a big, soft Silicon Valley, and that therefore, with enough suicide bombs, the Jews could be forced from Palestine, just as they had been from South Lebanon." Thomas L. Friedman, "Reeling But Ready," *New York Times,* 4/28/2002.

5. Friedman, "Suicidal Lies."

6. Among the most significant barriers to an enduring peace in the Middle East is the international community's rewarding of Palestinian terrorism. Were the Palestinians to achieve statehood as the result of their terrorism, that reward would only encourage more terrorism to achieve their stated goals beyond the establishment of a Palestinian state. For many Palestinians, these goals include "resolution" of the "refugee" issue in a way that would assure the eventual end of Israeli "occupation" of Tel Aviv, Jaffa, and West Jerusalem. If the Palestinians achieved their initial goal—statehood—by means of terrorism that was legitimated by the international community, what possible reason would they have for not seeking their ultimate goals by the same means? The only reason would be the loss of the lives of Palestinian suicide bombers. But enough of these terrorists seem willing, even eager, to become martyrs that this consideration is unlikely to serve as a deterrent. Nor would a Palestinian state be willing or able to control further terrorism from within its territory (to say nothing of further terrorism from Israeli Arabs seeking an end to Israel). No Palestinian leader could long survive if he genuinely cracked down on terrorists who were seeking to achieve goals supported by the majority of his constituents. A Palestinian state would not seek to maintain a monopoly over the means of violence. No Palestinian leader would ever do what David Ben-Gurion did when he had the Israeli Defense Forces fire on a ship loaded with weapons destined for the Irgun, Menachem Begin's paramilitary group.

7. *Meet the Press,* April 6, 2002; Thomas L. Friedman, "George W. Sadat," *New York Times,* 4/17/2002; Charles A. Radin and Sa'id Ghazali, "Hamas Deplores Youth of Bombers," *Boston Globe,* 4/26/2002.

8. The end of World War II occasioned mass expulsions from one part of Europe to another. "At the Yalta and Potsdam conferences in 1945, the victorious Allied powers decided to redraw the map of Europe by forcibly moving 12 million Germans, 2.1 million Poles, and hundreds of thousands of Ukrainians, Hungarians and other groups to create ethnically homogeneous states." Mark Kramer and Ana Siljak, " 'Separate' Doesn't Equal Ethnic Peace," *Washington Post,* 2/21/1999.

9. "Henry Morgenthau, Jr.—secretary of the treasury during World War II—

wrote a book called *Germany Is Our Problem* (1945), in which he urged that postwar Germany be partitioned and transformed into an agrarian society. Morgenthau called for the transfer of equipment and factories from Germany to the Allied nations as war reparations." Dershowitz, *Chutzpah*, pp. 137–38.

10. According to a Fox News report by Brit Hume on March 19, 2002, the Arabic version of Hitler's *Mein Kampf,* whose front cover features a swastika and a picture of Hitler, is a major best-seller (sixth on a recent best-seller list) in the area controlled by the Palestinian Authority.

11. Alan M. Dershowitz, "There's a Way for Israel to Deal with Terrorism," *New York Daily News,* 3/15/2002; Alan M. Dershowitz, "New Response to Palestinian Terrorism," *Jerusalem Post,* 3/11/2002.

12. Thomas L. Friedman, "Pull Up a Chair," *New York Times,* 3/20/2002; Friedman, "The Hard Truth."

13. Bennet, "Two-Edged Diplomacy."

14. Because religion plays a major role in creating incentives for terrorists (especially suicide terrorists), it becomes necessary to think about how to change religious doctrine. Obviously this will not be easy, as much of religious doctrine is believed to be God's word. Humans disagree about the meaning of God's word in every religion, and it is certainly possible to encourage the widespread dissemination of religious views that undercut the legitimacy of terrorism, especially suicide terrorism. There may even be legal ways of influencing religious attitudes, but any legal change will be difficult in countries like our own, where the Constitution mandates the separation of church and state and the free exercise of religion.

15. Brendan Koerner, "The Power of Technology May Help Prevent Another September 11. Yet There Are Challenges to Implementation," *Worldlink,* 3/19/2002.

16. For example, Article 15 of the Instructions for the Government of Armies of the United States in the Field, prepared by Francis Lieber and promulgated as General Orders No. 100 by President Lincoln, April 24, 1863, provides: "Military necessity admits of all direct destruction of life or limb of 'armed' enemies." Also, Article 23 of Part 4 of the 1907 Hague Convention (Laws and Customs of War on Land) provides that "in addition to the prohibitions provided by special Conventions, it is especially forbidden . . . [t]o kill or wound an enemy who, having laid down his arms, or having no longer means of defence, has surrendered at discretion." Hence, an enemy who has not yet "laid down his arms" can be killed.

17. Whether they are soldiers under the Geneva Convention is debatable. See Katharine Q. Seelye, "A P.O.W. Tangle: What the Law Says," *New York Times,* 1/29/2002; Thom Shanker and Katharine Q. Seelye, "The Geneva Conventions; Who Is a Prisoner of War? You Could Look It Up. Maybe,"

New York Times, 3/10/2002; Katharine Q. Seelye, "Rumsfeld Backs Plan to Hold Captives Even if Acquitted," *New York Times,* 3/29/2002.

18. "Clinton Ordered Osama bin Laden to Be Killed, Report," Agence France-Presse, 12/19/2001.

19. Israel intelligence mistakenly killed one innocent person.

20. Friedman, "Suicidal Lies."

21. *Meet the Press,* 4/6/2002.

22. Maimonides, Safer HaMitzvot, Negative Commandment 290, quoted in Nachum L. Rabinovitch, *Probability and Statistical Inference in Ancient and Medieval Jewish Literature,* Ph.D. diss., Institute for the History of Science and Technology, University of Toronto (1971), 411, 111.

23. Justinian's Digest quotes the Divine Trajan as having said: "It is better to permit the crime of a guilty person to go unpunished than to condemn one who is innocent." (Trajan was emperor of Rome from 98 to 117.) See *Fatico v. U.S.* 458 F.Supp. 388, 411 (1978).

24. Some of the earliest formulations in the Bible were premised on capital punishment being the penalty. In Genesis, Abraham articulates a form of the "better ten guilty" aphorism when he pleads for the people of Sodom and Gomorrah, whom God would soon kill. Later, Maimonides put the number at one thousand when those found guilty would be executed. In the Anglo-American tradition, English chief justice John Fortescue wrote in 1471, "In deede I woulde rather wyshe twentye euill dooers to escape deathe thoroughe pitie, thenne one manne to bee unijustlye condemned." In the seventeenth century another English chief justice, Matthew Hale, wrote that "it is better five guilty persons should escape unpunished, than one innocent person should die." Alexander Volokh, "*n* Guilty Men," *University of Pennsylvania Law Review* 146 (1997), pp. 173–216.

25. Or consider the detention of several Muslim men who had been found to have shaved off all their body hair, which is apparently an indication of anticipating imminent death, probably by suicide.

26. Bill Hosokawa, *Nisei: The Quiet Americans* (New York: William Morrow, 1969), p. 288.

27. Alan M. Dershowitz, "If Terrorists Attack the U.S., Our Own Legal Authorities May Inadvertently Help Them Achieve Their Objectives," *Penthouse,* 5/1986.

28. For more information on how the United States restricted immigration and citizenship on the basis of race, religion, political beliefs, and national origin, see GilderLehrman Institute of American History, "Landmarks in Immigration History," http://www.gliah.uh.edu/index.cfm.

      Although it is true that we cannot restrict immigrants and citizenship on the basis of race, religion, or sexual orientation (Gabriel J. Chin, "Is There a Plenary Power Doctrine? A Tentative Apology and Prediction for Our Strange but Unexceptional Constitutional Immigration Law," *Georgetown Immigration Law Journal,* Winter 2000), we still can—and do—restrict immigration on the basis of some political beliefs (8 USC section 1424, *Reno v. American-Arab Anti-Discrimination Committee,* 119 S.Ct. 936, 1999).

29. Sergio Bustos, "INS Chief Defends Troubled Agency in Hijacker Visa Approvals," Gannett News Service, 3/20/2002; Dan Eggen, "Moussaoui Probe Pushed U.S. Limits; FBI Wanted to Deport Suspect to France to Access His Computer," *Washington Post,* 1/31/2002.

30. "It is not surprising that several prominent police spokesmen are furious at Ashcroft for putting the interests of the gun lobby over those of potential victims of terrorism. Larry Todd, the police chief of Los Gatos, California, and a member of the International Association of Chiefs of Police, has characterized Ashcroft's decision as 'absurd and unconscionable,' accusing the Attorney General of having made it 'for narrow political reasons based on a right to bear arms mentality.' On the basis of his experience, Chief Todd has concluded that 'if someone is under investigation for a terrorist act, all the records we have in this country should be checked, including whether they bought firearms.' Or, as Matthew Nosanchuk, the litigation director for the Violence Policy Center and a former Justice Department lawyer, has put it: 'It is like there is a gun rights exception to the war on terrorism.'

"It is not in fact clear that current law prohibits the FBI from checking the gun records of terrorists. Current Justice Department rules provide that these records can be used 'for the purpose of investigating, prosecuting and/or enforcing violations of criminal or civil law that may come to light during NICS operations.' (NICS is the National Instant Criminal Background Check System enacted by Congress.)" Alan M. Dershowitz, "Why Is Attorney General Ashcroft Fighting for the Privacy Rights of Potential Terrorists?" *Penthouse,* 5/2002.

31. There may be technical solutions to this problem, such as allowing governmental agencies access only to the identifying aspects of the DNA print and not to other information associated with the print. Current technology can isolate only a part of the DNA, which would not give clues to anything other than the identification of criminals. The chief concern is that future technology will be able to draw information even from this limited genetic fingerprint of "junk DNA." See Samuel C. Seiden and Karine More, "The Physician as Gatekeeper to the Use of Genetic Information in the Criminal Justice System," *Journal of Law, Medicine & Ethics,* 3/22/2002; and Michael Higgins, "Acid Test," *ABA Journal,* 10/1/1999.

32. Phyllis Schlafly and Nadine Strossen, Letter to the editor, "Threat to Privacy in Driver's License," *New York Times,* 5/2/2002. In April 2002, a

panel of the National Academy of Sciences concluded that a well-run national ID system would provide some protection against potential terrorists, but that it also raised privacy concerns. Renae Merle, "Too Many Unresolved Questions on ID Cards, Study Panel Says," *Washington Post,* 4/12/2002.

33. See William Safire, "The Intrusion Explosion," *New York Times,* 5/2/2002; Robert Kuttner, Privacy and National ID Cards," *Boston Globe,* 5/1/2002.

34. See Dershowitz, *Chutzpah,* chapter 1.

35. ACLU associate director Barry Steinhardt, quoted in Mike Branom, "New Security Devices at Fla. Airport," Associated Press, 3/15/2002.

36. See *Brown v. City of Oneonta,* 221 F.3d 329 (2d Circuit 1999).

37. Jewish employees of some of our national security agencies were ethnically profiled following the arrest of Jonathan Pollard for spying for Israel. Former CIA lawyer Adam Saralsky has said he was fired from his job because counterintelligence officers accused him of spying for Israel, with no evidence other than his identification as a religious Jew. "Ethnic Profiling at CIA," *60 Minutes,* 2/6/2000.

38. Wendy Parmet, "AIDS and Quarantine: The Revival of an Archaic Doctrine," *Hofstra Law Review,* Fall 1985, p. 75.

39. Editorial, "Terrorists on Trial," *Wall Street Journal,* 11/16/2001.

40. *Ex parte Milligan,* 71 U.S. 2, 18 L.Ed. 281 (1866).

Conclusion: Are We Overreacting?

1. *Al-Risala,* 11/1/2001, translated by and quoted in Middle East Media Research Institute, Special Dispatch Series, no. 297, 11/7/2001, http://memri.org/; *Jerusalem Post,* 5/30/2000, quoted in Middle East Media Research Institute, Inquiry and Analysis Series, no. 73, 10/24/2001, http://memri.org/; *Al-Usbu',* 9/17/2001, translated by and quoted in Middle East Media Research Institute, Special Dispatch Series, no. 274, 9/21/2001, http://memri.org/.

2. If any Arab or Muslim leader in the world today possessed the military capability to destroy Israel (without itself being destroyed) and forbore from doing so *on moral grounds,* he would be deposed. Israel survives today only because of its superior military capacity and its deterrent capabilities. I have little doubt that if Arab armies were capable of defeating Israel's military, they would massacre the civilian population, rather than merely occupying the land. The evidence for these assertions is in the words of many Islamic leaders throughout the world and the actions of Islamic radicals in parts of Africa.

3. Ten days before September 11, 2001, French police, "who reportedly
   began investigating [Moussaoui] as a possible terrorist, told their U.S.
   counterparts . . . that he had ties to Al-Qaeda." This information, taken
   together with reports that he was "asking a Minnesota flying school for
   lessons in flying but not taking off or landing," should have provided officials with sufficient probable cause to secure a warrant to search his computer—a search that, in combination with other investigative steps, might
   have prevented the crimes of September 11, 2001, though that is not certain. Brian Knowlton, "U.S. Seeks Death Penalty for Sept. 11 Terror Suspect; Ashcroft Rejected France's Leniency Pleas," *International Herald
   Tribune*, 3/29/2002.

Acknowledgments

This book could not have been written without the help of Luke Bullock, who gracefully oversaw the production of the manuscript and provided invaluable assistance with the research. Thanks also to my student research assistants Owen Alterman, Daniel Volchok, and Mara Zusman, who are masters of Internet research and who were always available to answer my questions and provide me with the needed citation and support. Thanks as well to my colleagues Philip Heymann and Ariel Merari for their willingness to share with me their vast experience and brilliant insights. And a word of appreciation to Jane Wagner, my assistant who kept everything together while maintaining the hectic publishing schedule, always with a smile.

My thanks to my agent Helen Rees for encouraging me to write this book. Thanks also to Robert Flynn for inviting me to write it for Yale University Press and to Phillip King for his masterful editing job.

As usual, my appreciation and love goes to my family, who know how to balance just the right amount of encouragement, criticism, and love.

Finally, my unbounded admiration for the victims of terrorism who have never even considered resorting to this brutal and inhuman tactic in revenge.

Index